D1433827

# The
# Retirement
# Book

# Joan Adler

# The Retirement Book

A Complete Early-Planning Guide
to Finances, New Activities,
and Where to Live

WILLIAM MORROW & COMPANY, INC.

NEW YORK     1975

## Acknowledgments

My thanks to the many people of all ages who have been so generous with their time and with their knowledge. Unfortunately, they are too many to list here, but my special thanks are due to the National Council of Senior Citizens, the Gray Panthers, the American Association of Retired Persons, and the Senior Citizens Council. Without them, the information in this book could not have been forthcoming, although of course any misinformation is my own.

Printed in the United States of America.

1  2  3  4  5      79  78  77  76  75

**Library of Congress Cataloging in Publication Data**

Adler, Joan.
  The retirement book.

  Bibliography: p.
  Includes index.
  1. Retirement.  I. Title.
HQ1064.U5A63        301.43′5        74-26942
ISBN   0-688-02896-9

*Book design by Helen Roberts*

*To my parents with love and gratitude*

# Foreword

This book is about retirement and how to cushion its effects. The author has dealt with the complicated subject with sensitivity and creative common sense. She has researched many of the hazards of financing the retirement years and pointed clearly to the need for careful planning. She has also countered some of the undeniable hardships of decreasing income, declining quality of life, and zooming inflationary costs of survival with helpful and practical advice. Her options for new life styles, use of time and leisure, are attractive. Her counsel about maintaining optimum health of mind and body should be heeded.

The author obviously knows that Americans have widely different views and feelings about retirement. Her suggestions reflect these differences. What some regard as a disaster, others welcome with relief. Some count the days until they can enjoy "well-earned leisure." Many are "worked out," ground down in body and spirit, and desperately need the respite retirement brings. But to others retirement is the end of purposeful living, a traumatic experience from which they never recover. Far too many accept retirement from the *job* as retirement from *life!*

I hope many will ponder and act upon Ms. Adler's sound advice, but their action should be accompanied by some healthy skepticism and challenge of the underlying economic and social structures that make retirement mandatory and condition American workers to accept it without protest or outrage.

Gray Panthers and other groups concerned about age discrimination and social change have called compulsory retirement what it is— an enormous social waste of precious human resources—the experience, skill, judgment, and wisdom of the elders of our society. We call upon workers of all ages to fight the system that scrap-piles people as it does old automobiles.

Great multinational corporations put their workers "out to pasture" at 60, 65 at the latest. They accelerate social change and cultural dislocation for millions of workers and their families in the United States and around the world. With rapid urbanization and industrialization they contribute to the wealth of a few and the destruction of familial systems so that the elderly are isolated. (Even in Japan nursing homes are now a problem!) Furthermore, American workers have been sold on the pension goodies in union contracts negotiated on the basis of "30 years and out," lured by the argument that they are making a place for the young.

Scholars with long tenure are no longer protected from compulsory retirement by universities. Indeed they are fortunate if scholarly journals will publish what they write in retirement! Employment to age seventy is the best many can hope to attain.

To bolster profits and productivity we have built obsolescence into everything we make, from nylons to automobiles. Our penchant for making things not to last but to wear out has wasted natural resources and wasted people. The accumulated skills and experience of America's elders have been devalued and despised.

To reverse the trend of forced retirement at earlier and earlier ages, management, labor, and consumers have large personal and corporate responsibility. The present age-discrimination laws prohibiting discrimination in employment up to age 62 or 65 should be amended to make it illegal to discriminate on the basis of age at any age. There should be general public awareness about the placement problems that the existing laws create, even for middle-aged workers who have to find new jobs.

Personnel officers often reflect the same cruel biases and stereotypes held by society. Old and middle-aged workers are sterotyped as unproductive, inflexible, unable to change. These workers realize they are the victims of society's stereotyping, but they rarely register complaints or bring charges against the firm practicing the age discrimination.

When Gray Panthers have challenged employers to explain their bias against the older worker, the flagrant response has been that "retirement is the only way to get rid of the dead wood." Gray Panthers are not impressed by such reasoning and see it as a rationalization for ineffective personnel practices.

Old people have much in common with young people and are frequently plagued by the same identity crisis, and "put down" by people in positions of power.

We elders care deeply about our grandchildren and other young people who come after us. Therefore many of us are concerned about using our freedom, our knowledge and experience, to challenge and change the conditions and policies that demean and diminish people of all ages, and have the goal of improving life for the oppressed and powerless.

In this age of liberation and self-determination the elders of our society can develop many new freedoms: a) new life styles; b) new associations with people of other age groups, particularly young people; c) new uses of what we have learned through years of living as good neighbors, responsible consumers, and public citizens. We may be separated from our jobs and deprived of adequate income and status in society, but we do not retire from life.

If we are to have a liberated old age, we as liberated old people must put aside the old prejudices that once separated us from people different from us in racial origin, religious affiliation, or economic status. Since we are all aging, it is important to close ranks and be advocates of each other. This will be a new role for the elderly rich who do not know the rigors of living on small fixed incomes.

Responsible consumers are concerned about fraud and product safety as well as the sharp sales practices that victimize the old and handicapped. Hearing aids, for example, are frequently sold by profit-minded dealers to the hearing-impaired at exorbitant costs and without medical supervision. Legislation to regulate the sale of hearing aids and to provide for their sale only after proper medical advice and recommendation has been introduced in several states, but only after strenuous efforts by consumer advocates. It will take many more consumer advocates to overcome the powerful lobbies ranged against similar reforms in other industries.

Responsible consumers are also analyzing and protesting the high cost of medical care and the unavailability of home health care; they are also concerned with the prevention of mental and physical illness. Responsible consumers have become aware that American medical care is crisis-oriented and is more properly equipped to deliver "disease care" than health care.

Responsible consumers are concerned likewise about the high cost of funerals and the way in which the grief of the bereaved family member is exploited by morticians so that the extent of love is equated with the cost of the funeral. Gray Panthers are encouraging membership in memorial societies where death and interment can be dealt with by concerned undertakers.

Women's liberation is needed especially for the older woman. The plight of widows who have lived only in their husband's shadow is tragic. Women who have never discovered their own identity and goal need the consciousness raising and the support of the women's movement to save them from years of bitter loneliness.

Public citizens do not think merely·in terms of their own self-interest as many advocates of gray power seem to do. Public citizens are concerned about the larger common good and are willing to take the risks involved in working for legislative reforms in municipal government, state government, and the federal establishment. They are also working for the improvement of the courts and the administration of justice. In this age of rapid social change, it is crucial to build a supportive community of older and younger people who understand their own needs in relation to the needs of society and who are willing to work for justice and legislative reform.

Public citizens have determination and perseverance. They do not give up and go away. In their retirement years many older people are finding a whole new lease on life, working for the common good. They have nothing to lose.

MARGARET E. KUHN
The Gray Panthers

# Contents

# Introduction

The fact is that old age is honorable just as long as it asserts
itself, maintains its proper rights, and is not enslaved to anyone.

—CICERO, *De Senectute*

You have retired, or you are going to retire, from your job—the
job which since you left school has determined your answer to the
question "What do you do?"

What are you going to retire to?

For a lot of people that question has never come up. Many other
people envision late risings, golden afternoons—nothing concrete,
but certainly a new freedom. For still others the question stirs a faint
dread, because everything seems so blank beyond that unthinkable
day of retirement.

But maybe your response is different; maybe you have, if not detailed plans, at least a good idea of what you want to do. You will,
perhaps, spend a lot more time on your clock making. Or you intend
to be a volunteer worker for the blind. Or finally get that mobile
home and travel the continent—perhaps Mexico and farther south,
too. Or at last get yourself off to college for the anthropology courses
you have never had time for. Maybe you plan to have a second
career—as a consultant, perhaps, to the firm from which you have
retired. Or maybe you hanker after the totally unscheduled life, and
haven't the faintest intention of being tied down by plans.

But, whatever your intentions, unless you take certain facts of life
into account, your plans will founder among other unrealizable
dreams. Most obvious is the fact of income. Unless you are among
the nation's wealthiest 2%, your income will be less than it was during your working life. So, of course, will your expenses, but not (usually) to the same extent. The Bureau of Labor has estimated that you
need roughly 70% to 80% of your working income level to main-

tain the same standard of living after retirement. Since few people can count on that kind of retirement income, chances are that your financial arrangements must be overhauled. The various ways of doing this are considered in Section I of this book, which examines possible sources of income and ways of tailoring expenditures.

Where you live will at least partially determine what you can do, and vice versa. Section II of this book, therefore, details choices of accommodations, climate, environment, and society. Here again, financial considerations loom large, but they go hand in hand with equally powerful physiological and psychological considerations.

How your time is occupied will color every other aspect of your retired life; it's no use solving money problems only to be completely discontented with yourself. Nor can any book (or indeed any other source) presume to tell you what will make you happy. It is true and, given the nature of our society, not very surprising that most people are happier when they are busy. But you may be happiest in a rocking chair, watching the world go by; if so, your difficulty will be resisting everyone's urging you to do something. However, since most people's difficulty lies in finding what to do, Section III outlines some of the possibilities, together with some pointers about making your choices and carrying them through.

At the base of all this rearranging, planning, and problem-solving lies the assumption that you are reasonably healthy, both mentally and physically. How to achieve, or hold onto, health and what bodily changes to expect are discussed in Section IV.

The text is aimed at the "younger generation" of older people: those between the ages of 55 and 80. The differences between the 60's and the 80's are as great as those between the 20's and the 40's. Nursing homes, for example, have not been examined in detail because these most often concern people older than those addressed in this book. Development doesn't stop at any age, but the "older generation" demands a text unto itself and is beyond our scope.

# The Retirement Book

# 1
# Your New Scene

Most people stop earning a living, often under compulsion, after a 35- to 50-year working life. Usually they are then between the ages of 55 and 70. Retirement thus coincides with aging, and the two subjects have become quite inextricable.

Most of us feel twinges of aging in our 30's and 40's. Yet despite a sign here or a creak there—your back may ache a little sooner while gardening or your eyes get scratchy after a lot of close work—our physical and mental conditions remain at more or less the same level for the next 15 to 20 years.

Then, incredibly, it's your last day at the job: you've been retired.

Now, in some societies (ancient China was one) this would have been a form of graduation: you would have been deemed fit to seek wisdom, no longer having to immerse yourself in the daily trivia of earning a living. But we have a society in which youth, particularly the appearance of youth, is second only to money in desirability; where, as someone remarked, teen-agers are consulted about world affairs and older people are told to go out and play (but haven't enough money to get to the playground); where change has been so rapid over the whole of your lifetime that the experience of your own youth seems like that of another world; where your opinions and advice are judged to be out of date, and quite often are.

You stand a 50–50 chance of being forced to retire. You stand a 98–2 chance of a considerable drop in income. Your emotions at this graduation to freedom are therefore apt to go beyond pure delight that you don't have to get up tomorrow morning.

You begin, perhaps, to think that society could be right. After all, haven't you looked at retired people and felt a twinge of pity for their failing capacities? Not that you have actually *observed* them failing, of course, but what else could human capacities be doing under the joint circumstances of retirement and growing older?

1

After all, you think, there are a lot of younger men with families to support who will be glad of the job you have just vacated. And what right have you to stand in their way?—your own children are out in the world on their own six feet, your mortgage is paid up, your need for new belongings is just above nil. Of course, you could have used a few more years of work to build up your savings. It's going to be a bit tight on your new income. And what are you going to do with all that energy?

Still, there's a lot to keep you busy—house repairs you have managed to avoid for years; a pile of books you've been eyeing with anticipation for almost as long; this year you won't have to buy vegetables, you're going to grow your own; and your wife will be glad of help with the housework.

But you know it's not easy. A lifetime's habits are not shucked overnight. True, you've been through major changes before: you left school, started work, got married, had your first child, lost your parents. But it was easier to keep functioning then because you and your family got hungry otherwise. Now there's no real need to do anything. You'll get your Social Security check and (maybe) your pension whether you get up in the morning or not.

Well, of course, you can find that depressing; and indeed it is, if that's all it amounts to. But, after all, perhaps that's not all, perhaps there are other things to be, roles to play. You've got a mind of your own and, at long last, a choice of how to use it. So whether it's tomorrow morning after 65 for you now, was tomorrow morning after 65 for you last year or the year before, or will be 15 years from now, what can you do to get yourself together and do a phoenix act?

For starters, let's have a look at who your fellows are and where you all stand before embarking on the practical planning.

## SOME STATISTICS

**POPULATION**   The population of the United States in 1970 was 203 million, an increase of 154% since 1900, when it totaled 76 million. By the year 2000 the population will likely total about 270 million—enough to give you instant claustrophobia!

The increase has largely been due to decreased mortality rates among children and young adults. People born in 1969 will live an average of 70 years—about 20 years longer than people born in 1900. In the 18th century, American life expectancy averaged only about 37 years; and the world average is still somewhere between 40 and 50 years.

The life expectancy of older people is also increasing: in 1900 a man of 65 could expect another 10 years of life, a woman another 11; by 1969 the expectancy had risen to 13 years for men and 16 years for women.

Since more people reach the age of 65 now (a net increase of about 800 a day), their proportion to the rest of the population has been growing, giving them great potential as voter and consumer groups. One hundred years ago only about 3% of the population of the United States was over 64 years old; in 1900 the proportion was 4%; by 1970 the 20.1 million people over the age of 64 constituted almost 10% of the total population. By the year 2000, they are expected to number almost 29 million.

For every 100 girls, 105 boys are born. However, because mortality rates for females are lower and their life expectancy is longer, there are 138 women for every 100 men aged over 64. The disparity is less at the lower end of the age group (120 women to every 100 men), highest in the 70's, and lower again above the age of 80.

**LIVING ARRANGEMENTS** In 1972, 80% of men over 64 were married; less than 40% of women over 64 were married—a startling difference until you consider the far greater number of women than men in this age category. But in fact, 2 million more men than women over 64 were married, 40% of the men to women under 65. Almost 16% of men and 53% of women over 64 were widowed; 5.5% men and 6.6% women were single, having never married; and 1.8% men and 2.5% women were divorced. These figures make no allowance for the men and women living together in unmarried bliss for the sake of higher Social Security benefits. On the legitimate side of the fence, about 15,000 older women and 35,000 older men get married every year, not necessarily to each other.

Although New York, California, and Pennsylvania had the highest number of older people, this is only because these are the most populous states. The states with the highest proportions of older people were Florida, Arkansas, and Nebraska. The latter two are a surprise —especially Nebraska, which few people would define as ideal retirement country. A possible explanation is that the state's older people tend to stay put in familiar surroundings while younger ones leave (in Nebraska they claim that more of their population live longer for reasons yet unknown).

Older people were fairly equally distributed between central cities, suburbs, and nonmetropolitan areas, with a very small percentage living in farm areas. However, it seems all too likely that many older people living in the central cities were not there by choice. In New

York City, for instance, 51% of them were living in rent-controlled housing, and although their neighborhoods were deteriorating about their ears, they could not possibly afford to move out.

Most people over 64 were living with their families, usually spouses or children. The proportion of men living with their families was 82%, that of women 56%, but the actual numbers were nearly the same—just short of 7 million of each sex. This means that almost four times more women than men were living alone or with people other than their families. Only about 5% of women and 4% of men lived in institutions, a total of one million of both sexes combined, of which the majority were at the upper end of the age group.

**HOUSING**   About 65% of older people owned their homes, 80% of them mortgage-free. Most homeowners (77%) were married couples, but 39% of nonmarried men and 42% of nonmarried women also owned their own houses.

**INCOME LEVELS**   In 1971, a lucky 17% of married couples (850,000 of them) in which the man was over 64 were receiving $10,000 or more per annum. Another 32% (1.6 million couples) were getting between $5000 and $10,000 a year; yet 50% were getting only between $1000 and $5000, and 1% were getting less than $1000 per annum. These incomes averaged less than half of the average for younger families.

For single people the picture was less rosy still. Only 13% were getting over $5000 per annum (the percentage getting more than $10,000 was not worth noting); 18% were in the $3000 to $5000 bracket; 59% in the $1000 to $3000 bracket; and 10% under $1000. These incomes averaged about two fifths of the average income for younger nonmarried people. Incomes of older people are highest in the West, largely because a high proportion of them are working and partly because their wages are higher than elsewhere. The South has the lowest medians—Social Security benefits are smaller there because of lower average salaries, and wages, of course, remain low for those people over 64 who are still working.

The Bureau of Labor Statistics publishes estimates of the money needed annually by a retired couple at a low, an intermediate, and a higher level of living. The couple is assumed to live in an urban area, to own their home, to be in a reasonably good state of health, and to be self-sufficient. In the autumn of 1971 the lowest estimated budget called for $3,320, the intermediate one for $4,776, and the higher one for $7,443. Although the lowest-level budget supposedly marks the line below which real poverty sets in, most people are hard put to it to manage on the intermediate-level income.

On this basis, in 1971 some 22% (4.3 million) of older people had incomes below the poverty line. Well over half of them lived alone or with nonrelatives, and most of these single poor people were women, mainly widows.

Recent increases in Social Security benefits have raised the income figures; unfortunately, inflation has kept the real value of money down. The net result is no improvement of the situation.

**INCOME SOURCES**   Where did this income, such as it is, come from? While the latest available figures are from a 1968 Social Security survey of people over 64, it seems likely that income patterns remain much the same today.

In 1967, 86% were getting Social Security benefits. Appallingly, 30% of married couples and 60% of single people had no other source of income. Although almost half of the couples were able to earn money from work, and 27% were getting a private pension, only 10% had income from all three sources.

Nonmarried people were even worse off, with a meager 16% working, 12% with a private pension, and only 2% getting income from all three sources. Indeed, 9% had none of these resources and were dependent on public assistance, on Veterans Administration benefits, or on their relatives.

**WORK**   In 1900, long before Social Security, two out of three men and one in twelve women continued working after age 64. The First World War and the Great Depression make intermediate statistics unreliable, but these proportions clearly declined with the advent of Social Security in the 1930's and that decline has sharpened as benefit levels have risen and private pension schemes have slowly expanded. By 1972 one in four men and one in ten women were in the labor force. At first glance this would suggest a preference for retirement, even on a barely adequate income, and perhaps this is the case; however, one must take into account the increase in compulsory retirement policies in business and industry.

A large proportion of older working people (35% of men and almost 16% of women) were self-employed—probably reflecting the difficulties so many encounter in getting hired.

Most of the older labor force drops out at about 70, by the way. While some 42% of men and 17% of women worked between the ages of 65 and 69, only 18% of men and 6% of women continued to do so after age 70.

**HEALTH**   Even apart from the one million older people whose health or solitude confines them to institutions, only about 15% of the older population can be said to be free of chronic health impairments. "Chronic" means long-lasting; it does not necessarily mean serious, and it can include anything from having to wear spectacles to a severe heart condition.

It is not so surprising, then, to learn that despite the high incidence of chronic conditions, 80% of older people are perfectly mobile and not greatly discommoded by their particular health problem. Of the rest, perhaps 8% have a little trouble getting around, while another 6% need a mechanical aid such as a walker or wheelchair. Something like 5% of older people are homebound (apart from those living in institutions).

More older people are hospitalized over the course of a year (25% as opposed to about 12% of those under 65) and their stays in hospitals are twice as long (17 vs. 8 days). They also visit their doctors twice as many times as do younger people—about 6.7 times in a year. On the other hand, they visit dentists much less frequently.

## THE RETIREMENT PROCESS

The process of retirement has only recently come under much scrutiny, as the average period of retirement has grown to a 10- or 20-year stretch—a significant segment of a person's life.

What does retirement, often compulsory retirement, do to people? How does it affect them emotionally, physically, psychically? How long do the effects last and why do they pass, if they do pass? How do people cope with their altered circumstances and what changes are wrought in them and in their immediate circle of family and friends?

The answers to these questions are various, but from them a general pattern emerges: Retirement will probably have a temporarily depressing effect which, if severe, may have physical repercussions; however, most people adjust to their new situation in time and pull out to a normal state. The duration and severity of the effects probably depend on your all-round stability; if you have always coped well in crisis periods, you will continue to cope well. How well depends on the amount and kind of change you must face: financial straits after a comfortable standard of living can be oppressive; compulsory retirement for a completely job-oriented person can be a major blow.

How to avoid or at least mitigate these problems is the subject of a growing number of study courses, books, pamphlets, and pep talks. Retirement counseling is now a career for more and more people; the research and literature on the subject are developing at a fast clip. The consensus of advice is to keep busy, manage your financial affairs well, and keep in good health—laudable but not always practicable.

Another way to obviate the problems caused by the sudden onset of retirement would be to remove the cause itself, the sharp dividing line between working life and leisure life, and thus to encourage people to assign equal value to the latter. One of the more promising suggestions in this direction is to make working time longest for young workers and to gradually decrease it over the years until the workers choose to retire completely. In this way, the shock of the arbitrary break between full-time work and full-time leisure is avoided, because you get gradually accustomed to structuring your own time. In addition, should you suffer from health problems or a diminution of energy with the passing years, the shorter working hours would reduce stress.

A modified form of this scheme is already used in some industries, where your working hours are gradually reduced over the last five years or so before complete retirement.

Another interesting possibility is the retirement sabbatical. Though not likely to sweep the working world in the immediate future, it is a system which would make a lot of sense even now and will begin to look more practical as automation takes over many more jobs and work grows scarcer. Instead of retiring workers as they get older, the retirement-sabbatical scheme would pension off workers at various ages for various lengths of time. During these sabbaticals the worker would be free to pursue his own interests. He would retire permanently only after a certain age and only by choice or physical necessity. He would not be faced, as now, with a difficult period of total readjustment after a lifetime in one set of habits.

The proliferation of retirement counseling has not yet resulted in extensive planning for retirement among workers. Many firms and unions do have courses and pamphlets on the subject, but its importance is rarely emphasized and, of course, it is largely ignored by those workers who are most resistant to the idea of retirement—the very people who are most stunned by its advent.

But planning your retirement in advance is extremely important, and you are the only person who can do it. Nor is it a matter you can take care of in just a few weeks—good planning requires months, even years, of analysis and arrangement. The more attention you pay to your retirement before it overtakes you, the better chance you have of avoiding its more depressing aspects.

## THE AGING PROCESS

The subject of aging has remained mysterious for an unconscionably long time. What changes take place in the body and mind with the passing years? Why do they happen at all, and by what process or processes? Are these changes inevitable or can they be decreased or deferred among older people as they seem to be among middle-aged people now?

The questions seem obvious enough and of eventual concern to everyone. But it is only recently, with the growth of a large and comparatively healthy population aged over 64, that serious research has begun on any large scale. Hence, much of the medical information now available is tentative: the whys and wherefores of aging are now under a multitude of microscopes and are the subject of a plethora of theories.

According to one of those theories, deposits of amyloid, a hardened protein substance, form in certain body cells and impair their function; the longer you live, the more deposits you accumulate and the more deterioration occurs in your cell functions.

Thymosin, a hormone produced by the thymus gland, is regarded as a possible culprit in another theory, closely linking the hormone with the body's immunological system. The thymosin level in the blood falls off with age, our resistance to infection decreases, and we become increasingly susceptible to disease.

Still another theory has it that, with each illness or injury we suffer, the function of our body cells becomes less efficient, because repairs can never be perfect. Eventually, certain cells fail to maintain good health. The popular illustration of this theory is to compare our bodies to machines, which must finally wear out. But the fact is that our bodies are not machines and that some of our cells have apparently infinite renewal potential. The comparison with machines is obtuse, also, because it blinds us to the still relevant question of why living cells should suffer any degeneration at all.

As medical research continues, everyone as usual is hoping for the discovery of a single key which will open the door to a fountain of youth: Find the one cause of bodily aging, then find the way to remove that cause, and presto!

One theory, beloved of philosophers for centuries and advanced in detailed form about 15 years ago by Cummings and Henry in their book, *Growing Old: The Process of Disengagement,* is based on psychological rather than physical data. It suggests that older people are involved in simultaneous processes of disengagement from external ties and of engagement with their inner selves—and that the change from middle age is not just biological, it is as developmental as was the change from adolescence to adulthood. Cummings and Henry have held that this process begins at retirement for men and widowhood for women. Therefore, efforts to keep older people involved in active worldly pursuits are both mistaken and ineffectual.

This view has found little favor with most gerontologists, who have pointed out that if it were true, many older people would be spending 10, 15, or 20 years of their lives in what is essentially a preparation for death. They have also maintained that physical and mental health are much better in active, engaged older people than in more passive, withdrawn ones.

These are certainly valid objections, which can be backed by a wealth of statistical and personal observation. The disengagement theory, however, may be true for some people, particularly in the later decades of their lives, although not for all of them by any means. Most people in their 80's, for instance, are getting too frail for many physical activities, and with their frailty comes a contemplative turn of mind. Many of them report a falling off of emotional involvement with their previous concerns; if they are lucky, serenity arrives and death loses its fearful aspects.

Despite apparent drawbacks, the disengagement theory does point the way to possibilities for the combined aging-and-retirement process which are not immediately evident in statistical sources. It is obvious, looking back on life, that there are certain periods of great change. The difference between the child and the adolescent is marked; although it is the result of a gradual process, the process reaches a peak of change and turmoil in the years around puberty. The change from adolescence to young adulthood is similarly gradual and has a similar crisis period in the late teens and early 20's. The transition from young adulthood into middle age is another period of great change and, like the others, of great emotional and sometimes physical difficulty for many people. The change from middle age into the advanced maturity of old age has all the hallmarks of another major transition period. For some people it is smooth; for many others it is confusing, agitating, and painful in varying degrees.

To compound the confusion, many an older person is thrust into the process long before he is ready for it or in need of it, by the mere fact of his chronological age. You may never have had to give more than a passing thought to your years because physically and emotionally you have been in normal gear for middle age and could remain so considerably longer. Then you are abruptly reined in by retirement, say, and forced to change your way of life. This holds all sorts of implications which you may feel are not true for you and with which you are not yet equipped to cope.

At the other extreme, though less and less frequently nowadays, is the person who ages more quickly than the dictates of chronology allow. He may be faced with maintaining a level of output at work which he finds increasingly taxing; he will go through mental and emotional changes which he understands even less, because of their early advent, than if they were chronologically normal.

The rest of this book is devoted to detailed discussions of each aspect of change which may be necessary in the retirement/aging process and to practical ways of implementing those changes. But here we can take space to consider the process as a whole, as another metamorphosis in our personal life history.

Some physical and mental changes are readily visible to others. Far less appreciated, however, are the changes taking place in the developmental processes of aging—changes whose outward signs are not easily fathomed and are sometimes scarcely visible to anyone but yourself.

Your ability to "go with" the changes is crucial. If you balk at them or are blocked emotionally from moving on, your being will, so to speak, take its revenge. It is not possible to mark time for very long; the alternative to progress is regression—you will lose what you have already gained and your mental and physical health will deteriorate.

The characteristics of successful development at this stage are those which go to make a "whole" person: objectivity, good perspective, mental and emotional clarity, a balancing of reason and emotion, a shift from self-centeredness to detachment, self-reliance, understanding, and forgiveness. What they add up to, of course, are serenity and wisdom—the highest goals of old age, and perhaps of humanity.

Some people seem to have been born with a kind of grace which lets them attain these states in the natural course of their lives, without great upheaval. Most people have to struggle like chicks breaking out of eggs to make each step forward.

Certain types of action, however, seem to help bring changes about with fewer birth pangs.

If you practice one of the arts or crafts, for instance, you give direct, instinctual expression to a part of yourself to which you probably have no other access and whose nature may come as a complete surprise to you. Once released, however, that self will make possible actions and ideas of which you may previously have had only faint glimmers. This kind of creativity confers freedom to be yourself.

Education and travel open your mind to new ideas. Education also exercises your mind, quite literally, and keeps it in good working order. Travel demonstrates most vividly what education can only tell you: that the culture in which you live is not the only viable one and that other value systems have equal integrity. These kinds of knowledge unfold new possibilities which often point the way through otherwise impassable emotional country.

Community activities are a two-way street. What you give out in the way of good companionship and emotional and material support will come back to you in diverse forms. The very fact of being useful to someone is enough to make you feel worthwhile; those grim shades of obsolescence that loom at retirement are driven back. An active role in the community will bring recognition which is good growing soil for self-esteem.

All these activities will do their work a lot better if you pay some attention to your inner self. Self-analysis is difficult but highly educational and will often give you the means for sound judgment. It will also help to clear away a lot of outgrown debris and let you move on to activities more suitable to your real situation and potentials.

Needless to say, a healthy, well-exercised body will give you the best foundation for any activity, including psychological and mental ones.

But if self-development is assisted by certain kinds of occupation, it is hindered by others.

If you are forced to spend most of your time either getting or worrying about getting enough money to live on, you will have little time, energy, or inclination for any of the occupations just discussed. You will have little or no genuine freedom to choose your activities, and in any case this kind of basic deprivation leaves scant room for growth of anything except hunger and resentment. If you are threatened by this situation, you may have to undertake a total re-evaluation of what you consider necessary to a decent life; unless you have always lived on the edge of poverty and can trim your sails no further, it is well worthwhile to simplify your wants to real basics. At the same time, you should take all possible steps to secure a larger income.

While a certain type of introversion is necessary for self-knowledge, constant dwelling on your feelings can bring on emotional hypochondria. Faced with declining physical powers and perhaps with unfulfilled ambitions, and no longer occupied with a career, you may too easily fall into melancholy and dissatisfaction. The longer you let these states persist, the harder they are to escape; the eventual results can be either apathetic depression or demanding, nasty, self-centeredness. In these states of mind you will go nowhere but backward, and it is utterly essential that you fight your way out by any means possible—by exercising the strongest emotional control you can summon and by committing yourself to activities which will moor a large part of your interest to points outside yourself.

In the Western world older people, particularly retired older people, are often segregated willy-nilly from the society at large. They are then subjected to a discrimination based on fallacies about their mental and physical capabilities. Human credulity being what it is, these fallacies tend to be accepted by older people themselves. As a result they are no longer able to judge their own real capabilities, and they intensify their own segregation by further voluntary withdrawal.

But older people have an accumulated knowledge, and sometimes wisdom, about some areas of human experience, a knowledge unavailable to younger people except through their elders. The sense of perspective, the tolerance, and the kindliness of a good elder are badly needed by their descendants; it is an unrealized loss when older people are no longer an integral part of society. It is also a loss to the older person to have no one to teach and no proper function and effect in society. The only way out of this bind is to change the values of the society that rates youth above age. The people best equipped to bring about that change are older people themselves, with their experience and knowledge of their needs and ours.

# I.

# FINANCING
# YOUR
# FUTURE

One of the biggest changes that comes with retirement is the change in financial status. Unless you are particularly well-heeled, you will find yourself—along with 98% of the retired population—obliged to manage on much less money.

Of course, your expenses will undoubtedly be reduced: you won't need the same size or kind of wardrobe as when you went to work every day; you will spend less on restaurant meals; you will no longer have to pay for transport to and from work (and if you've had two cars, you can probably get rid of one).

Despite such obvious savings, however, the U. S. Department of Labor has estimated that most married couples need between 70% and 80% of their preretirement income to maintain the same standard of living after retirement.

Very few people achieve that percentage. Social Security benefits, the sole retirement income of some 30% of married couples and 60% of single people, are geared to mere subsistence levels. Work provides income for about 50% of retired couples and 16% of retired single people; it is the whole income for some 7% of these people—the rest work for extra income, and most of them don't find it worthwhile to earn more than the limit imposed by Social Security regulations. Private pensions are helping out about 27% of couples and 12% of single people. All three sources (Social Security, work, and private pensions) are available only to 10% of couples and 2% of single people; and, except for a few people whose private pensions are substantial, these are the only ones likely to achieve a standard of living which approximates their preretirement one.

This section is designed to help you plan (or reevaluate, if you are already retired) your retirement finances. It will show you how to take inventory of your sources of income and to adjust them, if necessary, for a higher yield. It will also help you to analyze your expenditures and to cut these down or out where necessary and possible.

The chart on pages 42–43 shows the basic budget sheet for both monthly and annual income/expenditure balances. As you work out your own figures, you can enter them on this sheet and get a clear idea of your financial status and of the adjustments you may need to make.

In addition to books mentioned in the text, you might find handy the U. S. Department of Agriculture publication *A Guide to Budgeting for the Retired Couple* and the Office of Aging publication by Virginia Lehmann, *You—the Law—and Retirement,* both available from the Superintendent of Documents (Government Printing Office, Washington, D.C. 20402). Other useful references are: J. K. Lasser's *Investing for Your Future* and *Your Guide to Social Security and Medicare Benefits,* both available in paperback from Simon & Schuster; Norman D. Ford's *How to Increase Your Retirement and Other Income* (Harian, 1968); and John Barnes's *Who Will Get Your Money?* (Morrow, 1972) and *How to Have More Money* (Morrow, 1974). From the American Association of Retired Persons (215 Long Beach Boulevard, Long Beach, California 90802) you can get the practical *Your Retirement Legal Guide.*

# 2
# Social Security and Pensions

## SOCIAL SECURITY

Social Security is a form of retirement, disability, or life insurance administered by the federal government through its Social Security Administration. During your working life a percentage of your income, up to a maximum amount, is taken from your wages to help pay for later benefits; your employer pays in an equal amount.

When you stop working because you retire, or if disability reduces your income prior to retirement, monthly cash payments are made to replace part of your lost earnings. If you should die, your family is entitled to a percentage of those lost earnings and also to a lump-sum payment intended to cover funeral expenses.

**JOBS NOT COVERED** Nine out of ten people work at jobs covered by the Social Security program. Those jobs not covered are certain kinds of family work: a child under 21 working for a parent is not covered; a parent doing household work for a child is sometimes not covered—your local Social Security office can tell you about specific cases. Also, wages paid in kind (for example, room and board) for work in private households or on farms are not covered.

**CREDIT SYSTEM** To qualify for full insurance benefits, you must have Social Security credits for a certain amount of work—that is, you 'must have been paying into Social Security for a certain length of time. You get credit for each three-month period since 1936 (or since you were 21 years old, whichever is later) beginning January, April, July, or October (calendar quarters), in which you were paid $50 or more in cash wages. Four of these quarters make a year of credit.

To claim your maximum benefit you must have one quarter of

15

coverage for, although not necessarily in, each year since 1950 (or since you were 21 years old, whichever is later), up to the year in which you became 62 years old.

Once you reach 10 years (40 quarters) of credit you can relax—you are "fully insured" no matter how little you work after that.

This works out in such a way that to claim full benefits in 1975, you must have six years (24 quarters) of credit; to claim in 1976 you need six years and three months (25 quarters) of credit; and so on up to a maximum of ten years of credit by 1991.

One and a half years (six quarters) of credit, earned within the last three years, are minimum for being "currently insured." If you are currently insured, certain survivors' benefits are payable at your death.

None of these credit quarters needs to be consecutive.

If you were in active military service from 9/16/40 through 12/31/56, you also earned Social Security benefits at a wage credit rate of $160 a month. For military service after 1956, you get a wage credit of $300 a quarter. You can use these credits to qualify for, or to increase, your benefits.

**SOCIAL SECURITY RETIREMENT BENEFITS**   Retirement benefits under Social Security are monthly cash payments paid out as a form of retirement pension. How much you get depends on: your average wages; when you start to collect (at age 62, at age 65, or later); and how much you are earning when you claim. Although the exact figure will be worked out for you by your local Social Security office when you make your claim, the information below will give you a rough idea of what you will have coming.

**Average Earnings**   These are figured as follows:

1. If you were born before 1930, count the number of years since 1956. If you were born after 1929, count the number of years since you reached age 27. Count the starting year and each year up to, but not including, the year of your claim.

2. List your covered earnings, beginning with 1951, as follows:

|        |    |         |     |      |         |      |
|--------|----|---------|-----|------|---------|------|
| up to  |    | $3600   | for | 1951 | through | 1954 |
| "      | "  | 4200    | "   | 1955 | "       | 1958 |
| "      | "  | 4800    | "   | 1959 | "       | 1965 |
| "      | "  | 6600    | "   | 1966 | and     | 1967 |
| "      | "  | 7800    | "   | 1968 | through | 1971 |
| "      | "  | 9000    | "   | 1972 |         |      |
| "      | "  | 10,800  | "   | 1973 |         |      |
| "      | "  | 13,200  | "   | 1974 |         |      |
| "      | "  | 14,000  | "   | 1975 |         |      |

(Since the wage base may increase in coming years, check for changes with your Social Security office.)

3. Cross off the years of lowest earnings until you are left with the same number of years as in (1). Add up the earnings for the years remaining in (3) and divide the answer by the number of years in (1). The answer is your average annual earnings. The amount of your annual earnings will determine how much you get in Social Security benefits.

Because benefits are geared to the cost-of-living index, your benefits may change periodically. But to give you a rough idea of levels of benefit payments: If you had retired at age 65 after June, 1974, and had no other work, you would have received $93.80 a month for an average annual earning of up to $924; $194.10 a month for an average annual earning of $3000; $236.80 a month for $4200 per annum; $278.20 a month for $5400 per annum. At the maximum annual earning of $13,200 you would get $469 a month, but this could not have been earned until 1985 (10 full years of credit at the maximum set in 1974).

**Claiming Before or After Age 65**   If you claim when you are 62 years old, your monthly payments will be 20% lower than your full benefit would have been at age 65, and they will remain 20% lower for the rest of your life. If you claim at age 63, your monthly payments will be 13⅓% lower; at age 64 they will be 6⅔% lower; they will remain at these levels for the rest of your life. In all cases, your dependent spouse or children (see below) would still get 50% of your full benefit, however.

If you delay claiming beyond age 65, your monthly payments when you do claim will be higher about 1% for each year of delay up to age 72.

**Present Earnings**   If after retirement you receive income from interest on savings, stocks and bonds, insurance, private pensions or annuities, rents, capital gains, royalties on works established before age 65, gifts, or inheritances, it will not affect the amount you get from Social Security *provided* you are not getting it by way of present business. For instance, if you are a stockbroker, stock dividends will count as presently earned income; but if you are not employed in stockbrokerage, then stock dividends will not affect your benefits.

Between retirement and age 72, you can earn up to a certain amount of money with no effect on your Social Security payments (see "Earning Limits," below). Above the set amounts, however, your Social Security payments will drop by $1 for every $2 you earn. Once you become 72 years old, you can get full Social Security payments no matter how much you earn.

**Dependents' Benefits**   If your wife (or your husband who is dependent on you for at least half his support) is 65 years old when you claim, he or she will get a benefit equal to 50% of your full benefit (based on your maximum claimed at age 65). Your dependent spouse who begins to collect at age 62 will get 37½% of your full benefit; at age 63, 41⅔% of your full benefit; at age 64, 45⅚% of your full benefit.

No matter what her age, if your wife is caring for an eligible child (see below) who is not collecting student's benefits, she will get 50% of your full benefit.

Your unmarried child under age 18, your full-time student child aged 18 through 21, or your disabled child of any age who was disabled before age 22 will get 50% of your full benefit when you become eligible.

Your dependent grandchild, if both its parents are dead or disabled, will get 50% of your full benefit under certain conditions.

**Survivors' Benefits**   These are monthly payments plus one lump-sum payment made to certain members of your family when you die. A widow or dependent widower who is 65 or older at the time of your death will get the full amount of retirement pension due to you. A widow or dependent widower between 60 and 62 years old when the benefits start will get 71.5% of the due amount; between ages 62 and 65, 82.9%.

A widow who has earned her own Social Security credits should check with the Social Security office to find out whether she will receive more money by claiming her own benefits or by claiming her husband's survivors' benefits.

A widow or widower who is disabled can start collecting on her or his deceased spouse's benefits at age 50, but the amount she or he gets will be permanently reduced.

No matter what her age, a widow or divorced wife who is looking after an eligible child (see "Dependents' Benefits," above) will get 75% of the basic amount unless the child is already collecting student's benefits. (This particular benefit may eventually be extended to cover widowers in like positions.)

If a widow remarries after age 60 or if a widower remarries after age 62, they will get 50% of the due amount.

A divorced widow may be entitled to payments under certain other conditions besides caring for an eligible child.

Unmarried children will get 75% of the due amount if they qualify under "Dependents' Benefits," above.

Your grandchildren may also get payments under certain conditions, usually if they were dependent on you for support.

Your parents, if they are over 61 years old and were at least 50% dependent on you for support, will also be entitled to payments. One surviving parent would get 82.5% of your due amount; two surviving parents would get 75% of your due amount each.

**Note** A maximum amount is allowed to a family each month. Therefore, if total payments would exceed this (as may a widow's with two dependent children), they will be reduced to fall within the limits.

Besides the monthly survivors' payments, there is a lump-sum payment called the death benefit. It is equal to three times your monthly benefit amount up to a certain maximum. It is paid (a) to a widow or widower living with the worker at the time of death; or (b) to whoever pays the funeral expenses; or (c) directly to the funeral home.

**SOCIAL SECURITY DISABILITY BENEFITS** These are monthly cash payments made to you should you develop a disability so severe as to stop you from working (earning a living) and which has lasted or will last for at least twelve months. Payments start in the sixth full month of the disability and continue for as long as you are disabled. You get the same amount as you would get at retirement at age 65, and when you reach age 65 the payment is converted to a retirement pension with no change in the amount.

If you are over 30 years of age when you are disabled, you must be fully insured and have at least five years (20 quarters) of credit during the previous ten years to qualify for payments. But if you were disabled before age 31, you'll have to check with the Social Security office because the requirements are different.

Your wife or dependents are eligible under the same conditions as those of a retired worker (see above). Disabled widows, dependent widowers, and divorced wives between ages 50 and 62 are eligible for payments between 50% and 82.9% of the due amount.

Anyone applying for disability benefits may be referred to his state rehabilitation agency for possible help with the disability.

**SELF-EMPLOYED PEOPLE** Almost all self-employed people are covered by the Social Security program.

Self-employed people pay a certain percentage of net earnings, up to the same maximum as the current wage base, as Social Security taxes. (The percentage is slightly higher than that taken from an employed person's earnings.) Earnings less than a certain minimum, investment income, and real-estate rentals which are not from your business are not taxed for Social Security.

If you also earn a salary, the taxable maximum remains the same, and your salary is taxed for Social Security before your self-employment income is taxed.

**MAKING CLAIMS**  To get Social Security payments, you must apply for them. The easiest way is to go to your Social Security office, taking with you: your Social Security card (or at least your Social Security number); your federal income tax withholding statement (Form W-2) for the preceding year; and proof of your age (birth certificate, passport, etc.). If you cannot get to the Social Security office, call them up and explain your difficulty and they will arrange to visit you.

**EARNINGS LIMITS**  If you are collecting Social Security benefits, until you are 72 years old there are strict limits on how much you can earn at a job or in self-employment without having payments reduced. Earnings are defined as wages and salaries; they do not include interest on bank accounts, dividends, gifts, inheritances, other pensions, insurance, annuities, capital gains, rents, or veteran's benefits.

Because the amount you are allowed to earn will increase with each automatic increase in Social Security benefits (an increase which is tied to the cost-of-living index), you'll have to check with your Social Security office for the latest limit. However, despite increases, the limit remains low—in 1972, for instance, you were allowed to earn only $2100 before penalties started; by 1974, this had increased to only $2400. If you earn above the prescribed limit in a calendar year, you will lose $1 of Social Security for every $2 above the limit that you earn.

But no matter what your total annual earnings are, if you earn less than a certain fixed sum (one twelfth of the annual limit for that year, therefore $200 in 1974) in any calendar month, you are entitled to your full Social Security benefit for that month. Thus, if you work spasmodically or seasonally, you are entitled to full benefits for those months during which you earned less than the set monthly limit.

For instance, say that in 1974 you work for a concessionaire at a holiday resort, earning $1000 a month for six months, while for the other six months you earn nothing. In this case you are entitled to full benefits for the six months when you didn't work—even though your total earnings for the year were $6000, or $3600 above the limit in 1974. At the rate of $1 deducted for every $2 earned, your excess earnings for the year total $1800; but this is deductible only from your benefits for the six months that you worked. If your benefits are, say, $195 a month, or only $1170 for all six months during which you worked, you are left with $630 (the difference between your $1170 in benefits and $1800 in excess earnings). This $630 cannot be charged against benefits for the six months in which you earned under $200 (in 1974), nor can it be carried over as charges into the following year. Thus, if you earn considerably more than the limit, you sacrifice less by working for fewer than twelve months of the year. (If your excess earnings had been less than $1170—$1000, say, this would have been charged against full benefits for your first five working months, and $25 against the sixth month, with no overage.)

In addition, for the six months in which you received no benefits because of earnings, your benefit amount is increased by $\frac{6}{12}$ of 1% —$\frac{1}{12}$ of 1% for every month you worked.

If you know that you will earn, in year-round work, more than the annual limit, you should work out just what you expect to earn during the coming year (or for the rest of the current year) and report it to your Social Security office. The Social Security service will then withhold payments in accordance with your estimates. If, at the end of the year, you find that you earned more than you thought you would, you will have to pay back the Social Security overage. If you earned less, you will get a check for the amount owed to you.

If your spouse or child collects Social Security benefits in his or her own right, the same limitations on earnings apply. If either gets Social Security benefits on the basis of your right, then your earnings will affect the amount received by the whole family.

You will be contributing to Social Security, whether or not you are also collecting it, if you are working at a job covered by Social Security. Periodically you should have your benefit amount re-estimated, particularly if you stop working altogether, since you may have earned the right to higher Social Security payments during the period in which you worked after retirement.

If you are self-employed, after retirement age your right to Social Security is determined on the basis of your involvement with your business rather than on how much you earn. You cannot get Social Security if you are "performing substantial services" in a trade, business, or profession. What constitutes "substantial services" depends on how much time you devote to your business, the kind of services you perform, how your services compare with those you performed in past years, and other circumstances in your particular case. The rule of thumb used is a limit of 45 hours a month, below which you are usually not considered to have rendered substantial services. But this can be lowered drastically if the total hours required for complete management of the business (or completion of the work) are normally less. Every case is decided on its own merits.

At age 72 you are entitled to your full Social Security benefits no matter how much you are earning.

## SOCIAL SECURITY INCOME (SSI)

This program provides a national minimum (albeit minimal) income for people who are over 64 years old or blind or disabled, and who have little or no income and limited resources. SSI replaces previous state public-assistance plans (where payments under the state plans were higher than SSI payments, the state makes up the difference so that no one suffers income reduction because of the new program). SSI is administered by the Social Security Administration, although it is funded by the federal government with supplements by the state governments, and not through Social Security contributions.

In assessing eligibility, certain limits are set on the amount of income and assets you may have, and certain types of income and assets are not counted in the assessment. The figures below were correct as we went to press, but your local Social Security office—where you must apply for SSI—can inform you of any recent changes.

**INCOME**   In 1974, the first $20 a month of income from any source and the first $65 a month of earned income did not affect payment; half of your earnings above $65 a month did not count, either. Work expenses of blind people and income for a federally approved self-support plan for a blind or disabled person do not count.

Income from Social Security benefits, veterans' compensation, workman's compensation, pensions, annuities, gifts, and other general sources reduce SSI payments (if they totaled above $20 a month in 1974).

**ASSETS**   A single person can own assets of up to a certain value ($1500 in 1974) and still be eligible; a couple can own more ($2250 in 1974). A home up to a certain value ($25,000 in 1974, except for Alaska and Hawaii, where the limit is $35,000) does not count. Personal effects up to a certain value ($1500 in 1974) do not count. Insurance policies up to a certain total face value ($1500 per person in 1974) do not count; above that face value, the cash surrender value counts. The retail value of a car, over a certain minimum ($1200 in 1974), counts unless you use it to get to a job or regular medical treatment.

## *VETERANS' BENEFITS*

If you served in World War I, World War II, the Korean War, or after January 31, 1955, you are a war veteran so far as Veterans Administration pensions are concerned.

As a war veteran, if you are over 64 and have an income below a certain fixed level (which is higher if you have dependents), you may very well qualify for a 90% disability pension from the VA (you may also qualify for the additional 10% if you really try). This is because VA assumes that anyone over 64 who is retired from full-time work is by definition disabled. (Disablement stemming from illness or injury, whether incurred during service or not, will entitle you to payments at any age if it prevents you from working and if your income is below the limits.)

If you do qualify, at your death your widow may be entitled to roughly two thirds of the amount of your benefit, depending on her financial situation at your death.

All private income plus 90% of Social Security benefits count in assessing your income; welfare aid and other VA benefits do not count.

This is certainly not to be shrugged off as a supplement to your other income; and if you think you may qualify, by all means get in touch with your local VA office.

Many state governments give special benefits to war veterans and their families. What is available differs from state to state, but property-tax exemptions are among the most frequent type.

VA benefits are also available for medical care, equipment, supplies, and drugs as well as for hospital care, outpatient care, and housebound care. If you need any of these, inquire at your local VA hospital or office to find out if you are eligible.

## *PRIVATE PENSION PLANS*

Private pension plans vary so much that they cannot be easily analyzed. Therefore what follows is a general discussion about possible types of plans and what you should know about them. For more detailed information, consult *You and Your Pension* by Ralph Nader and Kate Blackwell (Grossman Publishers, New York, 1973).

**WHO IS COVERED**  By 1970 about 55% of nonagricultural workers were employed in private industries that offered employees either private pension plans or deferred profit-sharing plans. Unfortunately, some 40% of these employees were not participating in the plans, mostly because they were short-term workers and therefore not eligible. Some were excluded for other reasons. As a result, of people retiring from private industry in late 1969, only one quarter of the married couples, one sixth of the single men, and one eighth of the single women were receiving a private pension.

If your work is in trade, services, or construction you are less likely to be covered by a private pension plan than if you work in mining or manufacturing. You are also less likely to be covered if you work for a small nonunionized firm than if you work for one of the large industries or for a small unionized firm that participates in one of the multiemployer pension plans. These last are most prevalent in the garment, construction, trucking, and mining industries.

In an attempt to widen eligibility, the private pension bill passed in September 1974 requires that existing and new pension plans be open to all workers over the age of 25 who have at least one year's service. But if you leave your job before your retirement, you will be entitled to accrued benefits only if you have fulfilled the conditions for vesting (age and length of service) set out in the plan.

**VESTING**   Under the 1974 bill, all pension plans must minimally meet one of three vesting standards: a worker is entitled to (a) 100% of his benefits after 10 years of service; or (b) 15% of his benefits after five years of service, increasing to 100% after 15 years; or (c) 50% of his benefits when his age plus his years of service equal 45, increasing to 100% over the next five years.

**HOW MUCH YOU GET**   This varies widely, but in general a blue-collar worker's benefit is a fixed sum and a white-collar worker's is a percentage (often 1½%) of his annual pay multiplied by the number of years he has worked under the pension plan. The resultant pensions range from well under one thousand to several thousand dollars a year, but the median is only about $1500 for 20 years of service, and not even $2000 for 30 years' service. This means that you may be able to count on only between 15% and 25% of your preretirement income.

**PORTABILITY**   A pension plan may be confined to one firm, to one region of the country, to one industry, or to a group of firms participating in what is called a multiemployer plan. But sometimes a plan is "portable"—that is, if you change employers, your pension credits go with you to your next job. This most often occurs within a union or within an industry in a certain area. Under the 1974 private pension bill, portability remains voluntary and is therefore unlikely to increase.

**FUNDING** Nearly all private pension plans are paid mostly or wholly by the employer and they can be regarded as deferred wages. About one quarter of private pension plans are partially paid by the employees and about 1% are totally paid by employees.

Some plans pay benefits out of a fund set aside for the purpose; this fund rarely has enough money in it to cover all pension benefits due to all employees at any one time. Other plans pay pensions out of the employer's current operating expenses.

Until the 1974 private pension bill, the employer was liable only up to the amount of money in the fund, if there was one (if the till ran dry, you might not get your pension). If the plan was unfunded, financial difficulties in the firm could reduce or halt payments.

The 1974 bill makes the firm fully liable for all vested benefits and makes certain levels of funding obligatory. To protect participants against loss of benefits if their plan is terminated, the bill established a pension benefit guarantee corporation. This is financed by premiums from firms with pension plans and is set up in the Department of Labor.

**WHAT YOU SHOULD KNOW** If you work for a company with a pension plan, it will pay you to get as much information as you can right away. The 1974 bill requires that all participants receive a description of their pension plan, and you should examine this closely for special conditions and to determine your benefit rates.

You should find out how the pension amount is calculated. Is it a fixed sum or is it geared to salary? If the latter, is it based on your pay rate over the last several years, during the highest year(s), or over the whole period of work? Is it affected by your age when you retire?

You may be able to increase benefit payments by opting to increase your contributions if you are in an employee-contributing plan; this is a useful form of forced savings if you are over 50 and if the plan is safe.

What are the vesting provisions (see above)?

How can you lose benefit rights? If you change union locals? If you work in the same trade or profession after retirement?

Is the plan portable at all and, if so, between which agreeing industries or unions? In what areas?

Does the plan have survivors' benefits for spouses? This might be an optional clause which you must activate yourself, and it might mean taking a cut in benefits during your lifetime. Sometimes you can increase the amount of survivor benefits by increasing your own contributions. Under the 1974 bill, a widow gets nothing if her husband dies in his late 50's. She gets 50% if he dies during retirement —if the plan has an activated survivor clause.

**RETIREMENT SAVINGS PLANS**   If you are a worker not covered by a pension plan, you can set up a retirement savings account of your own. You may set aside any amount, of course, but you can get tax deductions on the account only up to 15% of your annual income, to a maximum of $1500. The plan must be specially registered as such (ask your bank how to do this) and you cannot draw on it before retirement, although you can stop paying into it at any time.

Self-employed people can set up similar retirement plans on which they can get tax deductions of 15% of earnings, to a maximum of $7500.

# 3
# Annuities and Investments

This chapter will deal with income from the assets shown in the first part of the income side of the Budget Sheet on page 43. It also covers income from those pensions in the second part of the income side of the Budget Sheet which were not included in Chapter 2.

## ANNUITIES

Unlike life insurance, which is intended to benefit your survivors when you are dead, an annuity is a form of insurance which benefits you while you are living. For a sum of money you buy a guaranteed monthly income which starts on a certain date and, with some special exceptions, ends when you die. Annuities that end with your death are called "straight life annuities."

The date that the annuity starts is arranged between you and its seller. The date may be deferred and may be the date of your retirement or the day you reach a certain age. You can also buy an *immediate* annuity, starting, say, one month or one year from the date that you paid for it. You pay for an immediate annuity in a lump sum. You pay for deferred annuities in premiums over the number of years of deferment.

The prices for annuities are based on actuarial tables, which forecast the life expectancy of men and women of various ages. The older you are when the payments to you start, the lower your life expectancy on the tables and the cheaper the annuity, since the seller will expect to pay you for a shorter time. Because women live an average of five years longer than men, annuity prices for women are higher—an annuity for a woman of 65 will cost approximately the same as that for a man of 60.

If you live longer than your invested sum would last, you are guaranteed the set income anyway. If you live less than the expected time, the annuity company does not reimburse your heirs. Thus, unlike life insurance, an annuity does not require you to be healthy to qualify—rather the reverse, in fact.

**JOINT-AND-SURVIVOR ANNUITIES**   If you want to arrange for survivors' benefits, you can buy "joint-and-survivor annuities" rather than the cheaper straight life annuities. In the most expensive kind, your survivor gets the same amount per month as you were getting during your life. A somewhat less expensive form—a reduced survivor annuity—gives your survivor, say, one half or two thirds of the amount you were getting. Usually you would buy a joint-and-survivor annuity for a spouse or dependent close to your own age, since one for much younger dependents (such as children) would be costly.

**REFUND ANNUITIES**   For a higher price again, you can arrange for a "refund annuity," in which, if you die before your investment is all paid back to you, the remainder will be paid to your beneficiary —either in continued monthly payments or in a lump sum.

**CERTAIN-PERIOD ANNUITIES**   Another expensive kind of annuity is the "certain-period" one, in which the annuity company guarantees payments for a certain number of years whether or not you live for the whole period. If you live longer than the stipulated period, payments continue until your death. If you die before the period is up, payments continue to your beneficiaries for the certain period. The certain period can be anything from five years on up; the longer the period, the higher the cost.

**DISADVANTAGES**   The big drawback of annuities is their fixed-income aspect. Inflation has been fairly continuous for most of this century, and in all likelihood it will accelerate. Therefore, the income you get will provide less and less purchasing power. If you start buying the annuity with premium payments years ahead of the date the annuity will start, the dollars you pay now will most likely be worth much less when you get them back. This means that the income you have planned to get from the annuity may prove inadequate, however sufficient it looked when it was planned.

A deferred annuity is cheaper than an immediate annuity, but you will probably be better off if you put the annuity money into a savings account, where it will accrue interest until you actually need the income; then you can buy an immediate annuity. The money will earn higher interest in the savings account than in the annuity company account.

**VARIABLE ANNUITIES—A SOLUTION?** One way to over-come the problem of the fixed income of annuities is to buy "variable annuities." Here the annuity company invests your premium pay-ments in stocks, the returns from which fluctuate with the stock market. Your income, based on a percentage of the yearly investment value, will then increase with upward trends of the market and de-crease with downward trends. Stock prices generally rise during in-flation, but this does not always happen, and they might lag behind an increase in the cost of living, thus removing the variable-annuity advantage.

**WHO SELLS ANNUITIES?** Insurance companies are the com-monest sellers of annuities. Their rates vary considerably, and you would do well to shop around. Savings banks are another source, usually at lower rates than an insurance company's since they employ no salesmen. Some professional, business, and trade associations and societies offer group annuities to their members, usually at the lowest rates of all; if you are a member of such a group, by all means ask if they have an annuity policy.

**LIFE INSURANCE AND ANNUITIES** It is sometimes possible to convert all or part of a life-insurance policy into an annuity plan. In effect, you take the cash value of your insurance policy, or part of it, and reinvest it as an annuity payment.

Whether you want to do this will depend on the needs of your life-insurance beneficiary compared to your own needs during your life. It is certainly worth considering if your retirement income is unman-ageably low. If you must provide for a beneficiary, a joint-and-sur-vivor type of annuity can benefit you both.

Some life-insurance policies are combination contracts. For a high premium your beneficiary is guaranteed an immediate cash benefit. If you live, you yourself will receive a monthly income beginning at an agreed date—usually when you become 65 years old. You no longer pay premiums and you may, in certain contracts, be covered for death benefits for a few years after the monthly income begins.

## INVESTMENTS

If you are not yet retired and have some cash put to one side, you might consider investments. While you are still earning money you can afford to speculate a little with your savings. After all, during

money-earning years you can recoup losses by trimming your expenditures or putting in some extra hours of work.

For most people, retirement removes the trimming margin and also
the easy access to work. Savings then become a cushion in an emergency rather than money you can risk. If large enough, however, your
savings can earn you additional income through interest or dividends.

On the whole, if you are nearing retirement, it is better to be conservative about your savings, although you should certainly examine
what you might do with your cash to increase capital and income.
If you are investing the money in anything but a savings account (in
the stock market or real estate, say) it is wise to diversify the investment as much as possible so as to protect yourself against loss.

Do not let yourself be talked into such investments by any door-
to-door salesman; find a reputable stockbroker or mutual fund, or
consult your bank's investment counselors.

**SAVINGS ACCOUNTS**   The most convenient thing to do with
cash savings (apart from shoving them under the floorboard, where
the mice may get them and inflation certainly will) is to put them
into a savings account at a commercial bank, savings bank, savings-
and-loan association, or credit union.

**Commercial Banks**   These offer, besides savings accounts, such
services as checking accounts, personal loans, travelers' checks, safety-
deposit boxes, and sometimes investment and trust services. This
makes them very convenient since you can transact most of your financial business in one place.

Nine out of ten commercial banks are insured in amounts up to
$40,000 per depositor by the Federal Deposit Insurance Corporation,
a government insurance agency, so your money is perfectly safe.

The savings accounts with the highest rates of interest are those in
which you agree to leave your money untouched for a period of several years. You can get it out before the time is up, but then you
forfeit the higher rate of interest. A passbook savings account earns
less interest but the money is available to you at any time. In these
accounts the way that the bank computes the interest is important:
the best method is from day of deposit to day of withdrawal; the
worst method is that based on the lowest amount of deposit in the
account for the given term.

**Savings Banks**   These are mutual companies; that is, they have
no stockholders, being operated for the benefit of their depositors.
However, savings-bank depositors have no hand in management.
Savings banks are permitted in only eighteen states (mostly northeastern and middle Atlantic) and may be chartered either by the

state or the federal government. Like commercial banks, most are insured, some by the Federal Deposit Insurance Corporation, some by state insurance plans, for up to $40,000 per depositor.

Savings banks do not offer checking accounts (although an equivalent is being attempted in a few) but they do offer most of the other services to be found in a commercial bank plus mortgage loans and, in some states, life-insurance policies. Their branches are not so widespread as those of the large commercial banks; although you can usually make deposits by mail, withdrawals and other types of transactions may not be so convenient. Money in passbook accounts in mutual savings banks is as readily available as in commercial savings-bank accounts, and dividends (that is, returns paid to owners as opposed to interest paid to creditors) are usually higher.

**Savings-and-Loan Associations**   Also known as building-and-loan associations, these are cooperative banks or homestead associations. They, too, are mutual companies which are either federally or state chartered, and therefore they, too, pay dividends as opposed to interest. In many associations, depositors and borrowers have a vote in board of directors' elections.

About 70% of savings-and-loan associations are insured up to $40,000 per depositor. With the exception of checking accounts, many offer services similar to those of commercial banks. However, they tend to be local institutions and their loans are normally limited geographically. It is often possible to make savings deposits by mail, however, and you may be able to find higher dividend rates than you would in a nearby bank.

Passbook savings accounts are usually available, but in some you must give advance notice to make a withdrawal, and dividends are credited to the account. Investment savings accounts may require a minimum balance, often about $5,000 for a minimum period, and they pay dividends directly to the depositor.

Dividend rates on savings-and-loan association accounts run with the mortgage interest rates, because 95% of investments by the associations are in home mortgages. Thus rates nowadays tend to be quite high compared with those of commercial and savings banks.

**Credit Unions**   These are cooperative associations formed among people with some common interest—a trade union or a fraternal order, for instance. They are not insured and rely for safety mostly on the facts that their funds are used as loans to members, and members are also shareholders. Withdrawals are not so readily made as in the accounts already discussed, and a depositor may have to wait for funds to become available.

Credit unions offer loans, life insurance, and financial counseling, as well as savings accounts. Dividend rates tend to be high because funds are chiefly invested in high-rate consumer loans, and also because the credit unions are nonprofit organizations. However, since most have been formed since 1929, their safety in a real economic depression has not yet been tested. Therefore you should probably limit the proportion of your savings that you put into a credit-union account.

**GOVERNMENT BONDS   Series E**   You buy these at a percentage of face value, hold them for a certain number of years, and then cash them in (to the U. S. government only) for the full face value. You get the accrued interest only when you cash them in. You can hold on to your Series E bonds for a certain number of years beyond the maturity date at the same interest rate. If you cash them in before they mature, you get the purchase price plus accrued interest.

Denominations of from $25 up to $10,000 are available; they can often be bought through payroll or checking-account deductions, a fact which makes them an easy method of saving. Their yield is somewhat less than other types of savings investments but their safety factor is high and they are readily redeemed at most financial institutions.

Waiting to cash them until after you are 65 will probably save you at least part of the capital-gains tax to which you might be liable before 65.

**Series H**   These you purchase at face value, and interest is paid to you every six months. They are available only in denominations of $500, $1000, $5000, and $10,000. Maturity is reached after a certain number of years, at which point and for a certain number of optional years after, they yield about the same interest rate as do Series E bonds. Series H bonds can be redeemed after the first six months on one month's written notice. They are just as safe an investment as Series E.

**STOCK-MARKET INVESTMENT**   Investing in the stock market comes under the heading "Risky Ventures." You should undertake it only if you can afford to keep capital tied up during downtrends and if you are not absolutely dependent on that capital for an income.

If you have a few hundred dollars to spare, then you can spend many an amusing hour on the stock exchange, buying and selling with the best of them. If you get a lucky break, you will increase your capital. As much might be said for the races. If your emotional makeup is going to get you frenzied or plunged into despair with each roller-coaster swoop of the market, stay out of it. Even if you invest in a comparatively safe stock, you must be able to ride out downtrends, which can continue for years; if, for lack of capital, you are forced to sell during a down period, you stand to lose a lot.

If you do invest in the stock market, common stocks and bonds are the most straightforward kinds of investment. You can protect your investment by buying stock in very stable companies whose history is of a steady upward trend. Such stocks usually pay lower dividends, of course; they have tended to be about the same as a savings bank's, but in a blue-chip stock your capital investment itself appreciates over the years.

**Mutual Funds** Unless you have a large sum to invest you can buy stock only in two or three companies. One way to get more variation, so that a downtrend in a few companies has a better chance of being balanced by uptrends in others, is to invest in mutual funds. There are many kinds of mutual funds but, basically, you hand your money to a mutual-fund organization, which pools it with that of other investors and buys a variety of stocks and bonds. Investors receive dividends and capital gains in accordance with their percentage of the total investment.

The drawback of mutual funds is the high commission you pay the investment dealers when you purchase fund shares—usually over 7% of your investment as opposed to the less than 2% charged by an ordinary stockbroker for buying and selling stock. What you are getting for this commission is expert advice and handling of your investment; also, you usually pay no fee for cashing stock in, as you would with a broker.

**REAL ESTATE** Investment in real estate tends, with careful choice, to be relatively stable and to give high returns. However, you will be tying up a large sum of money in a form not readily liquified.

You can invest by buying unimproved land in or near a growing community. You can then hold onto it until you are offered a purchase price which ensures a good margin of profit. Alternatively, if you have extra capital that you want to invest, you can build on the land and sell it at a profit over your total costs.

In both these cases you must make very sure that the land has no bar to the kind of development upon which value increases depend— it is useless, for instance, to buy land with an eye to its industrial-development possibilities if it is in a restricted zone. The longer you hold land which is not paying you any income, the more you will lose in taxes and interest (the interest your investment would be accruing in a savings account). Try to buy land which will shortly be in demand—rural acreage is a much longer term investment.

Many factors enter into your choice of land: proximity to highways or main streets, accessibility of services, length of road frontage, type of land (rocky, hilly, forested) and its effect on development costs, and many others. Land suitable for residential development is the least risky investment; commercially and industrially zoned land is high risk, although you stand to make high profits, too.

If you are willing to invest time and effort as well as money, you can buy a residential property (a house is a surer bet and less demanding than multiple residences) in need of improvement, make the improvements yourself—choosing those which will most enhance value—and then resell at a profit as quickly as possible. Many people do this constantly, living in the property while they are making the improvements to save investment capital—but you must like moving!

You might consider buying a multiple residence (a two- or three-family house or a small apartment building, for instance), making the necessary improvements, and renting out the apartments at prices which will cover your outlay (for both improvements and continuing expenses such as taxes, repairs, maintenance, and landscaping) and leave you enough gross profit to pay for your supervisory services (and then some, if you can manage it). This kind of investment can give you good return if your choice of site is suitable and if you keep your management duties within tolerable limits.

Unless you are very experienced in the real-estate market, you should consult a real-estate broker in hunting for suitable property. However, remember that he gets his commission from the seller, not from you, and is more likely to act in the seller's interest.

# 4
# Other Assets

Besides income from the resources shown on the left-hand side of the chart on page 43 (Social Security benefits, pensions, annuities, savings, investments, and others), you probably own certain goods and rights which you may want to convert to cash.

## *IF YOU OWN YOUR HOUSE*

Whether or not your mortgage is paid up, retirement is an excellent time to reevaluate your living quarters. Perhaps your house is too big for you. Or perhaps you live where you do because it was necessary for your job; retirement will free you to move to a better climate, a less expensive area, a more congenial environment. You will find a full discussion of your housing alternatives in Section II ("Living Where You Like"); here we will consider how your present home might be used to increase your capital or income, or both.

**MORTGAGE BURDEN**   If you still have a mortgage, the chances are that it has only a few years left to run. With the drastically limited income of retirement, the payments probably are going to become a large percentage of your expenses. To avoid this burden, you might consider paying off the mortgage right away. You should, of course, try to arrange your finances so that you have some ready cash to fall back on, but any cash over and above this would probably be best put to use by paying off the mortgage—the interest you are paying on it is generally much greater than any interest your savings might be earning in a bank account or other investments. If you should need money at some future date, you could take out a short-term loan with the deed of your fully owned house as collateral; as a last resort, you could even take out another mortgage on it. Also, should you decide to sell your house later on, you can yourself accept a mortgage from the buyer and assure yourself of a high-interest steady income from the mortgage payments to you.

**SELLING YOUR HOUSE** Doing this after you reach age 65 will probably save you at least part of a capital-gains tax for which you would be fully liable before age 65. If you buy a smaller house or an apartment, the difference between the two prices can then be invested.

If you prefer to drop the responsibilities of ownership, you could rent a smaller place. You will have to allow yourself extra income to cover rent payments, remembering to offset against this your old allowance for repairs, taxes, and municipal services, which are probably included in the rent.

**CONVERTING YOUR HOUSE** If you cannot get a good enough selling price or if you want to hang onto your house because you like it there, consider converting it into two or more self-contained apartments, keeping one for yourself and renting the remainder. Much depends on what conversion would cost vs. what rent you could expect to get; and you would have to take on the duties and obligations of a landlord as well as the benefit of rent. But you would have a steady income, which, unlike the payments from mortgage arrangements, could be increased to keep pace with inflation. You would set the rent to cover the upkeep for the entire property, plus your salary for managing the rented parts. (You would also have an immediate neighbor for company and/or help when necessary.)

A large garage, barn, or other outbuilding may offer similar possibilities.

## WHAT ELSE DO YOU OWN?

**IF YOU OWN A MOBILE HOME** You can arrange short-term or seasonal rentals of your house while you travel rent-free in your trailer home.

**IF YOU OWN A VACATION COTTAGE** Consider staying in your vacation home for long stretches of time while renting your permanent home, or renting the cottage when you are living in your permanent home. Possibly the cottage could be converted for your permanent use, enabling you to sell your home.

If you seldom use your vacation cottage, consider selling it or renting it full-time. The shorter the period for which you rent it, the more rent you can charge. However, short-term rentals increase the work and attention you will have to give the place, since each tenant turnover must be supervised; you also run a higher risk of vandalism, and repairs will be more frequent.

**IF YOU OWN LAND** Most land accrues value steadily over the years, and you might realize a good profit if you sell now after a long period of ownership. Or, if it is suitable, you could rent it out as a campsite. Or you could build on it and rent or sell the improved land. This last possibility has been discussed more fully in Chapter 3.

**IF YOU OWN A CAR** If you own two cars you are less likely to need a second car once both you and your spouse are at home. So you can sell either your less favorite or the one for which you can get the most money.

If and when you need another car (once the current rattletrap has fallen to pieces) you might stick to a decent secondhand one; it's a much lower capital outlay and, often enough, no more trouble in upkeep.

If you live in the city or town center, or if public transport is available for your regular needs, you probably don't need a car at all unless you are given to frequent trips to the country. For occasional use it works out more cheaply to rent a car. (Public transport is often available at cheap rates for older people.)

**IF YOU OWN A BOAT** Think hard about whether or how much you'll really be using it. If you've been looking forward for years to taking off in it, then of course you will keep it and take off. But if that doesn't work out, or if you must honestly admit that the use and/or pleasure you get from it is minimal, talk yourself into selling it. If you have been using your boat chiefly for fishing, you might find it cheaper to join charter groups or to use rented boats when the weather is good than to keep your own boat year-round. This is especially true if you live in the north.

**IF YOU HOLD INSURANCE POLICIES** Investigate the fine print. Some life-insurance policies ("term" policies) provide for continuing premium payments until death, and these might be burdensome if your retirement income is low. Others are limited-payment policies—after you've paid premiums for a specified number of years, you have a paid-up policy. Still others are endowment policies which pay a certain sum of money after a specific number of years of premium payments.

As life-insurance policies are good collateral for loans from the insurance company, you may want to keep yours intact as a safeguard against an emergency. Otherwise, you might reconsider whether you need your life insurance in its present form.

You probably took out life insurance during your working life to protect your wife and young children against sudden loss of your income, their chief means of economic support. By the time you reach retirement age, your wife is probably eligible (or almost) for Social Security benefits and your children are, with luck, earning their own incomes. Their needs, therefore, are no longer so great. You should still be concerned about your wife, perhaps, because Social Security is miserably small to manage on. But you might be able to arrange for a joint-and-survivor annuity (see Chapter 3) which will supplement her income after your death, or yours after her death.

Lifetime-payment policies can often be converted to paid-up policies at retirement so that premium payments cease while the insurance continues, although carrying a smaller benefit than was originally agreed upon. Paid-up, limited-payment, and endowment policies can usually be converted to paid-up annuities if you want to buy a retirement income.

Social Security does pay a death benefit intended to cover funeral expenses. You should read Nancy Mitford's book *The American Way of Death* on American funeral practices. If you still want anything but a pauper's funeral after that, then arrange to keep enough of your life insurance to be paid at your death to cover funeral expenses.

**MISCELLANEOUS**   Consider all that elaborate camping equipment you haven't unpacked in years. What about the skis and ski gear stored away and forgotten? Remember when you used to collect stamps (brass keys, Chinese boxes, miniatures, dirty books)? Check out all of your miscellaneous collections and equipment and decide whether you want to engage in these activities again. Or could you happily sell your paraphernalia and bank the proceeds?

# 5
# Where the Money Goes

Outgoing payments—both regular and onetime—are summarized on the right-hand side of the Budget Sheet on page 42; here we will consider them in detail. The main categories of expenditures are housing, food, clothing, transport, medical care, and a catch-all category that we call personal expenses.

Some expenditures (insurance and taxes, for instance) involve regular and consistent amounts of money which can be easily budgeted. Others (such as food) are more variable but just as inevitable. Still others (such as gifts) are often difficult to avoid but can be dispensed with temporarily when things get tight.

The best approach to setting up a budget is to ferret out all your regular bills, total them up over a year, and divide by 12 to reach a monthly average. Food, clothing, and such miscellaneous expenditures as those for personal items are more difficult to estimate unless you have kept receipts over a reasonably long period. For these expenditures, keep a notebook for several months, jotting down each payment as you make it under an appropriate heading. At the end of four or six months you can get a monthly average for each kind of item, leaving out of your accounting total any extraordinary purchases (such as a new mink coat). A year's expenses would give you a more accurate figure, of course, but would be more of a nuisance to keep up. This note-taking will give you some clues about where all that money keeps disappearing to—but don't bank on being able to stem the flow.

Medical expenses can't be got at in this way because they usually crop up spasmodically. The best way to figure them out is to look back over your income-tax records (supposing them to have been accurate!) and see what your annual averages have been; then you can arrive at a sum to put aside each month for expenses to come.

If you have not yet retired, you will have to adjust some of your estimates based on current expenditure—some present expenses (travel to work, business or working clothes, restaurant lunches) will no longer exist. But new ones may arise. If you intend to satisfy your long-suppressed urge to travel, you will need a totally new kind of budgeting. Study courses will cost some money, if only for books and working materials. Section III will give you a good idea of other possibilities.

## HOUSING

According to the Bureau of Labor Statistics, you can expect to spend something like 40% of your annual budget on overall housing costs if you are a couple managing on a low or moderate income.

**RENT OR MORTGAGE**   These payments are easy enough to budget for, being regular monthly amounts.

**PROPERTY TAXES**   These are usually included in the total mortgage payment; if your mortgage is paid up, you have an annual or quarterly tax bill to allow for. Your state may have special property-tax concessions for people over 65 and for war veterans; check with your local tax office about this. Divide the annual figure by 12 and put this down on the Budget Sheet.

If your mortgage is paid for, incidentally, you can reckon that keeping up your house will be 15% to 20% less expensive than renting a small apartment (except in the northeast, where the difference is less).

**PROPERTY INSURANCE**   This includes insurance for fire, theft, personal liability, etc., which are often in the form of a comprehensive homeowner's policy, with a premium paid either quarterly or annually —so again you'll have to divide by 12 to get the monthly sum for these.

**FUEL BILLS**   Since fuel bills are higher in the winter, you should average out your annual cost over the whole 12 months so that you can put enough aside throughout the year and not be swamped by an unbalanced winter budget.

**Cutting Fuel Costs**   Double-glazed storm windows and doors keep in a lot more heat than do single-glazed ones; heavy curtains over them on winter nights prevent additional heat loss. On sunny days, keep the curtains back so that you get as much heat as a winter sun will provide—which is actually quite a bit if you have a lot of windows. If windows are loose, insulate them with weather stripping or caulking rope (the latter is very easy to apply and is removable in the summer, when you should get the windows tightened up permanently, if possible). Tack weather stripping around loose doors.

Rugs on tile or stone floors will probably help to keep you from shoving the thermostat up a notch or two on a chilly night. Roof and attic insulation are important in preventing heat loss. Close the dampers of fireplaces not in use.

If you have radiators, make sure they have adjustable valves; each season, before you turn on the heat, drain the valves so that the radiators can heat up properly. Move away anything that blocks heat circulation. A reflective surface (aluminum foil will do) against the wall behind the radiators will reflect heat out into the room instead of wasting it in the wall.

Hot-water pipes, steam pipes, and hot-air ducts near outer walls should be insulated.

If some rooms are not in use, close them off from the rest of the house and turn down the heat in them if you have room controls.

It is less wasteful of fuel to arrive at a constant day and evening temperature at which you can be comfortable rather than to keep altering the thermostat because you're too hot or too cold. If you are going to be away from the house for more than 24 hours, however, turn the thermostat down to about 55° F. for the period of your absence.

The thermostat should be placed in a central location so that it will register an average heat for the house. It is cheaper to live at lower temperatures, wear warm clothes, and keep moving than it is to lounge around in cotton clothes with the heat turned up. It is also healthier and it makes going outdoors less shocking to the system.

Nighttime temperatures, unless you are a nocturnal creature, can be lower than daytime temperatures. A ten-degree difference between day and night is about right. Remember that for every degree Fahrenheit above 70 you are adding about 3% to your fuel bill.

Get a humidifier, preferably one that links into the heating system if you can afford it. It helps you feel warmer at lower temperatures. This is because the level of humidity in a heated house is very low—about half desert level, in fact. The dry air takes moisture from wherever it can—including you—and the evaporation makes you feel chilly even at high temperatures. A humidifier also helps stop the furniture, wood paneling, and glue everywhere from drying out.

**UTILITIES**  Water, gas, and electricity are pretty constant expenditures. You might turn out the lights that you're not actually using;

## BUDGET SHEET

| | EXPENDITURE | | | | | | Annual | Monthly |
|---|---|---|---|---|---|---|---|---|
| | Annual | Monthly | Annual | Monthly | Annual | Monthly | | |

**FIXED**

Rent or Mortgage

Insurance: homeowner
automobile
life
health
(private & Medicare)

Taxes: federal
state
local property

**VARIABLE**

Food & drink
Fuel
Utilities: gas
electricity
water

Telephone
Medical care: doctors
drugs

**FLEXIBLE**

Property maintenance: building repairs
painting & decorating
appliance repairs

Furniture & equipment: purchase
repair

Transportation: automobile
public

Clothing
Other: gifts & contributions
education
personal

TOTAL

## INCOME

| | Capital | Annual | Monthly |
|---|---|---|---|
| **FROM ASSETS** | | | |
| Interest (savings accounts, bonds) | | | |
| Dividends (stocks, shares) | | | |
| Rents (real estate) | | | |
| **FROM PENSIONS** | | | |
| Social Security | | | |
| Private pension | | | |
| VA disability pension | | | |
| Other (royalties, etc.) | | | |
| **FROM EARNED INCOME** | | | |
| Salaries, wages, commissions | | | |
| Profit (self-employment) | | | |
| TOTAL | | | |

43

bake fewer pies and cookies (good for the waistline, too); run fewer baths and more showers. All of these will cut down on the utilities bills, if only by a dollar here and there.

The hot-water tank should be drained of about a gallon of water drawn from the bottom every month or so to keep it at top performance.

Leaking faucets should be repaired—one drop of water per second equals 700 gallons per year.

**MAINTENANCE AND REPAIRS**   Home-appliance repair costs can be reduced if you learn to do as many as possible yourself. It costs a small fortune to get a hairpin removed from the works of a washing machine, and that is surely not too hard to do oneself! Adult-education courses on appliance repair are becoming widespread and are often free to people over age 64. But even if you have to pay for the course, you will probably save its cost within the first year of your new knowledge.

The same thing applies to home maintenance and repair, although it's possibly a better idea to get someone else to do the scrambling across the roof.

## FOOD

Expenditure on food tends to vary from week to week but averages out over a few months. The Bureau of Labor Statistics estimates that a retired couple on a moderate income spends roughly 30% of their budget on food.

To cut costs in food buying you must become, if you are not already, a careful shopper. In addition to the tips given below, the information in Chapter 22 will also help you stretch your food dollar.

**MONEY-SAVING STORAGE TIPS**   As a first step, you might consider investing in a storage freezer, a good-sized one that keeps food at zero degrees Fahrenheit or below. With a storage freezer you must be able to spend, say, $20 extra this week to save you $30 over the next several weeks. The idea, of course, is to buy frozen and freezable foods while they are on special sales and to store them in the freezer against times of higher prices.

**Meat**   Prices vary considerably. Quantity buying for freezer storage can save you a lot of legwork from one sale to the next. Wrap the meat carefully to keep air out and avoid freezer burn. In a zero freezer, roast beef, roast lamb, and beefsteaks will keep well for up to twelve months; pork and veal roasts up to eight months; poultry and lean fish up to six months; chops of pork, lamb, and veal and fat fish up to four months; ground beef, lamb, veal, and shellfish up to three months; ham, sausage, crab, and lobster up to two months; and bacon up to one month. Precooked meats will keep for many months, although some loss of nutrients is bound to occur in the double-cooking process.

Fish can be bought fresh or ready-frozen and stored in the freezer. However, it is something of a waste to buy fresh fish for freezing; ready-frozen fish is usually a great deal cheaper than fresh fish.

**Fruit and Vegetables.** Frozen vegetables can be had at good sale prices if you keep an eye out. Make sure that you are getting a thoroughly frozen package. Certain fresh fruits and vegetables can also be stored in the deep freezer. They must usually be washed and, if appropriate, peeled before freezing. Some, such as peaches and corn on the cob, need special preparation. "Fresh Foods for the Freezer," Extension Bulletin 390, available from your County Agricultural Extension Service, gives full information on freezing techniques.

**Canned Foods** These are often available on sale. To avoid the risk of spoiled food, make sure the cans you buy are not rusty or dented.

**Dried Foods** These can be stored indefinitely in a cool, dark place. Dried peas and beans, of which there is a wide variety, are an excellent and very cheap source of protein if combined correctly in cooking (see Chapter 22).

**CUTTING FOOD COSTS** Although many fruits and vegetables are available year-round, those which are in season locally are lower-priced, fresher, more nutritious, and better tasting than those which have had to be shipped cross-country or stored for long periods before appearing on the stands.

Convenience foods (TV dinners, ready-to-eat cereals, baked goods, canned stews, and the like) are more expensive than those you prepare yourself; they are also lower in nutritive value. If you have more time than money it will pay you to make your own more or less from scratch.

Goods packaged by the store in which you are shopping will be cheaper than other brands it sells unless the latter are on special sale. Larger packages and can sizes may be cheaper than small ones, but check this closely for the occasional exception.

Powdered skim milk and evaporated milk are less expensive, less fattening, and just as nutritious as fresh whole milk. They are not as tasty, however, so the answer here is to use fresh (perhaps partially skimmed) milk for drinking plain, and the powdered or evaporated forms for mixed drinks and for baking and cooking.

Organ meats and ground meats are among the cheapest meats, and the former are high in protein (they are also high in cholesterol, so beware if you are on a low-cholesterol diet). Bacon and most sausage have high fat content, little food value, and large prices. Grades of meats refer to tenderness and juiciness; the lower-grade meats are just as nutritious. However, remember to add something to the price per pound to allow for fat, bone, and gristle.

You can use high-grade tuna for sandwiches and salads, lower-grade for casseroles; button mushrooms for sautéing plain, stems and pieces for stews; and so on.

Make out a shopping list before you go shopping and do as much as possible in one expedition. Don't go shopping while you're hungry —you'll find yourself with a three weeks' supply of truffles and no desire for them after the first orgy. Look out for food sale advertisements via your local newspaper and radio station. Save waste by serving at meals only food that everyone in your household likes. If you live where unit-price information is enforced, use it; it shows you plainly just how much you are paying for each brand of each product. Alternatively, take a little time and work out the price differences yourself. You should be careful to choose by the weight of the box or can rather than by its size.

Also, check the label for nutrients and make sure that you're not paying a lower price because the product has a high percentage of worthless filler. Some of these products are easy to spot—tomato sauces bolstered by corn syrup are a good example. But others—such as breakfast products claiming a high percentage of protein when, in fact, the protein is not in a form which can be absorbed by the human body—take more knowledge of nutrition.

**Group Buying**   This idea has sprung up in large cities where wholesale-food outlets are readily available, but it could be adapted by groups of consumers for various types of merchandise. Since buying in small quantities is always more costly than buying in larger quantities, you and your neighbors or friends can get together and pool your requirements. This idea can be extended to larger groups such as church or social clubs. If the group gets large enough, you can go straight to the wholesaler and buy at his prices. This needs organization, of course, but if you are interested in this kind of marketing you might well do the organizing yourself.

**GROWING YOUR FOOD**   If you have a garden you can, with a little effort, produce many of your own vegetables in season—you might even get to like it. Have your soil analyzed by the County Agricultural Extension Service. Then find out what vegetables will do best in your kind of soil and in your climate. Local libraries, nursery gardeners, and agricultural extension services are good sources of this kind of information. Samuel R. Ogden's *How to Grow Food for Your Family* (Barnes, 1973) might be helpful. See also "Gardening" in Chapter 14.

Poultry-raising is also a possibility if you are the adventurous type. Chickens, ducks, and geese are a good source of meat and eggs just as long as you don't get too fond of them in their live state. You must research the local zoning laws for this, though. You should also investigate the amount of equipment and work involved.

## TRANSPORTATION

All told, and not including long-distance vacation-type travel, the average retired couple living on a moderate income is estimated by the Bureau of Labor Statistics to spend 10% of their budget on transportation.

**YOUR OWN CAR** If you live in the country or in the suburbs, you probably have to have a car. In this case your transportation costs will consist of gas, oil, car maintenance, taxes, depreciation, license, and insurance; it is to be hoped you have your own garage. The costs of gas, oil, and maintenance will vary with the make of car, amount of travel, and the care you use in driving. Depreciation is how much less the car is worth with each year of use (about 30% a year, 2½% a month), and a depreciation fund set aside each month will eventually cover the cost of the next car.

Car insurance costs vary from state to state, though they are compulsory everywhere. In the no-fault system, being adopted in more and more states, premiums are less expensive; costs in some states, however, are still very high.

You will have to have another car about every eight years if you are reasonably careful and do only a moderate amount of traveling. A good secondhand car is cheaper and about as much trouble as a new one. Once you retire, it is very easy to become a one-car family; you can sell the second car and bank the proceeds.

If you live in the city, a car becomes a ball and chain once you no longer need it to get to work. Unless you take many drives out of town, it certainly pays to get rid of a car.

**PUBLIC TRANSPORTATION** Cities are usually well-equipped with public transportation; use it to save the hassle of city driving, as well as parking costs. One city and town after another is giving special fare reductions or exemptions for people over 65 traveling during nonrush hours. If your hometown turns out not to have special senior-citizen rates, perhaps you can lead the battle to get them— your chances of succeeding are very good nowadays.

## CLOTHING

The average retired couple's expenditure on clothes, as estimated by the Bureau of Labor Statistics, is about 6% of a moderate budget. This includes costs of buying, cleaning, laundering, repairing, and altering. Costs will depend largely on your way of life; if you do a lot of formal entertaining or attend many public functions you will need a larger clothing allowance than if you spend most of your time in the garden and drinking beer with close friends.

## MEDICAL

The Bureau of Labor Statistics estimates that an average retired couple living on a moderate income spend roughly 11% of their budget on medical expenses.

You are probably covered by Part A of Medicare. Since Part A is a deductible plan, you will have to pay an initial part of the costs if you have to go into the hospital.

To be covered by Part B you must pay a certain sum each month, which is deducted from your Social Security check before you get it. This coverage is well worth having. Part B is also a deductible: in this case you pay an initial part of doctors' bills and other insured items plus a percentage of the remainder.

To make sure that you will be able to pay the deductible should the need arise, you must put aside something each month.

Should you choose to have private medical insurance to supplement Medicare, your premiums (whether annual or quarterly) should be prorated on a monthly basis and put into the medical fund. This kind of coverage tends to be expensive for older people unless you are lucky enough to have a group health plan on your job that you can stay in after retirement.

Many medical items are not covered by Medicare or by most private medical-insurance plans. Dental, ear, and eye care, drugs, vitamins, and other such items will have to come out of the budget.

**CUTTING MEDICAL COSTS**   You can often cut down on the cost of prescription drugs by asking your doctor to prescribe in small amounts until you make sure that the drug is suitable for you. Ask him also to prescribe by the generic name of the drug rather than by brand name, whenever feasible. Unless a specific brand is the only correct one, the drug prescribed may have several manufacturers, some at much lower prices than others. With a generic prescription you can make sure the drugstore gives you the low-cost brand. Nonprescription drugs (such as aspirin and stomach remedies) and vitamins (particularly the multivitamins) are also much cheaper, and just as effective, under local or lesser-known labels.

Many drug-buying groups have been formed throughout the country, and membership in one of these can save a fair amount of money. Trade unions, retired people's clubs, senior citizens' organizations, consumer cooperatives, and group health plans are among the types of groups that organize drug-buying—your doctor or local health department can help you to find a group to join. Some groups sell the drugs themselves; others may have an arrangement for discount drugs and vitamins with a local pharmacist.

If you need to take medicine regularly for a chronic condition, it usually pays to join one of the big mail-order drug concerns. One of the biggest is run by the National Council of Senior Citizens, which anyone over the age of 50 can join.

## PERSONAL EXPENSES

This is the catchall heading for those things that you cannot find a proper place for elsewhere. According to the Bureau of Labor Statistics, about 8% or 9% of the budget of a retired couple on a moderate income goes for these items.

If you have a hobby or craft, then the money for your materials and tools will come out of this part of the budget. Books, writing materials, magazines and newspapers, entertainment, and television and radio purchases and repairs all should be included here. So also should such things as gifts and contributions, legal expenses, vacations, bank charges, toiletries, manicures, barbering, and other intimate items. Tobacco, alcohol, and other social drugs should also be included.

**CUTTING PERSONAL COSTS** Cosmetics and toiletries can sink anyone's budget, but many dermatologists and consumer groups are now exploding the claims for some high-priced products and advocating the use of cheaper products instead. Your library should have several books on this subject, including some with instructions for making your own cosmetics and toiletries from low-cost ingredients. In addition, as with drugs, many department stores, cut-rate drugstores, and other chains package toiletries and cosmetics under their own lower-cost labels, products which are similar or identical to high-priced ones.

Scents are trickier to duplicate, since many of their formulas are closely guarded secrets; and if you are so addicted to an expensive perfume that doing without it will plunge you into complete depression, perhaps you *can*, instead, do without a hairdresser by cutting your hair in a simple style. And if you must have that special soap, perhaps you can forgo that aftershave lotion. And so on.

You can stop buying books, even cheap paperbacks, and join the local public library. You may have to wait awhile to get the books you want, but you can always speed the process by reserving them. You can also cut out magazine buying and use the library's reading room instead.

Tobacco and alcohol can be cut down or out altogether with perhaps some pain but also great benefit to your health as well as to your pocket.

Movie and theater tickets are often cheaper during the day and/or on weekday evenings; there may be lower prices yet for people over 64, or for tickets bought in blocks for a group.

Recreational facilities at places like the YMCA and at public and private parks and zoos are often available for older people at cheaper rates during certain hours and on certain days. Facilities in state or national parks or forests—including golf courses, swimming, skiing, and other sports—are often great bargains. Many are free or low-priced for older people, and increasingly they are offering special facilities and programs for the blind and the handicapped. Subscriptions for social clubs, beach clubs, and other private recreational facilities may be lower for older people, with or without restrictions on the times during which you can use them.

Gifts within your immediate family and to friends and relatives plus any charitable contributions you make are another place to cut back. The cost of gifts can be reduced—by making them yourself, perhaps, or by foraging in antique and junk stores. So far as charitable contributions are concerned, you may, and quite rightly, feel that you have contributed sufficiently throughout your working life and can now stop. If you have a favorite charity or cause and are unwilling to desert it, you might consider giving your services rather than your money.

If you like to travel, see Chapter 14 for ways to cut costs.

If you like to drive and don't own a car, you can save your fare one way by arranging to deliver someone else's car for him at a point near where you want to go. There are agencies in several cities that coordinate pick-ups and deliveries. You can find them in the Yellow Pages of the telephone directory under the heading "Automobile Transporters & Drive-Away Companies."

# 6
# Taxes

## FEDERAL INCOME TAX

**SPECIAL EXEMPTIONS**   Certain provisions of the federal income-tax laws apply to people who are 65 or older:

**Nontaxable Incomes**   In figuring out your gross income for taxes you need not count the following: Social Security Payments; railroad retirement benefits; veteran's pensions; public-assistance payments; sickness or injury compensation; gifts and inheritances; life-insurance payments except that part of installment payments that constitutes interest on the total the insurance company owes you.

You need not file any income-tax return at all if the rest of your income for the year is under a certain level. The exact amount changes from time to time so consult the Internal Revenue Service for the latest figures. If you are living with your spouse and one of you is 65 or over, the level is higher; if both of you are 65 or over, it is higher still. However, if you received wages from which income tax was withheld, you should file a return if only to get your money back.

**Personal Exemptions**   If you do decide to file a return, you can claim the usual personal exemption *plus* another of the same amount if you are 65 or over. If your wife is 65 or over you can claim the double exemption for her also, if you file a joint return. If you file a separate return you can claim her personal exemption only if she had no gross income of her own and if she is not dependent on another taxpayer; if you are entitled to claim her personal exemption, you are also entitled to claim her age exemption (that is, you can claim the double exemption).

**Home Sale Exemption**   This applies if you sell or exchange your principal residence, defined as the property you have owned and used as your main living quarters for at least five years—interruptedly or continuously—out of the eight years just before the sale or exchange. After deducting selling expenses and commissions plus certain fixing-up expenses, you are left with an "adjusted sales price." If this price is under a certain amount you can omit the whole of it from your statement of gross income; if the price is over that amount, you can omit part of it. Since these amounts change periodically, consult the IRS for the limits prevailing in the year of your sale.

An exchange is treated as a sale and a purchase.

If you used only part of the property as residence, only that part of the sale price applies.

You can do this only once in your life and the choice as to when to do it is yours.

**Retirement Income Credit**  If you have retired, or are 65 or over, and have earned income over a certain amount in any of the ten previous calendar years, you can claim up to a maximum percentage of it as a credit against taxes. Earned income is defined by law as wages, salaries, and professional fees received for personal services— it does not include income from pensions or annuities, for instance. The following people cannot claim: those who receive Social Security, or any other excludable benefits above a certain amount, the amount being higher on a joint return; those who are under age 72 and have earned income above certain amounts.

**GENERAL DEDUCTIONS**  You should also take advantage of the deductions allowed to everyone.

## STATE AND LOCAL TAXES

The chief state and local taxes are: income tax, real property tax, personal property tax, sales tax, motor-vehicle registration fees, poll taxes, and gasoline taxes.

**INCOME TAXES**  Some states do not levy an income tax. Some of those that do use the same basis as the federal tax system; others have designed their own tax laws. Many grant the same exemptions as does the federal tax system; many have their own; some have no exemptions for older people. As these laws change frequently, consult an annually revised guide, such as J. K. Lasser's *Your Income Tax Workbook* (Simon and Schuster).

Some cities and local authorities also levy a personal income tax, but these are quite low except in New York and Philadelphia. The 23 counties of Pennsylvania also impose an income tax over and above federal and state taxes.

**REAL-ESTATE TAXES**  These, levied in all states, are usually based on the value of the property as decided ("assessed") by the local valuations officer. Thirty states grant special exemptions of tax credits or some other type of relief for older people. This relief is often tied to income levels and to the value of the property on which the tax relief is given; homesteads are the most frequent basis for relief.

**PERSONAL PROPERTY TAXES**  Personal and intangible property taxes are common throughout the states. The kinds of personal property most often exempted are household goods and furnishings and personal effects which are not used commercially. Intangibles such as bank deposits, cash on hand, mortgages, stocks and bonds, and public loans are sometimes exempt, particularly when they yield no income. In many places the state itself levies no tax but gives local municipalities the power to do so.

**SALES TAXES**  Most states have a sales tax; Alaska, Delaware, Montana, New Hampshire, and Oregon are among those few that do not. The most common rates are 3% and 4%, although some states such as New York and Kansas empower cities to levy an additional tax, sending the rates up. Food and clothing are sometimes exempt.

**VEHICULAR TAXES**  Motor-vehicle registration fees are imposed by all states at rates often depending on the weight or age of the automobile. Flat rates are also frequent and are usually annual. Some states also levy a onetime excise tax based on the retail price of the car. Gasoline taxes, common to all the states, take the form of a retail sales tax.

# 7
# Health Insurance

In addition to private insurance there are several public programs: two federal programs, Medicare Part A (hospital and related care) and Medicare Part B (medical and related care); State Medicaid benefit plans for the medically indigent; and Veterans Administration assistance, for which servicemen and their immediate families might be eligible.

## MEDICARE

Medicare is health insurance for certain people over 65 years old, and is administered in two parts. Part A, the Basic Plan, covers costs of hospitals and directly related care; it is paid for by contributions during working life; the employee, the employer, and the self-employed person each pay the same amount. The contributions are additional to Social Security contributions and are collected at the same time and in the same way as the latter.

Part B, the Supplementary or Voluntary Plan, covers medical costs and costs of directly related care. It is paid for by monthly voluntary contributions by people who are 65 and over.

**PART A—HOSPITAL INSURANCE  Eligibility:** The following people are eligible: people who (a) are over 64 and eligible for Social Security or railroad retirement benefits (you need not have retired, you must just be eligible except for the fact that you are working); or (b) are aged 65 before 1968; or (c) have three quarters of coverage per year after 1967 up to age 65 (for women reaching 65 in 1974 or 1975, one quarter coverage less is needed than for men the same age). People otherwise ineligible may buy the insurance for a monthly premium which will rise with hospital costs; they must also buy the medical insurance under Part B at the regular premium.

A quarter of coverage is a three-month period January–March, April–June, July–September, October–December) during which you earned above a certain amount. If you earned a certain net amount in one calendar year from self-employment or from farm work for cash wages, this counts as four quarters of coverage for that year.

**Coverage for Hospitalized Bed Patient** *Extent:* You are covered for up to 90 days within a benefit period (see below). You must make an initial payment (the deductible) toward hospital charges in each benefit period. After the first 60 days you must pay a certain sum per day. (Coverage for psychiatric hospitals is limited to 190 days for your lifetime.) You also have a lifetime reserve of 60 days' coverage that you can use as necessary to extend any 90-day period of hospitalization, and you must pay a certain sum per year for this reserve usage.

*Conditions:* Your stay must be in a participating hospital that meets legal standards and is the nearest one with an available bed that can deal with the emergency (emergency care for illness that began, or an accident that occurred, in the United States but which required care in a foreign hospital is covered under the same conditions as U. S. hospital care).

The stay in the hospital must be within a benefit period. A benefit period starts when you first enter the hospital after your insurance coverage has started; it ends 60 days after you have ceased being a patient in any hospital or extended-care facility.

*Examples of Benefits Covered:* Bed in semiprivate room or bed in private room if medically necessary; all meals; operating-room charges; regular and intensive-care nursing services; drugs furnished by the hospital; laboratory tests; X-ray and other radiology services; medical supplies (splints, casts, etc.); use of hospital appliances and equipment (wheelchairs, crutches, etc.); medical social services.

*Examples of Benefits Not Covered:* Extra charge for private room unless medically necessary; personal comforts or conveniences (telephone, radio, etc.); private-duty nurses; doctor's services (see Part B); noncovered care levels; first three pints of blood in a benefit period.

**Coverage for Extended Care as a Bed Patient** *Extent:* You are covered for up to 100 days. After the first 20 days you must pay a certain sum per day. If you are admitted again to the same or another extended-care facility within 14 days of your discharge, a new three-day hospital stay is not needed (see next paragraph).

*Conditions:* Your stay must be in a participating extended-care facility, and continued skilled nursing care must be required by your medical condition. Your doctor must decide this and order such care.

You must previously have been an inpatient at a qualified hospital for a minimum of three consecutive days for the same condition. You must be admitted to the extended-care facility within 14 days of discharge from the hospital; this may be extended to 28 days if no bed is available.

*Examples of Benefits Covered:* Bed in a semiprivate room or bed in a private room if medically necessary. All meals. Regular nursing services. Drugs furnished by the extended-care facility. Physical, occupational, or speech therapy. Medical supplies (splints, etc.). Use of extended-care facility's appliances and equipment (wheelchairs, etc.). Medical social services.

*Examples of Benefits Not Covered:* Same as those not covered under in-hospital benefits (see above).

**Coverage for Home-Health Agency Services** *Extent:* You are covered for up to 100 visits, which must take place after the start of one benefit period and before the start of another. Each service counts as one visit even if several services are given in one call at the home.

*Conditions:* The services you receive must be from a participating home-health agency. You must have been in a participating or qualified hospital for a minimum of three consecutive days. The continuing care needed must include part-time skilled nursing care, physical therapy, or speech therapy. You must be homebound. The doctor must decide your needs and set up the home-health plan within 14 days of your discharge from a hospital or from an extended-care facility. The care must be for further treatment of the condition for which you were an inpatient at the hospital or extended-care facility.

*Examples of Benefits Covered:* Part-time nursing care, physical therapy, or speech therapy. Plus, as long as any of these previous three are needed: occupational therapy, home-health aide's part-time services, medical social services, medical supplies and appliances furnished by the agency.

*Examples of Benefits Not Covered:* Full-time nursing care. Drugs and biologicals. Personal comforts or conveniences. Meals delivered to the home. Noncovered care levels.

**How You Pay** Payment under Part A of Medicare is claimed by the hospital, extended-care facility, or home-health agency whose services you have received. They will then bill you for services not covered. The Social Security Administration will notify you whenever it makes a payment on your behalf.

**PART B—MEDICAL INSURANCE** **Eligibility** Disabled people newly eligible for Medicare, plus almost everyone reaching age 65 after June, 1973, are automatically enrolled in Part B of Medicare. You can opt out if you wish but you must say so. You pay a basic premium per month into the fund which is matched by a payment from the federal government.

Anyone who was over 65 before July, 1973, and who has not enrolled voluntarily—or anyone who declined enrollment after June, 1973, but later changes his mind—may enroll during the first three months of any calendar year. His or her premiums will be increased over the amount of the basic premium by a certain percentage for every year during which he or she could have been enrolled but was not.

Any or all of the services listed below are covered if, all told, they total more than a certain amount in a calendar year. (See "How You Pay," below.)

**Coverage for Doctors' Services**  These are covered anywhere in the United States, in a hospital, at home, in the doctor's office, or elsewhere, as follows:

*Medical doctors and osteopaths* are covered for: medical and surgical services; medical supplies usually furnished by a doctor in his office; services of the doctor's office nurse; drugs and biologicals that cannot be self-administered; diagnostic tests and procedures. *Not covered* are visits for: routine physical checkups; immunizations unless directly related to injury; prescription drugs; patent medicines.

*Dentists* are covered for: surgery of the jaw or related structures; setting fractures of the jaw or facial bones; medical supplies usually furnished by a dentist in his office; services of the dentist's office nurse; drugs and biologicals that cannot be self-administered; diagnostic tests and procedures; all directly related to the surgery or fracture setting concerned. *Not covered* are visits for: care, filling, removal, and replacement of teeth; gum treatments; surgery or other services related to these.

*Podiatrists* are covered for: certain services legally authorized by the state within which they practice and all the attendant office services mentioned immediately above. *Not* covered are visits for: routine foot care; treatment of flat feet; treatment of partial dislocation of a foot.

*Chiropractors* are covered for certain limited services.

*Note:*  Certain types of medical visits are *not* covered. You cannot, for instance, claim visits to an optometrist for eye refractions or examinations for spectacles. Nor can you claim any examinations for hearing aids. Certain practitioners such as Christian Scientists and naturopaths are also excluded.

**Coverage for Outpatient Hospital Services**  These are covered when they are for: laboratory services; X-ray and other radiology services; emergency-room services; medical supplies (splints, casts, etc.); other diagnostic services. *Not covered* are outpatient hospital visits for: routine checkup tests; eye refractions and examinations for spectacles; immunizations, except where directly related to an injury; hearing examinations for hearing aids.

**Coverage for Outpatient Physical Therapy**  To qualify for payment, this therapy must be under your doctor's direct and personal supervision, or else under your doctor's plan and periodic supervision when it is furnished by a qualified hospital, extended-care facility, home-health agency, or public-health agency.

**Coverage for Home-Health Services**  To be eligible for this coverage, you must need part-time skilled nursing care, physical therapy, or speech therapy; you must be homebound; your doctor must prescribe the service, set it up, and review it periodically; and the home-health agency must participate in Medicare.

*Covered and Non-Covered Services:*  The same as those for home-health services under Part A of Medicare. These services under Part B are available in addition to those under Part A.

**Coverage of Other Medical Services and Supplies**  These must be medically necessary and prescribed by your doctor.

*Covered*:  Diagnostic tests by approved laboratories; diagnostic X rays in a facility or at home under the doctor's supervision; radiation therapy; durable medical equipment, rented or purchased, for use at home (wheelchairs, crutches, oxygen equipment, etc.); internal body-organ replacement (not dental), including corrective lens after cataract operation.

*Not covered:*  Prescription or self-administered drugs; hearing aids; spectacles; false teeth; orthopedic shoes or other corrective footwear except when a part of leg braces; first three pints of blood in a calendar year.

**Coverage for Ambulance Services**  To qualify, the ambulance service must be approved for Medicare. It must be used to transport you to a hospital or skilled nursing home when any other form of transport would endanger you. The facility to which it takes you must be the one serving your locale or the nearest equipped to give the care you require. These conditions also apply to ambulance service between hospitals, from hospital to skilled nursing home, and from hospital or skilled nursing home to your home if it is in the same locality.

**How You Pay**  Part B of Medicare is a deductible insurance plan; that is, you must make an initial payment (the deductible) toward your expenses in each calendar year. The insurance will then pay a major percentage of the rest of the cost.

The exceptions to this are the laboratory and radiology services required by your doctor while you are a bed patient in a hospital; for these the coverage is total—you do not have to pay either the usual deduction or the remaining percentage of the rest of the cost.

Expenses between October 1 and December 31 which can be counted toward your deductible sum that year can also be counted toward the deductible sum for the next year. Claims for services received from October 1 of one year through September 30 of the following year must be made by December 31 of the year *following* the September 30 date.

For this part of Medicare there are several ways to arrange for payment:

1. *Assignment Method:* Your doctor or supplier agrees to apply for Medicare payment and it will be made directly to him. The doctor or supplier agrees that his total charges will not exceed the reasonable charge set by the state Medicare claim organizations (known as carriers).

2. *Direct-Payment Method:* You make the claim yourself, whether or not you have already paid the bill. The claim has to be made on a proper form and you must enclose itemized bills if the doctor has not completed his part of the form. The claim is sent to your area carrier office. Forms and carrier addresses are usually available at the doctor's office or at the local Social Security office. Before any payment is made to you, your payment of the deductible must be on record. So send in medical bills as soon as they amount to the deductible sum or as soon as you know that the next bill will take you over the limit.

3. *Group-Practice Payment Plans:* In these plans, members pay regular premiums to the plans in advance, and get all the services the plans cover whenever necessary and without paying a separate fee for each service. The practitioners in the plans receive direct payment from Medicare for the services covered. As a plan member, you need make no claims except for services not covered by the plan.

If you are not able to pay the costs for which you are liable under Parts A or B, you should find out whether you can qualify for Medicaid or other special assistance plans (see below).

**SERVICES NOT COVERED**  The following services are not covered by either Part A or Part B of Medicare: services not reasonable or necessary for diagnosis or treatment of illness or injury; cosmetic surgery, except for prompt repair of an accidental injury or for improved working of a malformed body member; services for which you cannot legally be made to pay; certain services paid for by other federal, state, or local government programs; services of immediate relatives or members of your household.

## MEDICAID

Medicaid is available to people over 65 who cannot qualify for Medicare or federal-employee health insurance and cannot afford to pay themselves; or who get supplemental security income; or who are unable to pay their medical bills.

There is no one, basic Medicaid program; each state sets up its own to be administered by state, county, and city welfare departments and special agencies. However, the federal government does insist on certain minimum standards: every plan must cover some hospital, nursing home, laboratory, and X-ray services; and doctors' bills. Anything else covered is decided by the state. All the states (except Alaska and Hawaii) have Medicaid plans, and they often cover items such as spectacles and dental care which are not insured under Medicare.

Medicaid programs are financed by grants from federal, state, and county governments and are free to recipients. If you find that your money for food, clothing, and shelter is going to run short because of medical bills, by all means apply for Medicaid: local regulations will determine whether you get it. The local welfare office will tell you how to apply.

## VETERANS ADMINISTRATION

The Veterans Administration has many health services available to veterans aged over 64, or veterans of any age who are already receiving a pension and who cannot afford to pay the costs themselves. Among these services are hospitals; nursing homes; domiciliaries; outpatient medical and dental services; prosthetic appliances; and drug-rehabilitation programs. Rules for eligibility vary with the type of care. Consult your local Veterans Administration office for details on your own case.

## PRIVATE HEALTH INSURANCE

Many people are covered by Blue Cross and Blue Shield under group coverage at their place of work; for a slightly higher premium this coverage can be continued on an individual basis after retirement. Individual policies as well can usually be continued after retirement, again for a higher premium.

If you have never been covered, you can take out new insurance—but the premiums will be higher than in either of the previous arrangements. A policy for coverage to supplement Medicare would be cheaper than a total coverage policy, however.

Major medical coverage is insurance against most of the expenses connected with a serious accident or prolonged illness. This coverage is usually under a group plan and may continue for a few years after retirement if you keep paying the premiums.

If you can continue an already existing policy after retirement or find a supplementary type at low cost, by all means do so. Medicare plans are a great help but they provide only partial coverage, and a long illness can wipe you out.

A note of warning against those tempting advertisements for mail-order insurance policies: they are often aimed at older people, pointing out their frequent difficulties in getting adequate coverage from regular insurance companies. And the premiums are often low compared with those of regular companies. Before you happily plunge into a mail-order plan, read the fine print on the policy very carefully. If you cannot see it or don't understand it, get a regular insurance agent or a legal-minded friend to explain it to you. There are often well-hidden loopholes for the insurance company in that fine, dense print.

Before you even think of signing up, be sure the insurance company is licensed to practice in your state. Determine what the daily payments to you will be, which of your expenses will not be paid, and what medical exigencies are not covered at all. Check the premium rates and look for escalator clauses that can raise them. See under what circumstances the policy can be canceled, and also check the conditions for renewal.

# 8
# Legal Considerations

Perhaps you haven't made a will, feeling that you're not rich enough to warrant the effort. But this may not be true. If you own your house or apartment or a piece of land, if you own jewelry, a car, bank accounts, furniture, stocks and bonds, you are already a property owner. And if you own a life-insurance policy as well, your estate may total more than $60,000, the point at which it becomes liable to federal estate taxes. It will be liable to state inheritance tax at much below that figure in most states.

**IF YOU MAKE NO WILL** If you die without a will (*intestate*), your property will be distributed among your heirs according to the laws of the state in which you live; if you own property in another state, the laws of that state will apply to that property. These laws vary from state to state: in some a widow gets her intestate husband's property unconditionally; in others, the widow gets one third and the children two thirds divided equally among them. If you die intestate, the state or the court will appoint a trustee or executor to supervise the settlement of your estate. Most of your property, such as bank accounts, stocks and bonds, and safe-deposit box, will be "frozen"; that is, access to your property will be denied to anyone, even a joint owner, perhaps for several months. This can lead to hardship for your surviving spouse.

**DO-IT-YOURSELF WILLS** Be very careful if you decide to draw up your own will. Any will that you make is subject to the laws of your home state. About 25 states refuse to recognize a handwritten will. Many states that *do* recognize them insist on very stringent rules for validity: for instance, the will must be written entirely in your own handwriting, including the address and date; the will should have no printing on it. A written letter stating your wishes for your property will rarely stand up in court as a valid will on its own.

Printed will forms, in which you fill in the blank spaces for assets and heirs, and which you sign at the bottom, are even less likely to be valid than a handwritten will. Also, you run the risk of making mistakes, unless you understand the special meanings that words have in legal situations.

**USING A LAWYER**   The best idea, if you are going to make a will, is to have a lawyer help you to draw it up. His charges for a moderate estate will seldom be more than $100, often less. The fee is more likely to remain at this level if you can avoid numerous clauses. If you have a lot of small bequests of personal property, it is quite valid to attach a handwritten letter to the will detailing them. You should also arrive at the lawyer's office with all your information ready, so as to save his costly time.

For small estates, a lawyer may recommend that your wife, even if she has little property in her own name, make a will when you do. The terms of the two wills will usually be the same, each of you bequeathing to the other. This kind of arrangement should cost little more than a single will.

If you already have a lawyer, ask him if he is competent to draw up a will for you or whether he can recommend another lawyer who is. If you have no lawyer, you might ask around among your friends, or the trust department of your local bank.

Drawn up with the help of a lawyer, a will can have several advantages. For one thing, the lawyer can suggest ways of leaving your property, or even of disposing of some of it during your lifetime, that will keep federal and state taxes down to a minimum. You can make sure that your property goes to exactly the person or persons that you want it to. And you can arrange for an executor of your own choosing who can speed up the process of settling the estate after your death.

**ESTATE TAXES**   Federal estate taxes are estimated on the value of your total assets, including real and personal property as listed in the will, jointly owned savings and securities, life-insurance policies owned by you, and future payments due on annuities (whether or not jointly owned). The tax is deducted before the property goes to the heirs. If federal taxes are due, they are graduated from 3% up to 77%, depending on the taxable value.

Estates valued at $60,000 or less are exempt from federal estate tax. If you insert a "marital deduction clause" into your will, you can will all or part of your estate to your spouse; he or she will then not have to pay taxes on 50% of the estate's gross value. This means that, with a marital deduction clause, estates of up to $120,000 gross value can be exempted from federal taxes.

It is permissible to give up to $3000 a year to your spouse and to your children while you are alive without being liable for federal gift taxes; thus you can reduce the value of your estate so that it will not be as depleted by taxes at your death.

If an insurance policy on your life is owned not by you but by the beneficiary, it will not be included in the evaluation of your estate.

**TRUST FUNDS**   You can also set up a trust fund that will provide a steady income to its beneficiary at your death while leaving the capital sum intact. This may be a wise move where you are bequeathing a substantial estate to someone with no knowledge or inclination for business or to someone who you feel will dissipate the capital. The trust fund can be set up so as not to be counted as part of the beneficiary's estate at his or her death.

**STATE TAXES**   State taxes are levied on the amounts of the inheritances and not on the total value of the estate. The exemptions differ from state to state but are never so large as the federal ones. Your lawyer will be able to advise you on the best way to minimize state taxes.

**YOUR EXECUTOR**   When you make a will, you must name someone to settle the estate, the executor. The ideal executor is someone absolutely trustworthy and disinterested, who knows your affairs reasonably well, who is familiar with court and business dealings, and who will survive you.

Such a person, naturally, is hard to find, and it is becoming more and more common to name one's bank as executor, often in conjunction with either one's lawyer or one's spouse. The bank has a special department to handle wills and executor functions and its fees are usually moderate.

**CHANGING YOUR WILL**   You should review the terms of your will periodically, just to make sure that you want them to stand. You should alter your will to suit a change in your life such as another marriage (See "A New Marriage," below) or a radical shift in the value of your estate.

If you move to another state, you should contact a lawyer there and tailor the terms of your will to conform to the laws of your new home state.

**WHAT YOU CANNOT WILL**   There are certain things that you cannot do in a will. For example, you cannot will your survivor and death benefits from your Social Security to anyone other than the person entitled to them under Social Security law. Also, no matter how you want your property distributed, your creditors are usually entitled to payment of your debts *before* your estate is distributed according to your wishes.

Other dos and don'ts differ according to the state you live in. For example, in some states your spouse is entitled to a portion of your estate even if you do not wish it.

**JOINT OWNERSHIP** Joint ownership is sometimes used as a sort of "poor man's will," the assumption being that the survivor will have easier access to the property and that there will be no need to go through validating a will (*probate*) in court.

This is usually true of joint tenancy with right of survivorship; here the surviving joint tenant automatically inherits and probate is avoided. Death taxes, however, are still due on 50% of the value above the federal and various state limits. Also, the assets owned this way cannot be willed to or put in trust for anyone other than the surviving joint tenant.

"Tenancy by the entirety" is a form of joint tenancy which is valid only between husband and wife and applies only to real estate. Here again the surviving joint tenant automatically inherits without need for probate. An additional advantage is that the property owned in this way cannot be attached by a creditor of only one of the joint tenants; thus, if your spouse runs up fearful bills which you cannot pay, his or her debts cannot be paid by forced sale of a house held by both under a tenancy by the entirety.

However, joint tenancies are tricky, and whether the jointly owned property is or is not part of your estate may depend on the wording of the particular contract.

**SAFEGUARDING YOUR WILL** Don't leave the only copy of your will in the safety-deposit box at your bank, because, even if the box is held jointly with someone else (usually your spouse), it will be inaccessible to anyone after your death until probate hearings— often many months later.

A safe-deposit box in your spouse's name alone is the safest place for the original copy (and your spouse's original will should be in a safe-deposit box held in your name alone). Failing this, keep the will in a safe but accessible place at home and make sure someone (your spouse or executor) knows where it is. Copies should be kept with your lawyer and your executor. The original copy of the will, by the way, is the only valid one in a court of law, which is why you should ensure its accessibility.

Whether or not you make a will, you should for your survivors' sakes leave a memorandum listing your assets and liabilities, describing where various documents are to be found, and containing certain other information. The most important documents are your will (if you have made one), your birth and marriage certificates, your Social Security card (or at least your Social Security number), your military papers, leases, property titles, insurance policies, stocks and bonds, savings books, and federal and state tax records. If you use a safe-deposit box, make a list of its contents and state where the key is to be found. Name any debtors and creditors together with their addresses. Note what details you can remember (such as previous employers' names and addresses, and dates) of your employment in work covered by Social Security.

**A NEW MARRIAGE**   You may decide to get married—a decision that can, by the way, lead to a lot of strange reactions among your current offspring. If you own property, you might want to make sure that your children by a previous marriage get a share in it at your death. To avoid later questions of ownership you can enter into a special contract—called a prenuptial or antenuptial contract—with your prospective spouse; the contract specifies exactly who owns what and it is signed before the marriage.

Once married, you should think twice about transferring such things as your bank account into joint ownership with your new marriage partner. It sounds hardhearted, but you should bear in mind that many a marriage between older people (as indeed among younger ones) has lasted only until the money became available to the new spouse.

In some states your previous will is partly or wholly invalidated by a new marriage; you should therefore check your state laws with this and other possible effects in mind.

You should also check with your Social Security office to see if benefits will be affected, adversely or otherwise, by your proposed marriage. If a woman is drawing Social Security at a widow's rate or on the basis of her own earnings, she will probably find her benefits reduced by marriage to someone who is also receiving Social Security benefits. Because of this, many older people are forgoing the legal contract of marriage and living together without the dubious benefits of legality. Such an arrangement will also save a lot of flak from children and children's children on both sides, since their inheritances will not be threatened.

**LEGAL AID**   Other legal problems may arise in such areas as age discrimination in jobs and housing; losses in private pension plan benefits and in payment for poor nursing home care; denial of benefit in Medicare, Medicaid, and other public assistance programs; and involuntary commitment to state mental hospitals.

For people who cannot afford private legal service, the Office of Economic Opportunity has free legal aid, including paralegals specially trained in the problems of poor older people. You can get further information from OEO or from the National Paralegal Institute, Suit 600, 2000 P St., N.W., Washington, D.C. 20036; your local Office on Aging should also have information on local programs.

# II.
# LIVING
# WHERE
# YOU
# LIKE

Once you have a rough idea of your economic situation after retirement, you can make realistic plans about where to live.

Even with a limited income, retirement will give you a freedom of choice such as you have never had before. Your choice of areas is no longer determined by your job location. Your size and style of house, car, clothing, and behavior have always been dictated by the status requirements of your job, or your neighbors, by the standards you wanted for your children, by the appearance your community exacted. Now, at last, you can discard these compulsions. You can relax, forget about impressing others, please yourself. You are free. Well, almost free.

But before you chuck it all and head toward the nearest blue horizon, you had better consider a few facts which will help you make a right choice.

The perfect place probably doesn't exist outside our minds, but you can certainly have a shot at finding your version of it. The information given in this section should help you narrow down the possibilities and decide on the likeliest selection.

Additional information on climate is available from *Climates of the World,* a publication of the Environmental Data Service of the U. S. Department of Commerce, available from the Superintendent of Documents (Government Printing Office, Washington, D.C. 20402). Other aids might be: *General Climatology* by Howard J. Critchfield (Prentice-Hall, 1960); *Traveling Weatherwise in the U.S.A.* by Edward Powers and James Witt (Dodd, Mead, 1972); *Environment for Retirement,* and *Retirement Housing* available from *Retirement Living* magazine (150 East 58 Street, New York, N.Y. 10022); *Where to Retire on a Small Income* and other paperbacks by Norman D. Ford, available from Harian Publications (Greenlawn, Long Island, N.Y. 11740); *Foreign Retirement Edens* by Martha Ligon Smith (Naylor, 1967).

From the Government Printing Office you can also get the U. S. Department of Housing and Urban Development's *Buying Lots from Developers* and the U. S. Department of Agriculture's *Selecting and Financing a Home.* All About Houses, Inc. (25 Ritie St., Piermont, N.Y. 10968), publishes *How to Avoid the Ten Biggest Home Buying Traps.* You might also consult: *A National Directory of Housing for Older People,* a periodically revised paperback available from the National Council on the Aging (200 Park Avenue South, New York, N.Y. 10010); *Emphasis on Living: A Manual on Retirement Housing* by James A. Christison (Judson Press, 1970); *Guide to Retirement Living* by Paul Holter (Rand McNally, 1972); *The National Directory of Retirement Residences: Best Places to Live When You Retire* by Noverre Muson (Fell, 1973); *How to Buy Property Abroad for Vacation, Retirement, Income and Profit* by Patricia and Lester Brooks (Doubleday, 1974); or the annually revised paperback *Directory of Condominiums, Vacation, and Retirement Homes Around the World* by Glenn Fowler and Jerome E. Klein (Lehigh Books for Consumatics, Inc.).

*How to Choose, Buy and Enjoy a Motor Home, Van Camper, Tent-Top or Tent* by Clinton Hull, *All About Parks for Mobile Homes and Trailers* by Robert H. Nulsen, and *Let's Go Camping . . . Let's Go Trailering* are all publications of the Trail-R-Club of America; also helpful is the annually revised paperback *Woodall's Mobile Home and Park Directory* (Woodall Publishing Co.).

# 9
# The Ideal Environment

## *CLIMATE*

With the possible exception of the cockroach, the human race is the most adaptable of the earth's species. People may not be too comfortable in the arctic or on the equator, but one way or another some of them manage to survive in both. However, survival at such climatic extremes does take its toll of both body and mind. As we get older and our resistance to stress becomes more questionable, we often find ourselves automatically avoiding the sometimes serious discomforts of very high altitudes, very cold or very hot temperatures. In choosing a place for retirement, it makes sense to be methodical about finding a climate that will provide maximum comfort, health, and energy.

It is not, of course, possible to give a blanket specification for an optimum climate because people differ quite remarkably in their reactions to the same conditions. Your reaction may be the result of factors such as diet, past experience with climate, physical disability, cultural influences, or age. But some fairly consistent effects of climate —especially temperature, humidity, wind, atmospheric pressure, and sunshine—are well documented.

**TEMPERATURE** **Perception** Your body's perception of the temperature registered on the thermometer is altered by humidity level, wind velocity, and your own current metabolism—which in its turn is dependent on diet, exercise, and general health.

This alteration in perception is due to variations in the rates of conduction (transfer to other objects by touch), convection (transfer to moving air), and radiation (your body's own emission) of heat away from your body. It is also affected by the varying rates of moisture evaporation from your skin and lungs. In temperatures below 70° F.

71

evaporation is not usually significant, until you get well down into below-zero temperatures, at which levels heat loss through the lungs becomes a major consideration.

High temperatures, particularly if they are prolonged, sap both physical and mental energy. This effect is aggravated by high humidity, largely because a decent night's sleep becomes almost impossible. Under these conditions emotional outbursts become less controllable.

Low or falling temperatures are physically and mentally stimulating and increase the production of body heat. However, prolonged low temperatures prove enervating because all effort is needed to keep one's body heat balanced.

Optimum temperatures for physical well-being at a relative humidity of between 50% (night) and 80% (day) are in the range from 55° F. at night to 75° F. during the day. The optimum temperatures for mental energy seem to be somewhat lower outdoors and higher for sedentary work indoors. A certain amount of variability, both seasonal and from day to day, is necessary to prevent boredom.

**Adapting to Warmer Climates**   During the time you need to adjust, usually a few weeks, you may feel uncomfortable, lose your appetite, and lack energy. But once your body has adapted, you will be comfortable again. A few people, however, simply cannot adapt to some climates; if you are not comfortable within a year, you probably never will be.

During adaptation your body needs less oxygen but your sweat glands become more active and you feel greater need for liquids. Your total blood supply increases gradually as the capillaries near the skin dilate, a process that exposes more blood to the air and keeps you cooler. Take care to avoid protracted exposure to direct sunlight and heat, since your appetite and digestion may suffer and you may run the danger of heat exhaustion.

Unless you are accustomed to such a climate, you should avoid altogether humid regions where temperatures run about 98° F. for any length of time. You can, of course, stay in air-conditioned buildings during such heat waves, but this can be imprisoning.

Clothes should be loose-fitting to allow heat to escape from your body. Pale colors reflect sunlight whereas dark colors absorb it, together with its heat. Silk, cotton, and cotton-and-synthetic fabrics allow most air circulation; all-synthetic fabrics do not yet allow sufficient body moisture to escape. Headgear should meet the same conditions and should be brimmed to shade your face. Footwear is advisable to protect you from sun-hot surfaces (indoors you are better off without shoes), but it should be porous enough for good circulation —your feet are in the hottest climate!

**Adapting to Colder Climates**  In moving to a colder climate the body adaptations are the opposites of those for a warm climate and they take longer—sometimes several months. Your need for oxygen grows, your sweat glands become less active, your surface capillaries constrict and reduce the flow of blood, and your appetite increases. In addition, your blood thickens, its number of white cells increases, and your liver tends to enlarge. In cold climates, particularly if they are also damp, there is a higher incidence of arthritis and joint problems. Sudden falls in temperatures can strain the heart; and chilling lowers resistance to disease, especially in the respiratory tract.

You should therefore keep warm. Your house or apartment should be well heated and well ventilated, and you should be physically active and dress warmly. Clothing for cold weather is best made of a loose weave or knit. Several thin layers keep more warm air trapped near the skin than does one thick layer. Wool is the warmest material, although wool-and-synthetics run a close second. Silk next to the skin with layers of other fabrics over it works very well. With a layer of wool or wool-mix fabric next to the skin, you can wear all-synthetics as an outer layer.

Some ventilation is, of course, necessary. All of these layers should not add up to total imperviousness or you will feel great discomfort. Even outer garments should breathe a little, although they should be built to stop those icy winds. If your clothes get wet change them as soon as possible, because they have become useless as insulation.

**HUMIDITY**  Humidity is the water vapor in the air; relative humidity, the figure given in weather forecasts, is the amount of water in the air expressed as a percentage of the maximum the air can hold at that temperature (100%).

Humidity levels strongly affect the evaporation of heat from your body. If humidity is high, evaporation is less. Thus in high temperatures you will feel hotter with high humidity and cooler with low humidity. (This, incidentally, is why a humidifier is economical in a heated home.) The range within which relative humidity is comfortable at most temperatures is from 30% to 70%.

**WIND**  By increasing convection, wind cools you off. Thus it relieves high temperatures—although only up to 98° F., after which it will actually heat you up—but worsens low ones. A 45-mile-per-hour wind at 20° F. will produce the same effective temperature as a 5-mile-per-hour wind at −20° F. This effect, known as wind chill, is usually quoted in weather reports if it has reached a significant measure.

**ATMOSPHERIC PRESSURE**   Atmospheric pressure is lower at high altitudes than at sea level. The low pressure results in less oxygen for the brain and other vital organs. People who live at high altitudes develop greater lung capacity, larger chest cavities, and a higher pulse and respiratory rate to cope with the lower oxygen supply.

**Adapting to Low Pressure**   If you are not accustomed to high altitudes it will take time to adapt to the lower pressure. Up to 6000 feet you will usually be comfortable within one month, although complete adjustment will take about six months. Before becoming acclimatized you may find your mental and physical energy running low, you may get dizzy if you exert yourself, and you may even get nausea, headaches, and nosebleeds if the altitude is very high (above 6000 feet) or if your reactions are very strong. People with heart or respiratory diseases are advised to stay down; at least below the 6000-foot mark.

**Pressure Changes**   At any altitude, rapid changes in weather involve atmospheric pressure changes. These affect the circulatory, respiratory, and nervous systems and hence the emotions. The sudden onset of a storm, for example, which brings a sudden drop in barometric pressure, will stimulate a person in good health but will have an adverse effect on a sick one; someone with a respiratory problem may experience intensified symptoms; others may get muscle pains.

**SUNSHINE**   When people living in a cold or temperate climate are asked to describe their ideal climate, almost all include lots of sunshine as a major specification. In fact, however, constant sunshine is almost as depressing as constant rain and induces lethargy in most people.

In a variable climate, though, sunshine is definitely cheering. On the body, it has several effects. The infrared rays are absorbed by the body or its clothing and converted to heat. In moderate amounts the ultraviolet rays, in conjunction with the skin's oil, form Vitamin D and weaken bacteria. The pigment of a mild sunburn will protect the skin somewhat against a bad sunburn. If the temperature is high, the ultraviolet rays can encourage or aggravate cataract growth on the eyes.

The effects of the sun's rays are much reduced by smog and somewhat reduced by fog and haze. They are also less at morning and evening, when the angle of the rays is lowest. At high altitudes solar radiation is higher because the air is clearer.

**RAIN** Constant rain can be very depressing. But as a variable in a mostly sunny climate it is refreshing and will boost both physical and mental energy.

There is really no absolutely ideal clothing for wet weather. Completely waterproof clothing permits no air circulation unless it is very loose-fitting, which is awkward if the weather is also windy or if you need to move freely. Porous raincoats will not withstand a heavy downpour. The only thing you can do is choose the best compromise between weather, comfort, and activity.

**HEALTH AND CLIMATE** Climate itself is rarely the cause of a disease although it may aggravate an already existing one or activate a latent one. The diseases we associate with certain climates occur because particular disease organisms or carriers live in specific climates. Malaria, for instance, is carried by mosquitoes that can only live in tropical regions.

Dry air, wind, and dust irritate the skin and the respiratory tract, making infection in arid terrain more likely. Wind spreads more widely the pollen that causes hay fever and asthma. Smog is another door-opener to respiratory troubles, and this too is spread by wind.

Thus the ideal climate for a person in normal health is smog-free, dust-free, variable (with sunshine predominating), mild in temperature and relative humidity. If you find it, keep it. But don't expect it to cure all ills.

## THE SITE

Having decided among climates, you will next have to choose whether you want seashore, desert, or mountain living; the bustling activity of a large city; the reasonable space and greenery of a suburb; or the peace and isolation of rural life. While public transport is available in many cities, it is apt to be a problem in suburban and rural areas and you may therefore need a car. You might find it practical to compromise on a small town where staple goods and services are within walking or bicycling distance. Nowadays local cultural and social life in small towns—particularly if they are resorts or historic areas—may be fairly sophisticated. Resorts offer a change in pace and population with the on and off seasons, as well as a chance for in-season employment. Historic towns are increasingly popular, but since their charm depends on preserving the buildings in as original a state as possible, be sure to inquire about restrictions on altering the exterior (occasionally the interior too!) of any house you buy. Chapters 12 and 13 should help you pinpoint your choices. Then you can narrow down to the actual land upon which you will live and the site for your home, either yet to be built or already in place.

**GENERAL CHARACTERISTICS    Built-Up Areas**    If your chosen climate is a hot one, remember that expanses of concrete increase the temperature by absorbing heat during the day and radiating it at night. In a suburban area this effect can be mitigated by planting around the house both to shade it and to keep concrete surfaces to a minimum. In central cities this is not always possible (although many hot-climate towns are built to maximize cooling possibilities); air conditioning then becomes necessary.

**Valley Sites**    Avoid the floors of broad open valleys, which are hottest in summer and coldest in winter. Adjacent slopes suffer far fewer extremes of temperature, thanks to temperature inversion effects, and make much better building sites.

**Water**    Large stretches of deep water, such as the sea and big lakes, tend to level out temperatures, cooling the days and warming the nights; in moderate to warm climates their banks make good building sites.

Shallow water bodies on the other hand may worsen the climate. In hot weather they heat up more readily than deep water and, by evaporation, raise the humidity level. Since they also freeze more quickly in cold weather, they play no role in leveling off winter temperatures.

Sites on riverbanks may be subject to flooding. You should find out about the regional rainfall—what its average levels are, and whether it arrives all together in one week or is spaced out. Also, investigate the catchment or watershed area for the river as well as the flood history of the area and the amount of recent building that has taken place: large built-over areas increase runoff and flooding possibilities.

**Prevailing Winds**    These are an important consideration. In warm and humid climates wind is a help; in cold climates it is a curse. Sites on tops of hills, on windward slopes, and on plains are the most exposed to wind, and its prevailing direction, velocity, and humidity will directly affect temperatures.

**Exposures**    In the northern hemisphere, eastern and southeastern slopes get sun in the morning when it is cooler. Western and southwestern exposures get it in the afternoon at its warmest.

**ORIENTATION ON SITE**    The way the building is placed on the site should depend on the climate and on the force and direction of the prevailing winds. Except in extremely hot climates, wind tends to cool a building. In a warm climate, make sure that the broader side of the home faces the wind; in a cool climate you are better off with the narrow side facing the wind. The force of the wind can be cut by use of such windbreaks as clumps of trees and outbuildings between a house and the prevailing direction, though you must be careful not to create strong gusts by leaving direct channels between the windbreaks to the house.

If you do most of your cooking late in the day, your kitchen should face away from the hot afternoon sun, particularly in a warm climate. In a cold climate, the living room should be placed to get the afternoon sun; it should face away from the afternoon sun in hot climates. Northern exposures get no direct sunlight and are therefore lit fairly evenly throughout the day; this makes rooms facing north especially good for workrooms and studios. Bedrooms, unless you like to sleep late, should get morning sun—it is much cheerier to wake up to.

## THE HOME

**SIZE** The best size for your home will depend on your individual requirements. After retirement you will be spending a fair amount of time in your home, so don't talk yourself into small cramped rooms or two rooms fewer than you'd really like.

The best amount of land around a house will also depend on you and on the time and money you want to expend on its upkeep. If you've never much liked gardening, don't expect to develop a sudden passion for it once you've retired. Even if you do find yourself with an interest in growing, you can always extend a small garden indoors in planters. An avid gardener should have room for change and experiment; this can, however, be done in a space small enough not to be a hassle in upkeep. In either case, make sure that you aren't saddled with a large garden area that you will feel guilty about not working on. One quarter-acre is a good average for most requirements.

**GENERAL DESIGN** An ideal retirement dwelling would be laid out for easy access to all parts and would be on one level to eliminate staircases. It would be constructed from fireproof materials which require minimum upkeep and maintenance. Thresholds would be nonexistent or low, as would steps between rooms. Windows would be large enough for good lighting, good viewing, and increasing the impression of space; but they wouldn't be so large or so high as to present a cleaning problem. They would also be double-glazed for good insulation and thus would dispose of the need for storm windows, which would have to be hung and unhung every autumn and spring.

**INTERIORS   Lighting**   Either natural or artificial, this should be good throughout the dwelling—you should not have to grope along dim passageways or into dark closets.

Artificial-lighting levels will have to be increased if your eyesight is failing or if your eyes tire easily; you should probably double the ordinary level, particularly in those places where you do detailed work such as reading, sewing, writing, or carving. It is also less of a strain on the eyes to have general lighting as a background to area lighting.

Light switches should be at least three feet above the floor and placed just inside each entrance to a room or area; this will save fumbling and perhaps stumbling in the dark.

**Electric Outlets**   These should be plentiful and placed two to three feet above the floor so you don't have to bend to reach them.

**Heating**   The system should be good and thermostatically controlled, the thermostat being located in a central part of the dwelling so that the average temperature will regulate it. Hot-air heating systems detract least from the decor; but they are less efficient and less economical than hot-water heating. However, hot-water heating also has disadvantages: radiators in each room can be unsightly and may be dangerous for a person with failing eyesight or sense of balance.

**Ventilation**   It should be designed to avoid drafts and yet give sufficient air change so that rooms don't get stuffy.

**Floors**   Nonskid floors are desirable in uncarpeted areas. Carpets should not have a pile deep enough to trip you.

**Storage Space**   It should be plentiful and built-in. You should be able to reach it easily, particularly in the kitchen and workrooms where you use it constantly.

**Kitchen**   This should be as labor-saving as possible with ample, easily cleaned counter space of the right height to avoid either bending or high-arm positions. There should be knee space under the counters so that you can sit down while preparing foods. The dining area should be near enough so you won't have to carry full dishes very far.

**Faucets**   These should mix hot and cold water to prevent scalding. The hot-water supply should be thermostatically controlled at about 130° if you have a dishwasher and/or washing machine or at about 110° if you don't.

**Bathroom**   Grab rails in the bathtub and shower are useful (towel rails can be made strong enough to serve as holding bars). Nonskid bottoms on tub and shower are a good idea. So is a low lip to the tub so you can step in and out easily. A seat built into the back end of the tub or in a shower compartment is a convenience. Shower and bath faucets should be reachable from outside the water range for easy adjustment.

**Door Knobs**  If you have arthritis or rheumatism in your hands, hexagonal or octagonal rather than round knobs are easier to grip. Lever-type handles on doors are better still.

**Extra Conveniences**  There are many more refinements for convenient living—extra-wide doorways, roof overhangs for shade, automatic garage doors all come to mind instantly, and you can probably think up quite a list for yourself. But costs mount swiftly and usually draw the line for you. If you are building a house from scratch, you have a good chance, given an understanding builder, of getting many design factors and conveniences incorporated. If you are taking over an existing house, apartment, mobile home, or other dwelling you may be able to adapt some of these suggestions to make your life there easier.

# 10
# To Move or Not to Move

Financial, social and emotional factors will affect your decision on whether or not to move. But the reigning factor should be reason—look carefully at each aspect of your life and settle on what is best for you, not on what everyone else thinks is best.

## STAYING PUT

**YOUR PRESENT HOUSE** Most people (about 75% of retired couples and 40% of retired single people) own or are on their way to owning their own homes. Retirement is a good time to think about whether you really like your home, how convenient or difficult it is for you to keep up, whether you would prefer to live in another neighborhood, another town, another part of the country.

If you are near the end of your mortgage, think about paying the rest up before retiring (see Chapter 4), thus freeing yourself of a monthly burden during retirement.

Possibly you are still in the house you bought when you had two or three children to accommodate, and by now your children have left home. Your own activities may have spread out to fill up all the rooms, but even so you are burdened with a lot of cleaning, and upkeep. Chores will not grow fewer or easier; as the house gets older they will multiply; as you get older they will become more onerous.

On the other hand, the neighborhood kids may help you out on such things as gutter cleaning, lawn mowing, and leaf raking for a dollar or two. Perhaps, with more time at your disposal, you'll pick up on appliance and other domestic repairs yourself. Maybe you could get amateur help on such things as exterior painting (college students during summer vacation often do it). And maybe you could afford to pay professional help for the more skilled and arduous tasks like roof mending or floor laying.

80

Apart from size, the layout of a house is important. Steep stairs, high cabinets, and long treks to bathrooms are inconvenient and become increasingly so with age.

You must also take depreciation into account. How soon will major repairs be necessary? Do you have the skill to do them yourself or the money to have them done by someone else? And is it worth it?

**Conversion Possibilities**   If you want to stay in your present house, or are stuck with it for some reason, and can ill afford to keep it up as a single residence, several alternatives are possible. As suggested in Chapter 4, you might consider converting your home into rentable units. A large garage or barn, or a vacation house, might also be converted to year-round living quarters; you could then move into this new unit and rent out the main house, or vice versa. If you travel several months a year in a mobile home, you could rent your house during that period.

**YOUR PRESENT NEIGHBORHOOD**   This is a matter for concern from both social and geographical standpoints. In a stable or growing neighborhood your property value will increase; in a deteriorating one your house will not bring as much money in a few years. Also, it will get less and less pleasant to live in.

Access to shops and amusements has always been somewhat important, of course, but you may find as you get older that you are less willing to make constant efforts to get to outside activities. In deciding whether to stay, be careful that the location of your home will not lead to an eventual narrowing of your activities.

## MOVING

**YOUR NEW HOME   Renting**   Many people are glad to be rid of the responsibilities of ownership by renting a house or apartment. The disadvantages of renting are the lack of privacy (in apartments, particularly) and lack of a free hand with your accommodations. The same limitations apply to cooperative or condominium ownership, and the former leaves you with ownership responsibilities into the bargain. On the other hand, building maintenance is out of your hands and social advantages are often to be found in the very loss of privacy.

**Buying a Smaller House**   Perhaps you can get one that is in a place you like and that has built-in conveniences for older people— in a senior-citizen community, say, or built to your specifications. A smaller house has fewer rooms to clean and maintain, is cozier and more comfortable for one or two people, and costs less to heat, clean, and repair.

**BUILDING A NEW HOUSE** The possibility of building your own house is worth exploring. If you are handy and knowledgeable enough, you may be able to do it yourself—with a little help from your friends, perhaps.

Many people dismiss an architect-built or -designed house as too expensive, but in certain circumstances it could be the best alternative. For instance, you may already own land upon which to build. If you have very specific ideas about what you want in a house, you may have a hard time fulfilling them in an ordinary builder's house. A discussion with a builder can give you a good idea of what your ideal house might cost to build; this cost will assume an existing design plus specifications for measurements, layout, plumbing, wiring, drainage, sewerage, site clearance, and like expenses.

To get the design and specifications, you can go to an architect who will transform your original ideas into workable plans for the builder: this architect service will cost you an additional 10% of the builder's estimate. So if the builder's estimate plus 10% is not too much for you, you can afford an architect-designed house.

Alternatively, some builders use architectural consulting services, and within certain limits you can alter the builder's standard offerings to your own requirements. Or, if your requirements go no further than additional conveniences, you can try to find a builder in the area who is experienced in building specially for older people.

The ideal house for older people would take into account the possibility of increasing physical frailty and periods of illness, but, in fact, most people now approaching retirement age are not going to have to worry about these factors to any great extent; even now, unless they are very poor and are living in substandard accommodations, very few older people cite their homes as sources of trouble in their lives.

**Buying Land** A word of warning here about those ubiquitous advertisements for "retirement lots," usually in some dream haven and at a considerable distance from the point of sale: Certain promotional sales companies (usually those offering over 49 improved lots through the mails or by interstate commerce under a common promotional sales plan) are subject to "full disclosure" rules under the Interstate Land Sales Act, 1968. They must file a Statement of Record with the Department of Housing and Urban Development which contains information on the company's charter and financial statement; the land, local ordinances, facilities, and services; development plans; and supporting documents. They must also provide prospective buyers with a Property Report which contains a brief summary of the Statement of Record. Close reading of the Property Report should disclose all you need to know, but the salesmen often withhold it or include it in a mass of promotional material so that you don't see it before signing the sales contract.

People have found themselves stuck with land to which no legal access exists; on which the developer reserves the right to chop down all your trees or erect an oil derek on your lawn; and on which the costs of building a house with common services (sewerage, water, electricity) would be astronomical.

Never sign *any* piece of paper, even if you are told it is only an "option" or "reservation." Insist on a Property Report with complete specifications for the land (maps, contours, boundaries, etc.), on a list of legal encumbrances, and on a copy of the proposed agreement *and take them to a lawyer* knowledgeable about real estate. To do this, you need great sales resistance because the lures are tremendous— free meals or hotel weekends, low down payments, low monthly payments, and very persuasive salespeople. The whole idea is to get you to sign a sales agreement in a flush of enthusiasm. Even in those cases where you can see the land itself (and not just an "equivalent" plot), ask around among local real-estate agents to get general prices for land in the area; and always wait to see your lawyer.

If you think you have been cheated in a transaction since April, 1969, which is covered by the Interstate Land Sales Act, write to the Department of Housing and Urban Development/OIL SR, 451 Seventh Street, S.W., Washington, D.C. 20410. Give specific details and include developer's name, the name and location of the subdivision, and copies of any document you have signed.

**YOUR NEW NEIGHBORHOOD** If you wish to stay in the area in which you live, you already know it well enough to be able to hunt knowledgeably for another house or apartment. Don't forget to include costs of moving in your deliberations. These will include not only what you pay the movers, but also the new things you will inevitably need in another house plus the higher prices you will pay for repairs and supplies in the new neighborhood until you once more find cheaper sources.

Moving to another part of the country involves other costs. You should check the price of services—fuel, water, electricity, etc. Local and state property taxes, sales taxes, inheritance taxes, and others will be different. Cost of food and other staples, medical expenses, and local transportation may average higher or lower than where you are moving from. And, of course, the movers' fees will be higher for the longer journey.

Most of this information can only be found at first hand, which means you must either engage a local agency to get it for you or you must stay in the area for at least several weeks and get it for yourself. The latter is advisable because it will also give you a much better feel for the place and answer a host of questions that would never have occurred to you at a distance. All this costs money, of course. If you engage a search agency, you must pay them. If you go yourself, you must stay in a hotel and eat out for several weeks, and if you are traveling far you may have air, train, or bus fares to face. Unless you get very lucky and consummate the deal in short order, you may have to make more than one trip, particularly if you are buying property.

**Access to Supplies**   A shopping center about one mile away is just about ideal—it is near enough for frequent small expeditions—on foot! If you have a large refrigerator and freezer plus lots of storage space, you can afford to be somewhat farther from stores than if you do not. But you have to have either a good memory or an efficient way with a shopping list to avoid running out of toilet paper or light bulbs. You would also do well to calculate just how much of your time you spend moseying around stores and just how willing you are to give it up.

**Utilities and Services**   In outlying areas, your house may have its own well and fuel tanks. Make sure that suppliers are available and that you are accessible for deliveries in bad weather, when you are most likely to need them. You should also compare prices of suppliers if more than one is in the vicinity.

**Medical Services**   A doctor or hospital should be within easy reach —and not just by helicopter, either. Dental, eye, and ear services can be a little farther away unless you have a chronic problem which you know will need frequent attention. A telephone is, of course, an absolute necessity in an outlying area.

**Recreation and Amusement**   These facilities are important if you think they are. Some people have been going to a movie once a week all their lives and would feel deprived without them.

**Education**   Most cities, towns, and suburbs have adult education classes going nowadays, and many universities and colleges are opening their classroom doors to older people. If you need classes to pursue a particular craft or hobby, if you want to take classes in a particular academic subject, if you want to complete a truncated education, then make sure you can get to the right school without too much difficulty. Remember that most classes are given in the winter, many of them at night: you don't want to have to negotiate miles of mountain roads in a howling blizzard, nor do you want to have to skip classes for such contingencies; too many skipped classes inevitably mean a dropped course.

**Social Facilities**   These are largely a matter of personal preference. If you have always enjoyed being among people, you are likely to get very depressed without access to them. On the other hand you may be indifferent to all but a close circle of friends and relatives. Make sure you can get to what you want with a fair amount of ease.

**Religious Facilities**   If you care about these, you should check that the church of your choice is accessible.

**Family and Friends**   Proximity to your children and other close relatives and friends may be important to you. It is unwise to let it dictate entirely where you will live, but it will probably influence your decision. If, as is likely nowadays, you have fairly mobile children, it isn't much use spending your life's savings on a house around the corner from their present home—they could move to another state the year after. In any case, long-distance visiting is no longer alarming. Even if you can't afford the trip very often yourself, your children probably can.

Lifelong friends or relatives of your own age may also be near to retirement. If you have common notions about retirement, you might pool ideas, and even resources, and try to find a place as a group.

**Other Considerations**   Find out about zoning ordinances for the area at local municipal offices, usually the Buildings Department; the zoning will give you an idea of the fate of the neighborhood and future property values. This way you won't find yourself with an expressway outside your bedroom window in eight years' time! Avoid local nuisances where possible. Property is cheaper in the immediate vicinity of railroads, factories, airports, and major highways for very good reasons.

It is a good idea to investigate the possibility of part- or full-time work in a locale to which you may be moving. Whether you want to work for economic reasons or for interest's sake, you should know the local resources. If you can land a job before you move, you will be well ahead of the game.

The health of the local populace is definitely of interest—a high incidence of bronchial ailments, for instance, is fair warning to people with a weakness in that direction. This kind of information can usually be had from the local Board of Health or its equivalent or from local doctors.

Lastly, you should honestly appraise your own physical and mental capacities and admit to your limitations. Doing so will help to avoid bad choices and future disaster and may point you to the place that will suit you best.

If you are going to change location, allow a few months for your digestive system, sleep habits, and general equilibrium to catch up with you; unless you have been accustomed to moving around, it can be a (temporarily) discomfiting experience.

## FINANCING YOUR FANCY

**RENTAL HOUSING** If your income is low enough, you may qualify for public housing in a project built by your local housing authority. Until January, 1973, when all such programs were suspended for an overhaul (which has not yet taken place), the federal government helped with the capital funding of these local projects and also granted rent subsidies to needy tenants in them. Projects established before the moratorium are still supported, however. Inquire of your local housing authority about these and other, state-funded projects in your district, whether for the general population or specially for older people. Waiting lists are long, and the sooner you enter your name on the list, the better.

Until 1973, federal funding was also available for the building of multifamily rental dwellings by nonprofit organizations and for rent subsidies to needy tenants in those projects; a certain proportion of dwellings was set aside for older people; and qualifying incomes were set slightly higher than for public housing. Here, again, the moratorium persists but does not affect previously established projects. You can get information on the availability of such dwellings (built under Title I of the Housing and Urban Development Act, 1965, and under Section 236 of the National Housing Act, 1937, added by the Housing and Urban Development Act, 1968) in your area from the Department of Housing and Urban Development, Washington, D.C. 20410, or from its regional office. Waiting lists are long.

A third type of rental housing subsidized by the federal government is still partially in operation. Under Section 231 of the National Housing Act as amended in 1959, the Federal Housing Authority insures mortgage loans to finance the construction or rehabilitation of all kinds of rental housing for occupancy by people who are handicapped or over age 61. Public bodies and profit and nonprofit private organizations are eligible for the mortgage insurance. At one time public and nonprofit sponsors could obtain a contract with the federal government for rent supplements for needy tenants; this phase of the program has been suspended as of January, 1973. As a result, housing built under this section now rents at market-value levels. However, you can ask your regional Housing and Urban Development office whether such housing exists in your area; and if there is any, you can perhaps get your name on the list if you can afford the rent.

If you live in a rural area, inquire of the Farmers Home Administration about rental or cooperative housing under Section 515 of Title V of the Housing Act, 1949. Under this program, special low-interest rates are available to nonprofit sponsors of rental and cooperative housing for low- to moderate-income tenants or co-owners in rural areas. The Farmers Home Administration insures the loans.

**YOUR OWN HOME**   **Cooperatives**   If you are a cooperative owner of low- to moderate-income housing in a rural area, the Section 515 program just described may be available to your cooperative. It is also possible to form a cooperative and apply for these loans to buy and improve land for occupancy by low- to moderate-income cooperative owners, yourself included.

**FHA Mortgages**   Older people often find it difficult to get mortgages from private lenders, but you may be able to resort to Federal Housing Authority mortgage insurance through the Department of Housing and Urban Development or the Farmers Home Administration to get your loan.

The FHA insures private lenders (savings-and-loan associations, commercial and savings banks, insurance companies, mortgage bankers, builders, and individuals) against loss from inability to keep up payments on the mortgage. Interest rates are set by the administering government agency (Housing and Urban Development and Farmers Home Administration) and are lower than for conventional mortgage loans. Repayment periods are usually longer, and the FHA appraises the property for structural soundness and value.

Under Section 221 (d) (2) of the National Housing Act as amended in 1954, the Department of Housing and Urban Development insures mortgage loans for the purchase of proposed or existing low-cost one- to four-family housing.

For rural dwellers, a somewhat similar mortgage insurance is available under Section 203 (i) of the National Housing Act through the Farmers Home Administration. This insurance is limited to one-family houses (it must be a new house if it is a farm and must have at least five acres of land and be adjacent to a highway). The mortgage limit is somewhat lower than for urban homes, as is the length of the mortgage, but interest rates are about the same. Contact your local county office of the Farmers Home Administration for information.

**Mobile Homes**   You may be able to get help in financing a mobile home through the Department of Housing and Urban Development mortgage insurance, but only if the mobile home is to be your principal residence and if it is placed on a site that complies with FHA and local zoning standards. Down payments are low; interest rates are higher than for conventional housing; and mortgage lengths are shorter. You should be able to get information from a local lending institution or from your regional office of HUD, or from HUD's Washington office.

**VA Assistance**   In areas where there is a shortage of available credit for housing (as is often the case in rural areas, for instance), the VA makes direct home loans to eligible veterans. In areas with no such shortages, the VA insures loans from private lenders to eligible veterans on slightly less favorable terms than the FHA insurances described above. You may be considered an eligible veteran if you served in World War II, in the Korean War, or later. For information, check with your local VA office.

**Repair and Rehabilitation Loans**   If you need financial help for alterations, repairs, or improvements to your existing home, you may be able to get an insured loan from HUD through an FHA-approved mortgagor. Loans are at FHA interest rates and for up to 20 years. Your house must be at least 10 years old unless you are proposing major structural improvements. Consult your regional HUD office or a local approved lender for details.

# 11
# From Hotels to Houseboats

When you retire you may have new freedom to choose the kind of home you live in. The word "home" conjures up a house for most people, an apartment for a good many, a mobile home for some. But it can also be a room in a hotel, a duplex in a retirement village, or a houseboat.

## HOUSES

Privacy is the greatest single advantage offered by a house. A semi-detached or terrace house, of course, is only as private as the parting wall is thick, and in a crowded city you may have to put up with the sound of furniture falling down the stairs next door; with luck, that's just about all you'll hear.

Ownership of a house will let you make what alterations you wish to the interior and most of what you wish to the exterior—though local ordinances may inhibit installation of a fortune-cooky factory in your yard, and you usually have to get the permission of the local municipality for new building.

With privacy and freedom come responsibility. If you rent your house you are still responsible for all upkeep except structural repairs. If you own the house, these too are yours. Even day-to-day maintenance means time and money; there is no escaping the periodic major repair—roofs get old, gutters need replacement, basement floors crack. In addition, taxes must be paid.

As variety is much greater in the design of houses than of any other sort of accommodation, your choice is much wider. It is widest of all if you are having the house built to your own specifications.

## APARTMENTS

Apartments are great if you want to shed responsibilities for building maintenance. If you have had no experience in apartment living before, you should be prepared to strike a tolerant attitude to the many different standards of behavior with which you will find yourself at close quarters; and you will hear more noise within your apartment than you've probably been accustomed to in your own house. Most modern apartments are compact (too compact, often) and easily cleaned.

You should make sure when you take an apartment that the common parts are well kept and cleaned and that the building is structurally and decoratively well-maintained.

If the building is in a large city, a doorman is an excellent idea; in fact, the whole question of who has access to the building, when, and how should be carefully answered. An internal television or speaker system linking outer lobby and apartments allows you to see or hear the people ringing your doorbell before admitting them to the building lobby. In many areas, police give helpful advice about safety precautions.

**SIZE**   You can seldom expect to get as much space as in a house. Still, you must make sure that you don't get yourself cooped up in a bandbox. Remember that you will have no garden into which to escape. Stepping out of a house is easy; when you step out of an apartment you still have to negotiate hallways, elevators, and lobbies; this extra effort, small though it is, can prove enough of a psychological barrier to keep you indoors more.

For a retired couple, one bedroom, living room, separate kitchen with dining area, and one bathroom is probably adequate although a spare room for overnight guests is a great convenience. The rooms should be big enough to let you move freely and to avoid instant entrapment if you have to stay indoors because of bad weather or illness.

**LOCATION   Within the Building**   In a two-story, maisonette-type of building, the choice is simple: up—with stairs and farther from noise; or down—with no stairs and nearer to noise.

In taller apartment buildings, before elevators became common, the ground floor was considered most suitable for older people. Nowadays, the only drawback to high floors is that elevators are dependent on the area power supply: you are liable to get marooned every now and then. The ground floor nowadays is much less desirable. It is the noisiest floor—how noisy will depend on the local traffic—

and in a large city center it is also the floor most subject to robberies and open to dirt. The higher up a building you go, the quieter and cleaner it is likely to be, and the more expensive.

Noise from tenant and service elevators and from garbage chutes can be bad, especially in uncarpeted hallways; apartments nearest these services are noisier.

**Of the Building**   Apartments can be obtained in special retirement communities that range from apartment complexes, with special facilities in common, to retirement cities that are almost completely self-contained. Some of these communities rent out their apartments; others sell them outright (these are known as condominiums); others sell ownership not of the apartment itself, but of shares in the cooperative that owns the development. These various types of ownership are dealt with later in this chapter.

Low-cost housing projects, mostly apartments, are sponsored by local housing authorities; in these, certain apartments are usually set aside, sometimes especially planned, for older people.

**LEASES**   Rents vary sharply from one part of the country to another. Hawaii is the most expensive state; the Northeast runs a fairly close second.

When you rent an apartment you agree, usually, to take reasonably good care of the premises, including the landlord's fixtures and fittings, and to be responsible for decorative upkeep; the landlord agrees to hand over the apartment in good shape, and to be responsible for structural maintenance and major repairs to his fixtures and fittings (though not if you caused the damage by negligence). He is also responsible for decoration and upkeep of the common parts of the building such as hallways, elevators, staircases, laundries, and lobbies.

Lengths of leases vary from one year to about five years. Unless you are lucky enough to be in a rent-controlled apartment (an increasingly rare bird), the landlord will up your rent when you negotiate for a renewal of your lease. If your lease is a long one—say for three or five years—it may have a yearly rent increase written in.

You should check the lease for special clauses. Apart from extra responsibilities they may lay on you, you may find some that limit your right to own a pet or house a fellow human overnight. Noise restrictions may find you playing your records between 7 A.M. and 10 P.M., and you may never get to use your roller skates indoors at all.

## MOBILE HOMES

**TYPES**   Mobile homes are popular among retired people. Relatively inexpensive to purchase and maintain, and compact enough for easy upkeep, they are very appealing if your love of housework is as limited as your budget. The smaller ones are easily moved and appeal to lovers of the changing scene.

Many types are available, from the truck camper which fits on the back of a pickup truck to the double-unit mobile home bolted to a foundation slab in a trailer park. Here are described those you can live in with some degree of comfort. Those most suitable for vacationing are discussed in Chapter 14, although the smallest of the types below are also used as vacation campers.

**Truck Campers**   The really navigable ones are the truck campers and are comparatively small: six to eight feet wide, 12 or more feet long, high enough for decent standing room. At their cheapest they supply only the rudiments of living quarters, with bed, cooking facilities, electricity, and water. Truck campers are used by people who do not plan to stay beyond a few weeks in any one place. In them you can travel to your heart's content without an inordinate amount of trouble negotiating any but the narrowest or most tortuous roads.

**Travel Trailers**   As their name implies, these are made to be hauled along by either a powerful car or by a pickup truck. This fact alone makes them less maneuverable than the truck campers. They range from about six to eight feet wide and from about 12 to 35 feet long. The very largest are not maneuverable on many roads. On the other hand, they provide quite sumptuous accommodations and are suitable for permanent living quarters. Only a powerful car can pull the larger ones, and gas consumption runs well below ten miles per gallon for them.

**Motor Homes**   Here the driver's cabin is all of a piece with the home itself. Sizes range from six to eight feet wide and from 18 to about 30 feet long. Some of the larger ones have luxury accommodations and are almost completely self-sufficient. They are somewhat more maneuverable than the trailer types, despite their size, but are still denied access to many roads.

**Mobile Homes**   What we will call mobile homes are not mobile at all, or only minimally so. Their sizes range from eight feet wide and 29 feet long to 24 feet wide and 65 feet long. Not surprisingly, these units are more or less permanently parked once they have reached their site, often a trailer park. Some of the very largest, notably the double-width ones (20 or 24 feet wide, a size achieved by bolting together two 10- or 12-foot-wide units), have no wheels at all but are delivered by truck, assembled on site, and bolted to a concrete foundation slab.

A modern, good-sized mobile home is equivalent to a roomy efficiency apartment. It may contain a walk-in bathroom with a shower and tub; fully equipped kitchen; a living room with dining space; and at least one bedroom. A really large mobile home will have two bathrooms and several bedrooms and may be two stories high.

**BUYING YOUR MOBILE HOME** **Financing** If you can possibly pay cash down in buying a mobile home, do so. If you have to take out a loan to buy it you will find yourself paying astronomical interest rates, because mobile homes do not qualify as real estate in the eyes of bankers and cannot therefore be financed by a conventional mortgage. The occasional exception is the bolted-to-site unit which is already *in situ*. These may also be eligible for FHA or VA loans (see Chapter 10). Interest rates on loans are high, and many lenders use an add-on type of interest which practically doubles the quoted rate.

**Standards to Look For** In buying a mobile home or trailer, look out for quality of construction and try not to be dazzled by the glamorous installations in the showroom. You will need adequate insulation, sturdy fittings and appliances, and good, solid furniture, as well as adequate refrigerator space, water storage, and general storage.

Mobile homes sold in Florida are subject to minimum standards imposed by the state. Elsewhere, the seal of the Mobile Home Manufacturers Association or, in the West, of the Trailer Coach Association will usually indicate a decent product for the price.

It is wise to do your business with a reputable dealer the quality of whose mobile homes is not in any doubt. The dealer should also be able to guarantee and deliver service for repairs and maintenance. The dealer's membership in the Mobile Home Dealer's National Association will usually indicate his good faith (at least you'll have someone to complain to if the dealer lets you down).

**TRAILER PARKS** Parks for mobile homes now number well over 25,000 and are located all over the country. They are laid out in lots with a concrete or blacktop slab for the mobile home and perhaps another slab for an extension. If car parking is on site, there will be a third slab for this. The larger sites have additional space for a garden.

**Facilities** Each site is fitted with connections for electricity, gas, sewerage, water, and, in the more expensive ones, telephone. If there is no telephone on site, there will be pay telephones on the streets of the park or at the central office. Paved and lighted streets connect the sites, so a larger park resembles a conventional suburb. Recreational facilities vary with the type and cost of the park. Most new ones have swimming pools and a recreation building for such amusements as pool, card games, and club activities.

Many mobile-home parks are specially fitted out for retired people, and these usually have more elaborate recreational facilities such as golf courses, shuffleboard courts, saunas, dancing, bingo. Most parks for retired people are to be found on the outskirts of towns in popular retirement regions.

Many parks for mixed age-groups restrict families with children to special areas of the park to avoid disturbing other residents. This is a special problem because indoor space is limited in mobile homes and both adults and children must therefore spend a lot of time out-of-doors.

**OBTAINING A SITE**    Space is often set aside in mobile-home parks for trailers staying on an overnight or weekly basis. Not all parks accept temporary trailers but more and more are doing so. Despite increasing pressure to ban trailers from state and national parks and forests (and bans already operate in some of them), many still have power, water, and sewerage facilities for trailers.

Some mobile home parks rent lots, while others sell them to the mobile-home owner. Many of the newer parks, both rental and owner-occupied, limit the age of the homes they will allow on their sites—sometimes to about three years. Some insist on a minimum size, usually 45 feet. Some permit only the type that is bolted to the foundation slab.

In looking at trailer parks you should check out on the following: size and costs of lots; road widths, surfaces, and maintenance; slab surfaces and sizes; street lighting, parking arrangements; restrictions on visitors, children, and pets; landscaping and the general upkeep in the park; garbage-collection frequency and costs; mail service; recreational facilities; telephone service; laundry facilities if you need them; availability in the area of such facilities as shopping, churches, and public transport; and, very important, your impression of the management garnered from interviews with them and with the other residents and from the ambience of the park.

**Renting**    Older parks, naturally, charge lower site rentals than do newer ones. Frequently, they are the only ones that will accept older vehicles. These older parks, built before the mobile-home boom, tend to have small lots and narrow streets. Many of them are shabby and lack good services and utilities.

The highest rents come in the new parks with larger lots, often waterfront ones. The very highest rents are for really luxurious setups (private swimming pools, boathouses, large gardens, for instance) in a fashionable area. Like rents everywhere, those for trailer-park sites tend to increase year by year, a cost factor for which you should be prepared.

Changes in management have been known to make drastic differences in the policy and hence the livability of a trailer park. Since rental-park ownerships display an average turnover of three years, be prepared (stoically) for this, too.

Many trailer parks impose an admission fee, nonrefundable, to be paid to the park operator. Since demand for space in the better parks far exceeds supply most of the time, the mobile-home owner may find himself at the mercy of a ruthless rental-park operator: rules for living in trailer parks are stringent, and eviction is not hard to justify; a rapid turnover means more admission fees for the operator, and so it goes.

One answer to the insecurity and rent-increase problems lies in the municipally owned trailer parks with rented sites. Here security is about as good as it can get (in view of the number of rules to be broken) since the municipality is not out to make a big profit. Many of the municipal parks are, besides, very well managed.

**Buying**  Buying a lot in an owner-occupied park certainly removes the insecurity of renting. Against this, however, you must offset the fact that, once all the sites are sold, the park operator may quit and leave the operation in the hands of the occupants. A growing trend is for the park operator to sell the mobile home to the buyer rather than have the buyer bring in his own home. This will usually guarantee local services for repair and maintenance, and the admission fee to the trailer park will probably be included in the price of the home.

If you buy an empty lot, don't forget to add the cost of installing the slabs required in your deed of sale and of running power and sewerage lines from the developer's nearest connection point. Whether you buy a vacant lot or one with a mobile home already installed, you must allow for a monthly maintenance charge to cover water, garbage collection, sewerage disposal, night watchman, and public and recreational facilities.

Before finally deciding whether or not to buy, check the restrictions in the deed of ownership and think hard about your willingness to live with them.

Some states do not regard mobile homes as real estate and therefore charge an annual license fee, which is far lower than a real-estate tax would be. Those states that tax mobile homes as real estate usually rate them quite low. And almost all states have specially low rates for people over 64, if not outright exemptions. In some states you will also be subject to a personal property tax.

Finding a suitable mobile-home park is a matter of searching through the several national and state directories (available at local public libraries or through local mobile-home associations), looking under "Mobile Homes—Parks" in local Yellow Pages, talking to mobile-home dealers and suppliers, and reading the several mobile-home magazines now being published.

## HOUSEBOATS

With the advent of aluminum and fiber-glass hulls in the late 1950's houseboat living has at last become possible for the less hardy and adventurous. Now mobility is high, maintenance low, and comfort at least equal to that of a good mobile home. Prices have the same range as mobile homes, varying from low for the spartan set to a medium price for luxury and speed lovers. The advantages of houseboats are much the same as those of mobile homes: capital investment is lower, *quid pro quo,* than for a conventional home; compact accommodations make upkeep of living quarters easy and inexpensive; a change of scenery can be had without ever leaving home.

Useful references are: *The Wonderful World of Houseboating* by Duane Newcomb (Prentice-Hall, 1974); *The Complete Guide to Houseboating* by John W. Malo (Macmillan, 1974); and the books suggested under "Boating" in Chapter 14.

**BERTHING**   As houseboats gain in popularity, houseboat communities are springing up around the country. They provide the electricity, water, and sewage hookups to be found at any boat basin, plus clubhouses and various combinations of recreational facilities; much like trailer parks, in fact, but oriented to the water.

Boat basins, or marinas, with services and supply stores, are plentiful both on popular coastal stretches and on main inland waterways. Many kinds of boats berth at them, usually by the season but often just overnight in the course of a journey. You can anchor your boat offshore (moor it) or you can tie it up alongside a pier (in a slip). Costs do not differ greatly between the two on a seasonal basis and are fairly moderate.

As with mobile homes, migration is relatively easy from northern summers to southern winters with a seasonal berth at each end if you like. The journey down the Atlantic intracoastal waterway or down the several inland waterways can be a vacation in itself—twice a year.

Houseboats fall into two main categories: the pontoon type and the cruiser type.

**PONTOON TYPE**   The pontoon is basically a platform topped with a cabin and built across twin floating compartments, the pontoons. It is very stable, can carry a lot of weight, is easily handled and operated, and can be beached almost anywhere. It provides larger living space and costs less per foot length than a cruiser. Common lengths vary from 18 to 50 feet, the latter being at the luxury level. Speed is usually in the six- to ten-mph range, although it is possible to get a pontoon with a 30-mph capacity; at this point, though, you are using a lot of fuel.

Most pontoons have large outboard motors which consume an average of seven gallons of fuel per hour. They are less maneuverable than the cruiser type but excellent for easygoing cruises in quiet waters. Since the deck height above water (the draft) is small, pontoons are not suitable for unprotected coastal waters or for rough conditions on inland waters.

**CRUISER TYPE**   Cruiser-type houseboats are those whose hulls are built with a deep or modified V shape. This makes them very maneuverable and easy to direct, although handling and operation take time to learn. They are less stable than a pontoon and must usually be moored offshore at all but official landing places.

Eighteen to 50 feet are common lengths, although, because of hull construction and cabin positioning, cruiser types usually provide less living space per foot than do pontoons. They are capable of higher speeds with less engine power and, having greater draft, are more manageable in rough or coastal waters. Many of them are, in fact, fitted out and watertight to a good cruiser's standards so that they can be managed in rough coastal waters by an experienced person. Cruiser-type houseboats are usually fitted with inboard-outboard motors, sometimes twin engines, for added maneuverability and speed.

**OPERATING COSTS**   Operating costs depend on fuel consumption. Diesel engines cost two or three times as much as gasoline engines to buy, but they consume only half the amount of a cheaper fuel, last longer than gasoline engines, have a greater speed range, and are safer, since there is no danger of combustible gases building up in the bilge as there is with gasoline engines.

**WATERWAYS**   You can get guides and charts to inland and coastal waters from the Coast Guard, the Army Corps of Engineers, the Tennessee Valley Authority, and the state governments for the waters within their various jurisdictions.

For long-distance travel with a view to getting somewhere, the eastern half of the United States offers greater possibilities. It has the Atlantic seaboard intracoastal waterway; the northeastern Hudson–Erie Canal–Great Lakes–St. Lawrence–Hudson Bay system; the Midwest to South Great Lakes–Mississippi system; the huge TVA linked-lake system; the interior and coastal cruising waters of Florida; and the intracoastal waterways around the Gulf of Mexico.

Lake boating is the main type available in the rest of the country. Sometimes, as in parts of California and the region around Seattle in Washington, boating is linked by ship canal to the sea. Many of the lakes along the borders of Nevada and Arizona and in Utah and Montana are long enough to satisfy a moderate itch for getting somewhere else.

Southern California is a prime coastal boating region. There's a large coastal boating area south of Los Angeles and some smaller ones farther north.

**THE SAILOR'S LIFE**   Life on the water has a different ambience and pace, and you become very aware of and at home with the natural elements. It also has its own language, rules, and manners—and if you don't know them you must learn them. While cruising, there are "rules of the road" to observe every bit as specific as those on a hard-top, and standard waterway signs indicate such things as permitted speeds, channel routes, and types of recreational areas. Coastal navigational signs such as buoys and lights are used to signal weather and channel characteristics as well.

Weather lore is important—you should learn to recognize natural signs of weather changes as well as how to read weather maps and interpret weather reports. You should know some first aid—artificial respiration, anyway. There are certain safety rules to be observed in loading and balancing of the boat, boarding, and turning. If you want to know what maintenance men, harbormasters, and fellow boaters are talking about, bone up on some nautical terms. Last, but most, know how to swim.

## RESIDENTIAL HOTELS

Rooms, or sometimes apartments, in hotels wholly or partly catering to retired people are becoming increasingly available in urban areas, particularly in the South and West. The accommodations usually include room cleaning at least once a week, two or three meals a day, and recreational facilities of varying degrees of elaborateness.

Hotel apartments with several rooms including kitchen and bathroom come under the heading of luxury living. The more normal single room—with private bath and, occasionally, kitchen—will cost less. A double room will cost less again per person.

Some hotels require no guaranteed length of stay, though usually demanding a month's rent as security; others require a minimum stay of one month or longer; still others are run on a yearly rental basis, requiring two months' rent as security.

The better hotels have a registered nurse on duty and a doctor on call at all times.

In some states, New York for one, a hotel specializing in older guests may qualify as a Proprietary Home for Adults, more commonly known as a Senior Citizens Hotel, and thus be regulated by the State Department of Social Welfare. To so qualify the hotel must satisfy certain standards of safety features, fire protection, personal services, and planned recreation.

Many retirement hotels, converted from older commercial-type hotels, have been financed by FHA loans. This can often mean excellent location and a spaciousness hard to find in newer buildings. Since they are usually located in town, many facilities are readily available to residents, sometimes right on the premises.

Retirement hotels are an excellent idea for people who like hotel living, particularly single people. Residents must be ambulatory and in reasonably good health, and the management will require a doctor's certificate to this effect.

Properly run, these hotels can offer a social life otherwise hard to come by for a lot of people, especially older city dwellers. They also ensure regular meals and freedom from the onus of housekeeping. The extent of the recreational and social facilities varies considerably. The larger hotels may employ a social director. Or residents may organize most of the social life themselves. In the good ones space is set aside for games, meetings, or classes, and the liveliest social programs are often those run by the residents.

**CHOOSING YOUR HOTEL**   If the lobby is gray and bleak or if it smacks strongly of an institution, you'd be well advised to forget it right away. Armchairs full of silent, unmoving bodies are another strong hint to stay away. Bright colors, comfortable furniture, a little bustling, and a low hum of conversation are desirable.

When you visit a residential hotel that you might move into, the management will assiduously show you accommodations and quote prices. But make a note of how you were greeted as you entered the hotel, and when you have completed the Cook's tour, buttonhole a few of the residents (if the management makes it difficult for you to do so, that's a bad sign) and ask them how they like the place, what the problems are (there are bound to be some), whether the management lives up to its promises, how the staff behaves toward the residents, how the residents occupy their time. While they are answering, you can get a good feel for not only the place but also the kind of neighbors you would have.

The larger and better-run hotels will allow—often require, in fact— a two-week or one-month trial period of residence to ensure the satisfaction of both newcomer and management. Remember that your hotel room is going to be your home, so even if you plan to spend most of your time out of it, make sure the room is spacious and comfortable and a place you will be glad to come back to at the end of the day.

## RETIREMENT VILLAGES

The atmosphere most often sought by the developer of the completely self-sufficient retirement city or village is that of a country club; and the degree of his success is, as you might expect, determined to a large extent by the price you, the resident, pay.

The complex usually consists of apartments, duplexes, private houses, mobile homes, residential clubs, or a mixture of several, plus infirmary, clinic, nursing home, recreational and social facilities (golf courses, swimming pool, sauna, indoor amusements, exercise clubs, perhaps a movie theater). The very largest will have doctors in residence and a small hospital, and the population may be large enough to support the cultural, social, and shopping facilities of an ordinary town. Theaters, concert halls, recreation and meeting halls, schools, supermarkets, boutiques, churches may be found within the city's perimeter. Thus you may never have to set foot out of the area except for a specialized need.

Recreational and medical costs and facilities are included in the general charges for some and are optional and extra in others. Some smaller developments may lack on-site medical facilities and the more elaborate recreational and social arrangements; if they do, the development is usually set within easy reach of a community that does have them.

Many retirement communities are well guarded against the outside world; a visitor may have his identity, destination, and welcome checked at a gatehouse before he is allowed to penetrate any farther. With this kind of security control, residents can leave their possessions unguarded and stroll the streets and parks at any time of the day or night without fear.

Retirement communities used to impose minimum age limits of 50 or 55, but this age limit has been creeping down—to 40-year-olds in some cases, and perhaps with permission for a child over 17 to be in residence. In the newer developments, the trend is to impose no age limits for the community at large, but to set aside certain sections or buildings for the retired.

**TYPES OF OWNERSHIP**  Some properties are for rent only, with utilities and recreational facilities included in the rental. Here the resident has no maintenance responsibilities and needs no initial capital outlay.

Others have cooperative ownership; what you buy is not the living unit itself but a share in the cooperative ownership of the whole venture.

Condominiums are becoming the most popular form of ownership, but the term has been subject to such abuse that you should never enter into a contract without first consulting a knowledgeable lawyer. The appeal of a condominium is that the developer is often able to offer more desirable land and housing at less cost than you could afford by yourself, and amenities (such as a golf course) which are cheaper and more convenient than if you had to join local country clubs. After you buy your unit, the developer or subsequent management remains responsible for the facilities, buildings, and grounds, and you must pay a monthly maintenance fee as well as taxes and insurance. In condominiums that are investment-oriented, management rents the units, and sometimes owners may not even live in their houses or apartments (or may have to pay rental to do so and/or be restricted in their length of stay); the idea is that the owner gets back in rental his mortgage and tax costs (in addition, he has the benefits of tax deductions for depreciation and maintenance); ideally, investing in such a scheme well in advance of retirement enables you to have, with a minimum of attention and worry, a retirement home totally or partially paid up by the time you are ready to use it full-time.

But there are pitfalls. Unless a lawyer reads the fine print of your contract, you may be misled about the exact extent of your ownership and whether you are to get deed possession. If, as often happens, you are required to give a down payment before your unit is built, what guarantee do you have that the building will be built to specifications shown you? Have the developer's plans been approved, or are drastic changes likely before they meet local government regulations? Will your down payment be held in escrow? Are the recreational lands and facilities owned by the condominium buyers? Who makes the rules for these? If you are not interested in, say, golf, are you nevertheless required to pay golf-club membership? Will your electricity be metered, or how else will your fair share be calculated? What if other owners default on maintenance payments? How can you be sure management is not charging excessive maintenance fees, and what can you do about it if they are? (Needless to say, if your condominium is on foreign soil, the tax, insurance, and ownership questions are apt to be even more confusing.)

Outright ownership in fee simple is more common for single units on their own land than for apartments or duplexes. The ownership includes the land and involves a higher capital outlay than the previous two types. Recreational facilities are often an additional charge here, too.

**LIFE-CARE PLANS**   Often sponsored by churches, unions, and other special private groups, these may consist of a self-contained hotel or apartment-type building, or a small complex of separate buildings. Those of the hotel type may provide the same services as a residential hotel.

The life-care plan is intended to take care of retirees who can afford to buy the interest for the rest of their lives. The interest includes appropriate accommodations for any state of health, starting with an apartment or hotel room for the healthy and ending, if necessary, in a nursing home for the rest of one's life, although this may be restricted to the complex's own personnel and facilities. Thus medical specialists, for instance, may be at the patient's own expense. Nursing care may also be an extra charge.

The residents of life-care plan developments tend to be somewhat older than those of the retirement villages. This is partly because the more activity-oriented nature of the villages doesn't greatly interest most people getting into their late 70's. It is also because the fear and likelihood of illness grow in those later years, and the life-care plan gives security in all contingencies but one.

The life-care plan is, naturally, the most expensive of all these types of ownership. Usually there is the so-called founder's fee of from several thousand dollars for a single room to over $100,000 for a house in a luxury complex. This fee is the down payment for entry. Then there is a monthly charge for meals, recreational facilities, and services. Sometimes the contract provides for an annual increase (5% is popular) in monthly charges to cover increases in cost of living; often a 25% ceiling is placed on total increases from date of entry, thus protecting the purchaser against astronomical charges.

The facilities' accommodations and services are guaranteed for your lifetime; when you die your interest reverts to the owners of the complex, not to your heirs. Thus, if you die within a few years of entry, the facility has made a profit on you; if you live to a ripe old age, you're laughing.

**RESIDENT RESPONSIBILITIES**   Under most deeds of sale in retirement communities, once the developer has sold a certain percentage of the dwelling units, the residents become responsible for running the community and the developer's legal interest and responsibilities cease. This leaves the residents to manage the rest of the sales, maintenance of common land and buildings, organization of clubs and recreational facilities, security arrangements, and all the myriad aspects of a village's life.

More often than not the developer will try to prepare the residents for their future role by making sure that a residents' association is set up; the better ones will gradually shift the operation into the association's hands. Thus the development comes to resemble, in the end, a political entity in itself. Unless the development is incorporated, however, which it seldom is, the local municipality is ultimately responsible for the development's residents. This can cause friction where an irresponsible developer fails to provide adequate utilities (thus leaving the municipality to cope after his departure) or where the political weight of a large community of older people is felt to be discordant with the municipality's previous policies. Extra taxes for school needs, for instance, might be voted down by a large retired population against the wishes of residents outside the development.

The political upheaval, however, is seldom as great as feared, and the development's residents are rarely a burden on the rest of the community. Rather the opposite, actually, since they bring more purchasing power and require few, if any, special facilities (all of which are taken care of in the development).

**CONVENIENCE OF FACILITIES**   Retirement villages usually centralize their facilities. If you can get a home near the center, well and good. If not, make sure that transportation is good enough to get you there with ease; otherwise you may find yourself being bugged by the constant effort of traveling to social and cultural activities.

If your interests include live theater you may find (or found, for that matter) an amateur group in the community. If you need professional theater, make sure you can reach one from the development. The same applies to educational facilities: the development may offer courses in arts and crafts but it will seldom run to academic courses; for these you will have to be within reach of a college or university or some other course of adult education. Big-city shopping is a periodic must for most people, and you should make sure that you will be able to get to it when necessary. In other words, you should investigate the surrounding region and make sure it can provide what the development lacks for you.

**WHAT TO WATCH OUT FOR**  Don't sign any kind of agreement until you have carefully checked its terms—either by yourself at your own leisure or, preferably, through a lawyer.

The introductory tour of a retirement community can leave you in a rosy haze. You have been shown a model home, often furnished at a cost greater than you will be paying for the home itself. The apparent size of the model home may have been cunningly expanded by judiciously placed mirrors or by specially made small-scale furniture. You will have been taken through the most attractive parts of the complex. You will have been assured of the great resale value of the property.

You should try to dissipate the haze by talking to residents. Sometimes older residents, particularly in the more country-club-oriented complexes, are beginning to find the social life there unsuitable. People who retired as one of a couple may find the costs of living there too high once a spouse has died—this is particularly true of widows whose income is cut at the death of a husband. Both these groups are often looking to sell and, contrary to the agent's quotations, they are often selling in a buyer's market. If you really intend to move in, look for this kind of seller before plunging into the developer's sales contract.

Apart from life-care facilities, medical costs are usually the responsibility of the individual, although in some facilities medical insurance is available on an optional basis.

**PROS AND CONS**  The communities are age-segregated, which is not attractive to some people. Others may accept it with relief. Segregation is not limited to age. While racial segregation is seldom a policy, you will see few, if any, blacks or Chicanos in the developments. And an admixture of Jews and Christians is not frequent, either.

Security from crime and violent social disturbance is appealing to most people, although you must sacrifice a certain freedom in its achievement—your friends from outside cannot drop in on you unannounced (did I hear a cheer?) and the pressure against eccentric behavior is great. On the other hand, you can leave your house for several weeks in perfect confidence of its safety.

Most of the communities have regulations to which residents must conform. The number and type of pets may be restricted. How you paint the outside of your house may be controlled. Where you or your visitors park your cars, what you do with your garden, what size and type of television antenna can go on your roof, when your visitors can use the swimming pool—these and many more aspects of your life may be subject to regulation.

The character of the regulations plus the kind of setup plus the facts of segregation will together ensure a high degree of homogeneity in the people living in the developments. If a placid, regular life with people of your own sort appeals to you, fine. If you like variety, surprise, dissimilar people, then you may find the developments boring, despite their many organized activities.

# 12

# U. S. Retirement Country

As the world's population has become more mobile, certain places have become popular for retirement. Often climate is the attraction. Sometimes a specially built facility (such as a retirement village) or low property taxes or a low cost of living is what first draws retired people. Then, as more retired people come, the places begin catering to them and thus attract yet more retired people.

Although some of the more popular areas are described here, mention of specific developments or facilities does not constitute recommendation or endorsement (please refer to Chapters 9, 10, and 11 for a full discussion of factors you should consider).

## PRACTICAL CONSIDERATIONS

**CLIMATE**    The climate that appeals to most people is warm, sunny, and equable. As discussed in Chapter 9, this climate is easy on your body and allows for outdoor living and physical activity. Its economic advantages should be a major consideration if you are living on a fixed income. When temperatures rarely reach extremes, your house can be of light construction, with little or no insulation, without a basement (since the ground is never cold enough to warrant protection from it); and you will need little or no heating or air conditioning. Thus your house will be cheaper to build, rent, buy, and maintain.

You can also dispense with coats, boots, and other expensive protective clothing. Since you have no need to escape from extreme weather, you can vacation during the less expensive off-seasons. Lack of stress from weather extremes may even lower your medical bills.

**FACILITIES**    Retired people may be attracted to an area because of special conveniences—retirement developments or apartment buildings or hotels situated within easy reach of social, cultural, recrea-

106

tional, and medical facilities. Where facilities are chiefly for retired people, clubs, meetings, and classes can be held during the day instead of evenings or weekends as is necessary for a working population. Recreation may be organized with older physiques in mind. Doctors, nurses, clinics, and hospitals, accustomed to the problems of older people, may be better able to remedy these. Retailers may gear their hours and merchandise (supermarket meats, for instance, will be packaged for one or two people) to the preferences of retired people.

A preponderance of older people in a community means a generally quieter atmosphere (although too great a preponderance can be sepulchral) with an easygoing pace. Rush hours tend to be nonexistent; night life closes down early; and weekends, with an influx of visitors, may be the only time the shouts of children are heard in the community.

**COST OF LIVING**   A generally low cost of living will attract retired people because of their fixed incomes. Real-estate taxes, state or municipal, are another consideration. In some regions retired people are at least partially exempt from taxes on their homes and personal property. In a few, no personal income tax is levied by the state or municipality. Some of these benefits are mentioned below; others can be found by writing to the local Chamber of Commerce or its equivalent.

Cheaper food may be a lure in a farming area, or the need for costly importation might be a deterrent in some isolated rural areas and on some islands. Clothing, with the possible exception of native items in some nonindustrialized areas, tends to cost about the same everywhere.

## THE U. S. MAINLAND

Most states have a Department of Commerce or its equivalent in the capital city where you can write for information on vacation areas, cost of living, population, industrial and commercial development, taxation, medical facilities, and so on. You should also be able to get the names of licensed real-estate agents in the areas you ask about.

As a rule, vacation areas are good places to investigate for possible retirement—the less seasonal their appeal, the better for year-round habitation.

**FLORIDA**   Much of Florida consists of highly commercialized vacation land which attracts many people while repelling many others.

**Climate**   Generally subtropical; rainfall averages about 50 inches

a year, most of it in summer and autumn. The southern half of the
state, below the frost line, is more humid, hot, and stormy (with a
very occasional hurricane) than the north. Winters in the south are
milder, averaging about 70° as against the north's 55°.

On the eastern coast, offshore breezes go a long way toward
ameliorating summer heat and humidity. The northwest and Panhandle areas, with Gulf Coast climate and character, have higher
humidity, warmer summers, and more luxuriant vegetation than the
rest of the state.

**Cost of Living**    Florida has no state income tax, low personal and
property taxes, a generous homestead allowance for retired owner-
occupiers on its property taxes, and real-estate prices that run a good
bit lower than equivalent properties elsewhere. Prices are high along
the southern coasts, especially the Atlantic, and higher still along the
Keys. Florida's climate makes few demands on clothing or heating
budgets.

**East Coast**    The Atlantic side of the state is dotted with famous
resorts—Miami, Miami Beach, Fort Lauderdale, Boca Raton, Palm
Beach—which have long catered to the retired. Although the beach-
fronts and the centers of these resorts tend to be more expensive than
the inland areas, retirement hotels and apartments (often run by
church groups) are usually available at moderate rates.

A host of developments, many reserved for retired people, offer
apartments and homes for rent (becoming scarce) or sale. Some
private developments, often with standardized houses built on small
plots of land around centralized recreational and social facilities,
attempt to be fairly self-contained communities (such as the Deltona
Corporation's St. Augustine Shores). Others, such as the many new
high-rise condominiums, may provide some recreational amenities but
depend on the local town for services. Some developments are union-
or organization-sponsored (such as the Steelworkers' Vulcan Village
at Daytona Beach) and limited to members. Religious-sponsored
facilities vary; some prefer their members or create an atmosphere in
which nonmembers would feel out of place, while others (such as the
Methodist-developed Wesley Manor Retirement Village in Jacksonville) are actively nondenominational.

Florida, particularly in the southeast, is having problems with air
and water pollution, power and water supplies; by 1973 over 40
communities in the state had moratoriums in effect on sewer hookups,
and by 1974 many towns were casting about for other ways to limit
growth. Building your own home, setting up a mobile one, or buying
an inexpensive new home is therefore increasingly difficult. New developments stand the best chance for approval if they promise low

density, good taste, and some evidence of ecological concern, such as a bird sanctuary—all of which means expense. Thus, while Deerwood Villas up in Jacksonville can still hold down the price, most of the new condominiums in the south (at Juno Beach, North Palm Beach, Pompano Beach) are well over $50,000. Many go over $100,000 (Suntide on Hutchinsons Island or the Club on Sailboat Key at Cocoanut Grove); villas at La Coquille Club Village, south of Palm Beach, start at $100,000; and at Lost Tree Village on Singer Island prices go well above $200,000. For modest budgets the best bet is therefore to look for a resale in one of the older developments.

**West Coast**   Fort Myers, Punta Gorda, Sarasota, St. Petersburg, Bradenton, Clearwater, Tampa, and Lakeland, besides being popular retirement cities in themselves, are near neighbors to a multitude of retirement developments, some of which are cities in their own right (Cape Coral, Port Charlotte, Lehigh Acres, Sun City Center, New Port Richey). Many mobile-home parks are here, some quite elaborate. Prices in general have been lower here than on the Atlantic coast, but overbuilding became such a problem that in 1974 St. Petersburg tried unsuccessfully to force the last 25,000 settlers to move back out! As a result, developers either turned to less congested areas (such as Deltona Corporation's Marco Island project) or to types of building capable of absorbing the additional costs (such as the new condominiums at Clearwater, Belleair, Fort Myers, or Sarasota).

**Central Florida**   Here humidity, winter temperatures, and general cost of living are somewhat lower than in the rest of the state. Orlando and Winter Park are the two most popular retirement centers, but apartments, retirement hotels, and other special facilities for older people are available throughout the area, as at Clermont, De Land, Kissimmee (with Orange Gardens, a 500-home retirement community), the Lake Wales area (with the garden-style apartments of the Nalcrest Foundation retirement community), and Sebring (where the Florida Brethren Homes, Inc., has retirement apartments, lakefront cottages, and mobile-home sites). Similar facilities stretch north of Orlando, through Leesburg, Ocala (where the Amrep Corporation developed Rainbow Lakes Estates, a retirement community, and Silver Springs Shores, for families as well as the retired), Gainesville, and Live Oak. Deltona (northeast of Orlando) and Citrus Springs and Spring Hill (both west of Orlando) are Deltona Corporation communities which have also attracted retired people.

The area can supply ample lake boating, fishing, and other recreation as well as considerable cultural activity. And at no point is one or another coast more than 75 miles away.

**The Panhandle**    Inland, this Deep South strip along the Gulf of Mexico is characterized by mild winters and hot, high-humidity summers; the number of high-heat days doubles as you move west from Tallahassee toward the Alabama border. But along the "Miracle Strip" —100 miles of beaches and resorts stretching from Panama City to Pensacola—offshore breezes mitigate the discomfort. The Deltona Corporation has another of its planned communities, Sunny Hill, just north of Panama City, and the area has many trailer parks. Although this area was once moderately priced, costs have been rising steadily (at Bay Point, a modern condominium resort on St. Andrew's Bay at Panama City, prices start about $50,000).

**CALIFORNIA**    California, rivaling Florida as a retirement center, offers more varied climate, some of which (such as at the southern coast) is very nearly ideal. But San Francisco, Los Angeles (whose air pollution, carried on Pacific breezes, affects large areas to the east and southeast), and San Diego are all suffering urban ills. Air pollution is intensified by the coastal fogs. Water pollution is created not only by industry (such as oil spills in Santa Barbara Channel) but also by houseboats (as at Sausalito) and by motorboats jammed into developed waterways (as at Redondo Beach Marina). Forest fires, earthquakes, and shore erosion are other factors you should consider.

In addition, although the overwhelming migration to California that characterized the 1960's has ended, the resident population is shifting (especially southward), so that today many communities are instituting or contemplating growth controls. New but weak controls on desert lands are expected to be strengthened soon. Marin (short on water), Orange (inheriting the Los Angeles sprawl), and San Diego counties can also be expected to impose restraints.

**Cost of Living**    This is generally high, particularly along the southern coast, in urban areas, and in desert resorts. It is, of course, possible to find moderate housing, but you have to search diligently. Mobile-home parks here are sometimes quite plush and expensive (rentals can run double what you would pay in the East). You should be prepared to pay more for food, taxes, and incidentals (including medical services); heavy dependence on an automobile also adds to your expenses.

**South Coast**    The coast from San Diego up to Santa Barbara offers a most attractive climate. Summers average fewer than 25% cloudy days, and even in rainy season the sun shines over 50% of the time. Night fogs are frequent but usually clear up by midmorning.

San Diego has many apartment complexes for retired people

(Buena Vista Garden Apartments, Grace Towers, Luther Tower, St. Paul's Manor, and the Wesley Palms Retirement Residence are examples). Nearby Ramona and Spring Valley, and, south of the city, Coronado, and La Mesa are also good places to look. North of the city, Rancho Bernardo is a 5800-acre retirement community; El Cajon has the Ivanhoe Village Apartments; and La Jolla, on the coast, has apartments built by the Pacific Homes Corporation and other private concerns, as well as White Sands of La Jolla, a project on the beach built by Southern California Presbyterian Homes (which has facilities in other areas, too). Inland at Escondido there are the Escondido Village Apartments and Lawrence Welk's Country Club Village.

North along the shore, San Juan Capistrano has retirement developments; at Laguna Beach is the 7000-home Laguna Hills retirement village; inland, other large developments with homes, apartments, and mobile home sites are Del Webb's Sun City, Sierra Dawn, and Sun Park, south of Riverside.

While Los Angeles has a wide choice of apartments, apartment hotels, and other retirement facilities, it was also the site for several "new towns" and other planned communities, many of which are now difficult to distinguish from the city's suburban sprawl. Virtually every community—Van Nuys, Burbank, Tujunga, Glendale, Eagle Rock, Pasadena—has apartments and other projects for the retired; at Altadena, the Quaker Retirement Center is open to all faiths. Claremont has several apartment and garden-apartment complexes. Eastward, in Alhambra, one of California Lutheran Homes' projects includes rental and health-care units, and nearby Covina, Pomona, San Dimas, Redlands, and other communities also offer facilities. Among Santa Monica's accommodations are high-rise apartments overlooking the ocean.

South of Los Angeles you might want to check out Long Beach (with retirement hotels, mobile-home parks, and apartments) and Seal Beach Leisure World (which, like many of the area's developments, has a minimum age of 52). Inland, at Stanton are the Quaker Garden apartments; at Anaheim, the Luther Home Association of California sponsors rental units and at Satellite Mobile Home Estates sites can be rented or homes purchased.

North of Los Angeles, on the coast at Ventura, are waterfront developments such as Ventura Keys, and the Pacific Coast Senior Citizens sponsor the Ventura Hotel. The National Retired Teachers Association apartments, Grey Gables, are at Ojai, and the California Teachers Association sponsors Vista del Monte at Santa Barbara. Here, too, is the American Baptist Homes development Valle Verde and several other apartment and hotel facilities. Inland, Solvang is a pleasant city, unusual in having retained the mark of its Danish founders.

**Midcoast**   North of Santa Barbara on up to the San Francisco Bay area the coastal mountains begin to run close to the shore resulting, above Morro Bay, in the famous scenery of Monterey County. Because of cool currents, the ocean is chilly for swimming.

The towns in this lovely area, such as Grover City and San Luis Obispo, tend to be expensive, but at Pacific Grove the Episcopalian-sponsored Canterbury Woods or the Methodist-sponsored Forest Hill Manor, or the Congregational Homes project at Carmel, might be possibilities. Santa Cruz has apartments at Garfield Park Village and the Casa del Rey retirement hotel. At Los Gatos, Wedgewood Manor Association offers condominiums for people over 50 and the Episcopal Homes Foundation's Los Gatos Meadows is pleasant. At San Jose, The Villages is a large adult community. Valley Village retirement community at Santa Clara is church-sponsored, as are several other facilities in towns in this area, and Springtown at Livermore is another development for people over 50. The Sequoias in Portola Valley near Palo Alto is church-run but open to all faiths. San Mateo has several retirement apartments (such as Park Tower and Pilgrim Plaza).

In San Francisco it is worth checking with religious organizations, because Northern California Presbyterian Homes has facilities in and near the city; American Baptist Homes of the West, Inc., sponsors Grand Lake Gardens, Piedmont Gardens, and other projects in Oakland; the Episcopalians have built St. Paul's Tower on Lake Merritt in Oakland. In addition, the nonprofit Lesley Foundation sponsors several projects, including apartments at Belmont, Half Moon Bay, and El Solyo Village. Private developments include the Tamalpais high-rise apartments at Greenbrae and the huge Walnut Creek adult community east of the Bay.

**North Coast**   At about the Monterey Peninsula the change to cooler climate begins; it becomes increasingly evident north of the San Francisco Bay area. Communities are small and tucked away in valleys that run down to the coast; a few, such as Mendocino, have become art colonies. Retirement and other developments (such as Shelter Cove Sea Park, Ltd., at Whitethorn) have gotten a late start here, so this is best for the individualistic retiree who does not require built-in amusements. Inland, despite projects such as Coyote Dam which produced Lake Mendocino, the Russian River resorts (Monte Rio, Guerneville) remain relaxed. Living in this area is not unduly expensive.

**The Mountains**   The mountain climates (above 2000 feet) are, as you might expect, cold in winter, and as much as 16 feet of snow often close the Sierra passes. The Sierra foothills, however, often provide better climate than does the valley below them.

Most built-up is the beautiful Lake Tahoe area (over 6000 feet), ringed with year-round resorts, homesite developments (such as Tahoe Keys at South Lake Tahoe), and ski lodges. But Sierra roads to other recreational meccas are also favorites with builders and land-sale companies (much of the previous lumbering land has recently been subdivided here). For instance, near Calaveras Big Trees State Park (between Lake Tahoe and Yosemite) there are planned retirement and recreational communities (such as Meadowmont Village and Big Trees Village).

**The Sacramento–San Joaquin Valley**   The great central valley is a very fertile, flat, agricultural region with hotter summers (frequently 100° days, in the 60's at night) and colder winters (50's days, 30's at night) than the coastal regions. Only at the San Francisco Bay inlet do cooling winds from the Pacific break through the mountains, causing milder temperatures than elsewhere in the valley. Rainfall occurs mostly in winter, about 15 to 20 inches in the north (Sacramento Valley) and about 10 inches in the south (San Joaquin Valley).

The valley bottomlands are not the most attractive regions physically, unless you plan to take up wine growing or fruit-and-vegetable farming on a commercial scale. However, in the surrounding foothills of the Sierras and the coastal range are tucked many lovely valleys, fertile and mild in climate, where living costs are moderate.

In the San Joaquin Valley, Fresno's recreational and cultural lures have made it a popular retirement center, offering homes, apartments, and hotel-style rooms within the city; the California League of Senior Citizens built Senior Citizens Village here (preference given to those with low incomes); a unique feature of the Sierra Sky Park development (no age limit) is that you can taxi your plane to your door. Facilities for the retired branch out into every direction—north through the wine country as far as Lodi, and south to Hanford (with Luther Village for people over 55) and Bakersfield (a development for people over 50).

In the Sacramento Valley, although most towns have at least a couple of accommodations for older people, and Oroville's thermal belt is enticing, most retirement projects are concentrated toward the Bay area, in towns such as Vacaville (with the large Leisure Town) and Napa. If you're an independent, outdoor type, you might prefer the far north of this valley, where Redding is the gateway to the magnificent Shasta-Cascades country.

**The Desert Regions**   Rainfall in the Mojave and Death Valley area is only two inches average a year; thus summer afternoon temperatures, usually around 100°, are made more bearable by the low humidity. Winters are more pleasant—about 70° during the day and in the 40's at night.

The hot springs in the San Bernardino area, originally used by Indians and later as stagecoach stops, became focal points for spas. Palm Springs/Palm Desert, with over 30 golf courses (several of tournament caliber), is most chic. Luxury condominiums here, such as Ironwood and Rancho Mirage, can run as high as $100,000, with a few almost double that; and the better mobile homes (as at the celebrated Blue Skies Park, opened by Bing Crosby) can run well over $50,000. Nevertheless, here and in the nearby resorts (Desert Hot Springs, Twentynine Palms, Indio, or Thermal on the Salton Sea) are many modestly priced facilities. Between the San Bernardino and San Jacinto mountains are over 300 mobile-home parks, many exclusively for retired people, which include some of the fanciest in the United States.

Farther north, in Lancaster, the Retirement Housing Foundation has built the Mayflower Gardens apartments. California City in Antelope Valley, with no age restrictions, has been planned as a self-contained community. Less ambitious homesite and mobile-home developments also dot the area.

Farther out into the desert, Barstow is one of the fastest-growing centers in San Bernardino County. And Needles, on the Colorado River, is attracting fishermen with marinas.

**THE SOUTHWEST** New Mexico, Arizona, westernmost Texas, and southern Utah are also popular for retirement. Many people consider the landscape here—with its canyon lands, painted deserts, mesas, and towering pine-covered mountains—among the most spectacular in the world. Many others are attracted by the extraordinary heritage of Indian and Spanish culture, and find themselves becoming archaeology buffs or experts in exotic cactus and geology.

The main appeal here is a very high proportion of sunny days—the sun shines 85% of daylight hours in most of the area—plus an informal, easygoing way of life. Elevations are mostly high, although some valleys in southeast Arizona and southern New Mexico are as low as 1000 feet. Low humidity makes the high summer temperatures (about 100°) more bearable, but most houses have air conditioning. Although winters are mild (45° to 60° in the day, dropping to the low 30's at night), central heating is necessary at higher altitudes. The late-summer storm season brings the most rain, although some also occurs in winter. Water is in chronically short supply, and even irrigated areas must pay a premium for their water. Respiratory and rheumatic diseases are often eased in this climate, particularly where thickly planted gardens are not the rule. But beware the high altitudes which give the heart and lungs extra work; elevations between 500 and 2000 feet are more suitable for older people.

Housing costs somewhat less in Arizona than the average for the country as a whole. In New Mexico, higher housing costs are to some extent offset by lower state taxes than in Arizona. In both states, mobile-home sites are plentiful, stretching for acres along the highway approaches to cities or ringing the older sections of towns to form suburbs; a few of the costly California-style parks, with swimming pools and other amenities, have also appeared.

Arizona and New Mexico are undergoing such rapid development, often not in the best taste and at inflated prices, that a few inquiries should flood your mailbox for months with descriptions of "estates" and "cities" being carved out of the desert. Some of these consist of nothing more than an optimistic name—or perhaps signs neatly laid out among the sagebrush to indicate where streets will be; so be sure to check what guarantee you have that water and other facilities will actually be brought to the site. It might also be smart to investigate whether local residents have organized to delay or obstruct construction of any development you are considering.

In Arizona, one of the building booms has hit the Phoenix–Tucson area, and both cities have apartments, mobile-home parks, and other accommodations especially for the retired. Nearby are dozens of age-restricted and nonrestricted developments: Sun City (with 28,000 retirees), Mesa (with apartments, mobile parks, homes), Youngtown, Desert Carmel at Casa Grande, Toltec at Eloy, Corona de Tucson and Tucson Green Valley at Tucson, and Arizona Sunsites at Pearce. Another boom has hit the Colorado River, where Golden Shores, a retirement development at Topock, and Holiday Shores, offering homes, building and mobile-home sites at Bullhead City, are examples.

In New Mexico, similar real-estate ventures began near Albuquerque, with developments such as Paradise Hills and Rio Rancho Estates, and are proceeding north via Cochiti Lake toward Santa Fe— from where trailer parks and developments are spreading south. Santa Fe (and Taos), with Spanish- and Pueblo-style homes, is a vigorous cultural center favored by many artists and craftsmen. You might also try Deming (Kingdom of the Sun Retirement Center) or Roswell (Sunny Acres Senior Center, Inc.) in the southeast.

In either state, it's hard to find a town without a small colony of retired people—perhaps in mobile homes or in a few buildings put up by a local builder—and this might be more satisfactory for people who don't like developments.

**THE PACIFIC NORTHWEST**   Though they lack a sunny climate, Oregon and Washington are very beautiful and subject to fewer temperature extremes than their latitude might lead you to expect.

**Climate**   Because ocean breezes penetrate the central valley, the area west of the Cascades has a fairly homogeneous climate except for the heavy rainfall of the Olympia Mountains (where the 140-inch annual average is, fortunately, atypical). Summer coastal temperatures range from the high 70's during the day to the 50's at night. In Puget Sound they sometimes reach the 90's during the day, while in the Willamette Valley they often reach 100°.

Rainfall is light in summer and heavy in winter. Along the coast it averages 75 inches a year, but little of it falls during June to September except in the rain forest. In the Willamette Valley it ranges from 30 (in the south) to 52 inches (in the north); up toward Puget Sound it reaches 63 inches.

Winter coastal temperatures are usually in the 40's during the day and 30's at night, but the heavy rain and constant ocean winds aggravate the cold. In Puget Sound, nights are lower, sometimes to zero. Willamette Valley ranges from the upper 30's in the day to single figures at night, except where sea breezes through the Columbia River inlet even them out somewhat.

Coastal fog and gray skies are winter characteristics. If you can escape the winters, the Pacific Northwest is an ideal spring-summer-autumn place to live.

**Oregon**   Oregon has very few facilities especially for the retired. The Willamette Valley has some mobile-home parks and retirement apartments; at Salem, Salem Town is a planned adult community; and in and near Portland are several apartment and home complexes which cater to retired people (The Village Retirement Center is an example). A few planned developments—King City, south of Portland, or Christmas Valley, southeast of Bend—also lure the retired, although they impose no age restrictions. But for the most part you're on your own to settle in with the regular population in an appealing town—say, Ashland, with its mineral springs and Shakespeare festival, or Klamath Falls if you like fishing and the outdoor life. The coast, with much land reserved in state parks, has many resorts which make the most of beautiful stretches of sandy beach wedged between rocky headlands and backed by craggy pine-clad mountains. New housing is moderately priced.

Several large cities (Eugene, Portland, Salem, Medford) provide a metropolitan life style yet are clean, since large-scale industrialization is chiefly confined to the Portland–Columbia River area. Taxes are moderate—with exemptions for retired people—as are food, clothing, and medical costs. You do need winter underwear, though.

Oregon is very ecology-conscious and its inhabitants fight hard against the encroachments of industry and urban development. It contains well over 200 state parks, plus state and national forests and the unique Crater Lake National Park.

**Washington** Greener and lusher than Oregon, Washington also has a coast of sandy beaches set amid spectacular mountain scenery. On the northern coast of the Olympic Peninsula a stretch of low rainfall (16–20 inches) lies in the rain shadow of the Mount Olympia rain forest.

Seattle and Tacoma represent the largest industrial belt, but both are relatively clean cities set in lovely surroundings. Seattle, a colorful seaport of architectural interest, is the starting point for an unusually large variety of cruises and land tours. Spokane, Bellingham, and Olympia are also attractive; but since few other cities have more than 10,000 inhabitants, and many towns consist of only a few hundred souls, life is oriented to the outdoors.

Panorama City at Lacey is one of the few private developments in the state. Seattle does have the Four Freedoms House of Seattle, Inc. (lakefront apartments for older people), as well as residences and apartments sponsored by church groups (Lutheran, Methodist, Roman Catholic, Baptist, Presbyterian, United Church of Christ), as do Spokane and other large cities. But, as in Oregon, for the most part you're on your own to find an independent niche.

To sum up, if you can put up with wet, cold, sunless winters or find a home in the drier, milder places; if you like the outdoors and informality; and if you like mountains, think about the Pacific Northwest. If you are prepared to do your own work around the house and in the garden, you may find the cost of living no higher here than it is in Florida.

**THE GULF COAST** Also popular for retirement has been the Gulf Coast, which extends from the Florida Panhandle (see above) to eastern Texas. This coast was once the resort to which plantation owners and the wealthy of New Orleans and Mobile fled to escape heat and epidemics, so great summer houses lined much of the shore. But hurricane damage and inflation caused these to give way to resorts that were, on the whole, fairly cheap. However, waterfront property is now hard to get, and in the desirable sections costly condominiums are on the way.

**Climate** This subtropical coastal plain below the snow line has mild winters; but only on the coast do breezes relieve the summer heat (most often over 90°) and humidity (often around the 90% mark, particularly in the mornings). Rainfall, fairly constant throughout the year, is heaviest in summer, when it is often accompanied by thunderstorms. This summer rain is heaviest along the Alabama coast, lessening gradually toward the west until, in Texas, it is down to about 30 inches a year. Mosquitoes and termites, chief among the insect inhabitants, can be a nuisance. So can hurricanes, although only about 15 in 55 years have actually reached land and caused damage; warning systems are excellent, so that injury and property damage have been decreasing.

**Cost of Living**    It can be as low here as it is in Florida. Fresh seafood abounds, locally grown fruit and vegetables are cheap, and clothing is informal and requires little seasonal adjustment. Housing can be cheap, and winter heating by local natural gas is low in cost.

**Development**    One reason retired people have come here is that income levels have been low; in fact, poverty has been rampant. Now, eager for economic advance, the Gulf states have encouraged industry (such as oil) which has met environmental opposition in states that could afford to be more particular. Port Charles and New Orleans are already highly polluted; offshore oil drilling lines the entire Louisiana and northern Texas coasts. In addition, oil "superports" are planned for Port Fourchon, Louisiana, and Freeport, Texas. Dirty refineries and petrochemical plants, plus a rising need for sewers, water, housing, and other necessities for workers employed by the new facilities, will make this area less and less attractive for retirement.

At present, the short Alabama shore has enticing little resorts— such as Fairhope, with crafts shops, or Point Clear—and fine beaches on Dauphin and Pleasure islands. How much of this area remains desirable, and for how long, depends on how successfully the city of Mobile horns in on the oil bonanza. Mississippi's coast is also short; as it is serviced by a major highway, most of the towns (Pass Christian, Bay St. Louis) are highly developed, with the greatest crowding between Biloxi and Gulfport. The offshore islands—such as Deer Island, where legends promise buried treasure—can be reached only by boat. In Louisiana, inland towns which have previously attracted some retired people (such as Morgan City, accessible to the Intracoastal Waterway) will undoubtedly be affected by oil development; and urbanization is already spreading north of New Orleans to towns above Lake Pontchartrain.

About 120 miles inland from the Gulf, at a 700-foot elevation, San Antonio forms a nexus of retirement living in Texas. Its winters and summers are mild, humidity is a pleasant 54% annual average, and the weather is sunny two thirds of the time. Housing suitable for retired people is plentiful and moderate in cost.

**SOUTHEAST STATES**    From Virginia to Georgia, the past lies deep all around you, with proud ports, famous gardens, and noted historical towns. Despite pockets of both expensive and cheap living areas, in general prices are highest in the north and get lower as you move south.

The coastline is lovely, with hundreds of offshore islands, some only accessible by boat but many connected to the mainland by causeways. Once the summering place for inland plantation owners and later industrial barons, the islands and coasts are now a popular retirement and vacation area for people of all economic levels. They offer a variety of resort centers, fishing hamlets, and state and national recreation centers.

In the past, the only facilities available for older people were small homes, usually run by religious groups (often Lutheran and Methodist in the Carolinas, and Baptist and Presbyterian in Georgia). But as Florida's development reaches saturation point, real estate projects are moving north through Georgia and south from Virginia.

The beautiful inland mountain areas boast many small towns which are centers of lively cultural and social activity, particularly in the summer holiday season.

**Climate**    High humidity combined with summer temperatures, which average about 80° or 85° but often reach 100°, can be oppressive in the midlands. Along the shore, sea breezes reduce the effect. The mountains are comfortable most of the year but winters can be bitter, with snowfalls averaging about four inches. Winter daytime temperatures average in the upper 40's in Virginia (upper 20's at night) and 55° in Georgia (seldom below the 40's at night). Occasional cold spells are common; about three a winter will blow down from Canada. Rainfall, much of it in summer showers, averages about 48 inches in Georgia and lessens somewhat as you go north.

**Georgia**    In addition to resort and mobile-home parks along the coast, large inland cities (such as Augusta) offer retirement apartments and hotels. Old cities, such as Savannah, have been rejuvenated with large new rental complexes that attract retired people even though they have no minimum-age restrictions. Atlanta has been particularly active in building new apartments, including some especially for the retired.

You might also want to consider the mountain recreational area, which is well supplied with lakes and rivers. Most of this area, within a two-hour drive of Atlanta, is undergoing rapid development. Big

Canoe is a giant project near Casper; a more expensive, golf-oriented complex is Kingswood Country Club near Clayton. Because Georgia has been slow to pass environmental or consumer protection legislation, you might want to check with experts at the University of Georgia's School of Environmental Design or the North Georgia Mountains Authority (in Unicoi) before investing in land.

**South Carolina**   The state offers a good choice of fine beaches, coastal resorts, and some inland antebellum towns. You will find housing costs relatively little. Retired people have been attracted to the communities and mobile-home parks along the coast. The most famous is the Sea Pines Company development of Hilton Head Island which received a Citation of Excellence from the American Institute of Architects; most homes are well over $50,000, but the living is gracious. Despite tasteful projects in the area, there has lately been some grumbling about overdevelopment. The older resorts (Myrtle Beach, Isle of Palms, Edisto) are attractive and offer a wide range of prices.

Much new building has taken place in older communities (such as Beaufort or Charleston), which offer attractions to retired people who are looking for a quietly secure or relaxed metropolitan way of life. Toward the mountains the population is less culture-conscious, but both inland and along the coast, life is easygoing, with southern charm and hospitality always at the ready.

**North Carolina**   Most of this state is eminently suitable for retirement living. In addition to beautiful beaches and boating in sounds and inlets, the coast is famous for offshore fishing. The low Sand Hills are a favorite retirement spot for the better-heeled golfer. Condominiums at Pinehurst, over $50,000, come with golf and other resort privileges.

Very popular for retirement, too, are the attractive highland towns near the Blue Ridge Parkway and south of Asheville (which itself has some special retirement facilities such as the Manor Retirement Club). Many of these (Hendersonville, for example) cater to retired people; others have built developments especially for them; but you might want to check into zoning and other controls, because commercialization is ruining many towns here. While in much of this area winter can be severe, thermal belts create warm pockets where temperatures seldom drop below freezing. However, prices in thermal-belt towns (such as Tryon) naturally tend to be higher. Educational and cultural life is richest in Asheville or nearby towns such as Brevard.

North Carolina has a reputation for being an up-to-date Old South state, and its cultural and intellectual life is hopping. It is still notable for its southern manners and mountain-crafts tradition. Living costs vary greatly, but reasonably priced housing is available almost every-where, and some jobs can be found. Excellent state facilities are matched by taxes to pay for them, although some exemptions are given to retired people.

**Virginia**   This state is very conscious of its past, and a list of its towns sounds like a roster of historical firsts. Virginia is also hot on culture. Many people here have retired early from military or government service, and retirement clubs are often exceptionally lively and well traveled. This tends to be especially true in the expensive Alexandria–Richmond axis. Cheaper are some of the fairly old-fashioned towns on the Chesapeake Bay and in the muggy interior plain. Prices in the beautiful Shenandoah area and south along the Blue Ridge Parkway vary tremendously; here costly enclaves alternate with moderately priced hamlets and cheap rural hideaways.

**THE MIDEAST**   New York, New Jersey, Pennsylvania, Maryland, and Delaware in their entirety are too industrialized to be charming, but in certain districts all offer attractive options. Harsh winters in western Pennsylvania and northern New York are another deterrent; hot, somewhat humid summers can be escaped only in the mountains or on the coasts; spring and fall are, however, delightful. Prices are high, of course, in the metropolitan regions; in outlying areas cheap land is still available, although, for the most part you must look hard to find rural life offset by tourist or cultural life.

**New York**   The tempo of life in southern New York is fast, exciting, and for some dangerous—not the place for curing high blood pressure or stomach ulcers. It is also expensive. Nevertheless, many retired people enjoy New York City, and a few retirement facilities have been built nearby (such as the Springvale-on-Hudson Apartments at Croton-on-Hudson). The most popular area is Long Island, where rather expensive condominiums have been built at beach resorts such as Southhampton, and where moderately priced housing is available in many developments; Leisure Knoll (near Brookhaven) is an example of a community geared to retirees.

In the part of the state toward the Great Lakes the countryside is flat and unlovely. To the east, the great forest region of the Adirondack Mountain Preserve offers moderately priced recreational resorts, where winters are harsh and jobs scarce, but quite a few people have retired to Saratoga Springs. South of the Mohawk River, centers such as Cooperstown have drawn large numbers of retired people, as has the Catskill Forest Preserve; these are attractive vacation areas.

**New Jersey**   Overspill of population and industry from metropolitan areas has made much of this state expensive and polluted.

Northwestern (popular for vacation) and central (farmland and the Pine Barrens) New Jersey contain public recreational facilities and land is still decently priced. West of Cape May, the Delaware Bay shoreline is also not yet urbanized. On the highly developed Atlantic coast, Atlantic City, Asbury Park, and other resorts offer retirement apartments; many of the old commercial hotels have also been converted to retirement living. The sandbars rimming the shore are connected by road to the mainland, are highly developed, and are high-priced (except for a slight decrease at the central section). The largest planned community is Rossmoor Leisure World at Cranbury; Cedar Glen Homes, Inc., at Toms River, is a tenant-owned retirement village; a few church groups sponsor facilities open to all races and religions, such as the Navesink House in Red Bank.

**Pennsylvania** The Appalachian Mountains, highest in the west, descend to foothills in the east and southeast of the state. Both eastern and western Pennsylvania are heavily built up and industrialized. In between (from the Wellsboro area south through the center of the state) lies farming country with hamlets where the living is not expensive. Winters here are deep in snow, summers warm and pleasant. Special facilities for retirement are usually run by cities or counties for local people of limited resources or are sponsored by religious groups. Some retired people seek out the homesite and other developments near recreational facilities, such as Wild Acres Lakes and Dingman's Ferry or Big Bass Lake, Inc. at Goldsboro.

**Maryland** With so much of the state fronting on the Chesapeake Bay, Maryland has lured many boatmen and fishermen. On the western shore, Annapolis is charming though expensive. On the eastern shore, a building boom that threatened to engulf the quiet fishing villages was slowed when many communities placed moratoriums on sewer hookups. Worth special mention is Columbia, between Washington and Baltimore; unlike many developments which dub themselves "new towns," Columbia is the real thing—built after much study of European models and expert advice. It was described and extolled by Vance Packard in *A Nation of Strangers,* worth reading if you are considering a planned community.

**Delaware** Beachfront property here is virtually unobtainable, but for relaxed living within reasonable distance of great cities, some retired people have chosen Dover, Lewes, and other small towns here.

**NEW ENGLAND** For a lively, independent kind of retirement the small towns of New England are ideal—the countryside is easily accessible, most facilities are within walking distance if you live in town, many areas are redolent with historical and cultural life, and several large metropolises are within easy reach. Although most areas have senior citizens clubs and activities, specific retirement developments or villages are rare since most older people prefer to be part of the regular community life.

**Climate**   Summers are hot, particularly in the southern reaches, often humid, and given to brief thunderstorms. Winters are cold, damp along the coast and with heavy snowstorms inland. Spring sometimes gets lost between a rainy winter and a hot summer, and Indian summers are common in the fall, which is probably more beautiful here than almost anywhere else at all.

Pollution is bad along the southern coast and near the industrial complexes, but where tourism is big business, as in Vermont, anti-pollution controls are stringent.

**Connecticut**   Suburbanization afflicts much of southern and middle Connecticut, and most of these suburbs are expensive. The countryside is rolling and wooded, even in the suburbs. The coast and the industrial Hartford–New Haven complex are heavily polluted. A few attractive old towns (Mystic Seaport, Guilford) exist, as do pockets of reasonably priced land and houses (particularly toward the north). The few developments for the retired tend to be in good taste but rather high-priced: award-winning Heritage Village (Southbury); beautifully landscaped Canaan Close (New Canaan) with luxury townhouses; and Lyme Regis (New Lyme), built to blend unobtrusively into the old town. Connecticut, close to New York City's attractions, is nevertheless locally strong on cultural pursuits, too.

**Massachusetts**   Here, where the American Revolution began, are villages of great charm intent on preserving their heritage; yet about equally prevalent are drab manufacturing centers (often set in lovely valleys) you'd do best to avoid. Accessible to Boston are historic towns and seaports in which you'll have to search hard for a property bargain. South, the beautiful beaches of Cape Cod have created high-priced resorts and a few condominiums (such as Tide Watch Village); on the islands of Martha's Vineyard and Nantucket, environmental concern restricts development and has raised prices pretty high. In central Massachusetts, where woods and ponds abound, the cost of living is lower. In the west, the Berkshire Mountains are a center for fairly sophisticated year-round tourist activities with an emphasis on the arts; in the country towns, of great visual appeal, you'll again have to look hard for inexpensive housing.

**Rhode Island**   Except for a few of the coastal towns, most of Rhode Island's landscape has been marred by industrialism, and pollution levels are high.

**Vermont**   With the Green Mountain National Forest running down the center of the state, Vermont is one of the foremost year-round resort areas of the Northeast. Condominiums and independent Alpine-style lodges are for sale in and near most of the ski resorts; check for water and sanitary problems in these, as some have been overbuilt. Southern and much of middle-Vermont are expensive; craft activities are good here, and some old villages—such as Woodstock—are extraordinarily appealing. A typical project is Quechee Lakes, a picturesque village being restored, with limited new building. Farther north, costs are lower, and if you can stand the harsh winters you'll find many undiscovered hideaways. This tourist-conscious state has taken a tough stand on environmental control.

**New Hampshire**   Neither the short, highly developed coastline nor the smallish industrial cities of the south are particularly appealing, and some people feel the central lake region has suffered from uncontrolled development. But the beautiful White Mountains toward the north are a handsome year-round resort. Prices and population density are generally lowest the farther north you go.

**Maine**   With its long, spectacularly rocky coastline, its offshore islands, and its vast tracts of inland forest, Maine presents the wildest aspects of New England life. Winters are rugged, and much of the interior is scarcely touched except by timber companies. Thanks to a year-round arctic current, swimming can be chilly. Despite, or perhaps because of these features, parts of Maine are very popular for retirement. The fishing villages (Wiscasset, Damariscotta) are especially appealing, and the islands attract their share of individualistic retirees.

**OTHER PLACES**   Particularly in mountainous country that is not too far into the northern latitudes, searching will often turn up specific places—a valley or group of valleys, a small community, a district—where the climate is more favorable than in the surrounding region, where development has not (yet) run away with itself and where prices are therefore still low, where the scenery is beautiful, and where the population and way of life are attractive to you. The climate will probably not be so desirable or the elevation may be higher than most people would like. Or perhaps lack of development means that amusements are not organized, so that you are thrown on your own devices. Thus a town such as Jackson, Wyoming, which is too cold and too high for many people, might attract you with its out-and-out tourism, liveliness, and scenery. But since so many personal exceptions cannot be covered here, below are a few general areas where retired people have congregated:

**Ozarks**   At the point where Arkansas, Oklahoma, and Missouri meet are the Ozark Mountains and, just south of them, the Ouachita Mountains. Summers are apt to be humid and hot—both figures hitting the 90's. Except for an occasional cold spell, winters are in the 40's during the day and 20's at night; snowfall is between 6 and 12 inches for the season; and the sun shines over 50% of the daylight hours. Rainfall is some 50 inches, fairly evenly spread throughout the year, and summer rain is brought mainly by thunderstorms.

This scenic country, whose rugged mountains, lovely valleys, and extensive series of lakes and reservoirs have long drawn vacationers, is a favorite retirement area for people of modest means. Land is still relatively cheap and building costs moderate. So are food and state taxes. Activities tend to be on the folksy side (square dances and the like), but summer brings a variety of seasonal theater and other attractions, and cities such as Tulsa and Little Rock are close enough for occasional excursions.

In the Oklahoma Ozarks, you might search the towns from Tahlequah (former capital of the Cherokee Indian Nation) north through Claremore (whose waters have long been visited for rheumatic ailments), and in the Grand Lake area. In Missouri, Branson and Lake Ozark are among the liveliest resorts, but historic towns such as Ironton have also attracted retired people. (Other possibilities in Missouri, of course, are Clarksville and other scenic Mississippi River towns within easy reach of St. Louis.) In Arkansas, Eureka Springs is the oldest spa, but the area around Harrison and Bull Shoals Lake has many retirement homesites, apartments, and other facilities; if you're culturally inclined, Fayetteville, with the University of Arkansas and a Fine Arts Center, might be more appealing. In the Ouachitas, the city of Hot Springs, surrounding Hot Springs National Park, offers golf courses and other recreational facilities in addition to ample housing; rock hounds like this area, as well as the diamond-hunting grounds near Murfreesboro.

**Appalachians** In Kentucky, Tennessee, and West Virginia are some of the most beautiful rural areas in the United States. To find them you must avoid the pockets of great wealth (such as the bluegrass horse country around Lexington, Kentucky) and the scarred coal-mining areas. For the most part the cost of living in these states is low—the population is poor and geared to rock-bottom living. In the cheapest sections, housing consists principally of small mountain cabins or mobile homes on enough land for a good-size vegetable garden. Although there are some small (and often shoddy) attempts at tourist development, the state governments have not yet attempted large-scale tourism, and real-estate booms have yet to hit here. Medical facilities are scarce in some districts, so check their availability.

In West Virginia, you would do best to avoid the industrialized western sector and concentrate on the area around Martinsburg, Berkeley Springs (which claims to be the oldest spa in the nation), Shepherdstown, Charles Town (not Charleston!), and Harpers Ferry, which will allow you to get into Washington occasionally. White Sulphur Springs is pretty chic, and Morgantown is the university center; by searching the small towns between them and east of them, you might find cheap, though isolated, living.

In Tennessee, TVA dams have created so many lakes that the state calls itself the "Great Lakes of the South." Public recreation lands are beautiful. Memphis, proud of its cultural facilities and cleanliness, has a Deep South character. Nashville, with 13 colleges and universities, has been undergoing rejuvenation. But retired people seem to prefer the Smoky Mountain area, where they can live in magnificent countryside yet be within reach of the cultural and other facilities of Chattanooga and Knoxville (both cities suffer from pollution). Unfortunately, however, there has been little attempt at environmental control, so unless you enjoy living amid motels and souvenir shops, avoid the centers of tourist towns such as Gatlinburg.

In Kentucky, you'll want to keep away from the southeastern coal-mining district (Ashland to Middlesboro) and from the oil and industrial towns (Owensboro, Elizabethtown, Glasgow, Greenville) toward the west. Instead you might want to look in the Land Between the Lakes National Recreation Area, with the resort towns of Murray, Aurora, and Cadiz; Gilbertsville, being closest to Paducah, is most developed with homesites and planned communities, but there are some chemical plants nearby. The other pretty region is the bluegrass country near Lexington; though Lexington itself is surrounded by wealthy horse farms, nearby are quiet villages (such as Nicholasville to the south), the sulfur-spring resort of Harrodsburg (west), and three tranquil college towns: Berea (south), which also has a hand-weaving industry, Morehead (east), and Georgetown (northwest). The Lake Cumberland region, with attractive towns such as Albany, is another possibility.

**Colorado**   For people who can take fairly severe winters and can pay moderate to high prices, the Rocky Mountains, justifiably famous for their beauty and almost equally famous for their active cultural life, are a possibility. Snow lasts from December through late spring, which makes for a long skiing season and also for limited traveling. Winter days may reach the 40's, but readings in the teens are standard at night, with subzero on occasion in lower altitudes and frequently in higher ones. Summer days are usually in the 60's and 70's, and the 40's and 50's at night. Humidity is low, rainfall about 15 inches a year. Frequent, brief thunderstorms occur throughout the area. Year-round resorts abound, and a building boom has made prices high. Water supply is becoming a problem. As a result, Boulder, Aspen, and other cities are now trying to limit population growth.

Denver and its suburbs have a number of retirement facilities, such as Sunny Acres retirement community or the bungalow-style apartments at Geneva Village in nearby Littleton, as well as communities open to people of any age. Condominiums are popular here, with the Summit House East and the Anaconda apartments (near the Copper Mountain ski lifts and golf) typical of those commanding higher prices. Slightly north, Boulder, Longmont, and Greeley (with the nonprofit Bonell Good Samaritan Retirement Community) are also popular. South, Pueblo and Colorado Springs have been chosen by trade unions, religious groups, and private developers as retirement sites. In the foothills and mountains just west of these cities, so-called new towns and other developments are going up at a fast clip.

Some of the most expensive condominiums are being built near Aspen; examples are the apartments at Concept 600 (near Buttermilk Mountain), cedar chalets at The Gant (Aspen Mountain), and the luxury Top of the Village units (*above* the lifts at Snowmass). At Vail, the apartments at Sundown, clustered housing around pools at Valley of Vail, and the new village of Lion's Head are representative. Grand Junction, to the west, was chosen as site of the Monterey Park Apartments by the Foundation for Senior Citizens, Inc.

Southern Colorado is the latest area to be developed; condominiums such as Tamarron in Durango have already been built, but much other land here has been subdivided for future building.

**Idaho** Sun Valley, whose recreational facilities include golf, tennis, skiing, and swimming, has branched out into many new condominium clusters. Some of these are most attractive; while prices of some new units can go well over $100,000, more reasonable housing is also available.

**Nevada** The glamour of Las Vegas has always been an attraction, and condominiums are still rising here. Less expensive is nearby Boulder City, with the facilities of Lake Mead National Recreation Area. At Lake Tahoe, the Boise Cascade Corporation built Incline Village, Inc., and many other developers have ringed this area west to Carson City and north to Reno.

## U. S. ISLANDS

**HAWAII** In climate and topography, Hawaii is probably the nearest (except for the Virgin Islands) you can get to paradise in the American hemisphere. But it is expensive. It is especially expensive if you want all the modern conveniences in an urban environment. If you can do without these, live on local food and off the beaten track, forswear dressing up, and do a bit of your own building and maintenance work, you might just make it on a moderate (not on a small) income.

The islands are very healthful; water is pure; local fruits, vegetables, and seafood are various and plentiful. Imported food costs about 25% more than on the mainland. State taxes are high, although retired people get certain income- and property-tax exemptions. Trips to the mainland are expensive—it's a long way, after all—and you must take this into account if you think you'll need to make them.

**Topography**   Seven of the major islands are inhabited, the eighth is not; an additional 124 minor islands stretch across miles of ocean. All the major islands are volcanic in origin (one of the two volcanoes on Hawaii is still active, though not alarmingly so).

**Climate**   The islands are in the path of the northeast trade winds, which kindly deposit most of their moisture on the northeastern slopes of the mountains. This leaves the rest of each island with climates varying from subtropical to semiarid. Hawaii Island also gets southwest trade winds, which give it a higher rainfall than the others. Rainfall on mountaintops ranges from 200 to 480 inches (*ulp!*) a year. On the northeast coasts it ranges from 32 to 64 inches, varying with the island. Sheltered sides of the islands average about 15 inches, except for Hawaii and Kauai, which get up to 64 inches in some spots.

Coastal temperatures average 78° in summer (and seldom get above 85°) and 72° in winter (and seldom fall below 60°, even at night). Inland, temperatures cool with altitude and it is even possible to find snow on the highest peaks in midwinter.

**Population**   Hawaii, the largest island, is by no means the most developed, thanks perhaps to its rainfall. It is Oahu, the third-largest island, which has the greatest population, with a very large urban conglomeration around Honolulu and Waikiki Beach. This, the biggest resort, has many homes and apartments suitable for retirement, but it is expensive and polluted. On Maui, the second largest island, condominiums (such as Lahaina Shores or Whalers Village) are no cheaper. But away from the resort areas property is moderately priced.

The tourist season is year-round, with a slight falling-off between January and June. Residents are of many racial origins, of which Japanese and Caucasian form the largest proportion and Hawaiian one of the smallest.

**THE U. S. VIRGIN ISLANDS**   St. Thomas, St. Croix, and St. John are U. S.-owned and located in the Caribbean, east of Puerto Rico.

These islands are beautiful, with rolling, wooded hills and lovely beaches. The other 40-odd islands and keys of the group must be reached by boat from the larger islands; many of these are uninhabited (and uninhabitable) or present other difficulties (Buck Island is a national monument, for instance, and land cannot be bought on Water Island but must be leased from a company which in turn leases it from the U. S. government).

**Climate**   In this subtropical climate, temperatures are usually in the 70's during "winter" months and in the 80's at the height of summer; at night they might fall into the low 70's. Humidity is highest in autumn but well controlled the rest of the year by northeast trade winds. Rainfall averages 45 inches and arrives in brief showers, mostly at night, throughout the year.

**Development**   St. John is largely national park, and any available private land is at a premium. Development on St. Thomas, which has the highest population, started before that on St. Croix, but now both islands are host to heavy condominium construction. (On St. Croix, the south shore is least desirable because of oil and other industry.)

Housing prices are high, because building materials must be brought from the mainland and because much new construction is now on land which must be leveled from hillsides or which presents some other expensive obstacle. In fact, the cost of living is just generally high, with most food costing about 20% more than on the mainland. Jobs are to be found, particularly in the tourist trade, but wages are low. Taxes are at U. S. federal rates; they are paid into the coffers of the island government, thus obviating the need for state taxes. Water is so precious that each house must have its own rain-gathering system. Medical facilities are good.

Although whites are still a minority of the population, their numbers have increased recently. Racial and political tensions have been growing, and if you are considering a move you should investigate closely the current state of affairs.

If you want a U.S. standard of living in a perfect climate, this is it —if you have an income well above the average.


**PUERTO RICO**   The climate of Puerto Rico is approximately that of the Virgin Islands except that in the mountainous interior temperatures are a good 10° lower. As the mountains milk most of the moisture from the prevailing northeast trade winds, rainfall is much heavier on the northeastern coast and mountain slopes than on the southwestern. Rainfall averages about 50 inches a year at the midway point between the two extremes.

San Juan, the capital, offers a wide spectrum of social, cultural, and sporting activities. The other old towns are quieter and a lot cheaper to live in. Outside San Juan are many new housing developments where prices are about the same as for equivalent property on the U. S. mainland. The Sea Pines Company, which developed Hilton Head Island, S.C., is building the planned community of Palmas del Mar; no cars will be allowed (only electrified vehicles and bicycles), and half the land will be preserved in park and forest.

Income taxes are a little lower than on the mainland. Work is available only for special skills but starting your own business is a possibility—the tourist trade is large.

# 13
# Foreign Retirement Country

## PRACTICAL CONSIDERATIONS

**COST OF LIVING**   Until recently, a prime reason for retiring abroad was to take advantage of a lower cost of living. Unfortunately, unless you are prepared for isolated, perhaps primitive, living, there are few places left where you can make much of a savings. Inflation and the building boom have hit most other countries even harder than they have the United States, so that living abroad now costs nearly as much as it does here; in some places it costs even more.

This is most certainly true of the Caribbean Islands, many Far Eastern and northern European cities, and increasingly of southern Europe. Mexico, Morocco, Ireland, Madeira, and Greece still offer some possibilities outside the fashionable enclaves. New Zealand and Australia are still a hair less expensive than the United States, although they were never notably low.

Two books that might help your choice are *All You Need to Know About Living Abroad* by Eleanor B. Pierce (a Pan American Airways publication distributed by Doubleday & Co., Inc.) and *I've Had It— A Practical Guide to Living Abroad* by Robert Hopkins (Holt, Rinehart and Winston, 1972).

**CLIMATE**   If you are starting from scratch in your choice of a foreign domicile, the first thing to consider is the climate (see Chapter 9 for the effects of climate). Remember that July is the height of summer in latitudes north of the equator, and January south of the equator. Climate for selected areas is described below; for other parts of the world consult the appropriate references in the introduction to Section II.

**THE RECONNAISSANCE TRIP**   Unless you have spent some time in the place very recently, and certainly if you have never been there, you should take an advance trip to the land of your dreams and stay there as long as you possibly can—several weeks at least, several months, even a year if you possibly can.

Before you go, write to or visit the tourist bureau, consul's office, or embassy of the country in which you are interested. These are usually in Washington, D.C., and New York City, and are happy to supply you with information on visa regulations, income requirements, tax regulations, job restrictions, cost of living, popular foreign tourist and settlement areas, climate, and topography; they will give you sources for further information and can usually suggest ways of finding competent real estate agents in specific areas. Two American agencies that handle international properties are Previews, Inc. (49 East 53rd Street, New York, N.Y. 10022), and Panorama International Ltd. (810 18th Street, N.W., Washington, D.C. 20006); both, however, handle the more expensive properties.

Once there, you should carry out the same sort of investigation you would for a new area of the United States (see Chapter 10). Go to the local Chamber of Commerce or its equivalent and check out rent levels, home-purchase prices, and other costs. Talk to both foreign and native residents, particularly foreigners who are leaving—they will usually give you a good rundown of the disadvantages. Find out if there is a foreign colony, where it is located, what its makeup is, how it lives, whether it has skyrocketed property prices in its area. Also inquire about possible restrictions on land ownership by foreigners.

Check on the nature and extent of the local medical facilities: the number, quality, and accessibility of doctors, clinics, laboratories, and hospitals. In the United States you are accustomed to an overall high standard; abroad this may not be so. If your chosen country has tropical climates, you will need a whole set of inoculations before you go; even if you mean to settle in a temperate area, you may need to travel in other parts.

You should also—gloomy note—investigate what might happen if you die abroad. Are you particular about how and where you will be buried? There may be mandatory burial times in your host country; can your family get your body out in time if you want to be buried in the United States?

Visit the American Embassy and get its opinions of local conditions. Walk around a lot, sit in local cafés, get a feel for the atmosphere. Read up on the history and cultural life of the area.

**INCOME**   You can arrange for your Social Security payment to be sent to you; the U. S. Embassy usually does the distributing within the country. Similar arrangements can also be made for private pension, annuity, interest, and other regular payments.

Find out what will happen to money which you transfer into the currency of your host country. In some nations it is difficult to get permission for it to be reconverted into dollars.

Jobs are not likely to be available; most countries have a hard enough time finding work for their own nationals and working papers are consequently hard to get. The only exception is if you have a skill that is rare and necessary in your host country. For additional details, see "Jobs Abroad" in Chapter 17. Starting your own business may prove easier in some places. Even so, you must investigate local regulations very carefully before you plunge into any commitments.

**VISA REGULATIONS** Most countries require you to get an immigrant's visa either before you go or within a certain period after getting there. These are obtainable from the immigration department in the country itself or the country's consulate in the United States.

To get the visa you will have to supply certain documents, which may be any or all of the following: a currently valid passport, a medical certificate, proof of economic stability, vaccination certificate, police certificate of good conduct, statement of intention to transfer money. Some countries require a certain minimum income for retired people; how much depends on the general cost of living in the country.

You should also check on whether you will need an exit visa to leave the country again and, if so, how difficult it will be to get.

**TAXES** Unless your income falls below the taxable limit, you will have to complete a yearly income tax return for the U. S. Internal Revenue Service. You may have to do the same thing for your host country as well. If you are lucky in your choice, the country will have a treaty with the United States not to tax the same money twice. Some countries tax Social Security income, some tax other pensions. The United States will usually allow deduction for taxes paid to the host country. Get hold of *Tax Guide for U. S. Citizens Abroad*, published by the IRS (publication Number 54) and revised annually.

**CUTTING LIVING COSTS** As a North American you have enjoyed a degree of comfort not common to most other countries (although now increasingly to be found in more developed nations). In your new country you may have to pay premium prices for a centrally heated house, for stereo sound equipment, for dry cleaning, for gas for cars, for bourbon. If you can do without and substitute what the locals use, you can cut living costs. In general, expect locally produced goods and services to cost less and imported ones to cost more.

In most foreign countries (though not all) the following items tend to cost less than in the United States: public transport, entertainment, domestic foods and drinks, restaurants, tailoring, medical and dental supplies and services, reading matter, domestic help, and personal services.

On the other hand, the following things are usually more expensive than in the United States: private transport, imported and frozen foods, imported drinks, mortgage rates, home appliances, gas for cars, and ready-made clothes.

Remember that although medical care is usually less expensive than in the United States, you will not be getting Medicare. A few countries, mostly northern European, have an equivalent health service; most do not. You should therefore have enough money set aside for medical expenses. Your emergency fund should also include a sum for possible legal expenses, especially if you are buying property. It is probably better to stash your emergency fund in the United States, preferably in such a way (in trust, say) that only you or your heirs can get at it.

On a cautionary note: there is a high rate of repatriation among people with only moderate or low fixed incomes who have tried to live abroad. Make very detailed investigations into what your expenses are likely to be and a very realistic estimate of what you are willing to live without. If you do go broke, the U. S. government will ship you back to the States—but you will be in debt to it for your fares and expenses. And it can be very bad if you come back to nothing. If you are adventurous by nature you will probably risk it and take what comes; if you are not, you may find such consequences very painful.

**LOCAL CUSTOMS**   Out of sheer courtesy you should bone up on the social and cultural history of your host country before you move. You should then familiarize yourself with local customs as quickly as you can after you get there. This will be a lot easier to do if you have taken the trouble to learn the language. Your knowledge of the language or attempt to gain it after you get there will also be much appreciated by the natives. They are only too accustomed to having to learn your language; as a resident, the least you can do is talk to them in their own.

Americans are brought up to value material possessions and to evaluate other people by their material success. In many other countries this is not so much the case—the emphasis may lie more on ancestry, learning, or social ease. As a foreigner you will probably be evaluated on your own personal merits since the natives will have no other frame of reference for you. This fact presents many people with great difficulties; it presents many others with great opportunities.

## SELECTED RETIREMENT AREAS

What follows is a brief survey of a number of countries throughout the world that present some attraction for retired people. The information given is—necessarily—incomplete and sketchy; the subject demands several books in its own right.

With the exception of Morocco, the countries of Africa are not discussed. This is not to say that no retired American would find them attractive. Kenya, Zambia, Southern Rhodesia, and South Africa are all climatically and scenically very desirable in certain parts. But the political situation is uncertain in some of them; the attitude toward nonworking white people (if white you are) may be problematical in others—or in the same ones; and if you are black you would automatically exclude such countries as South Africa.

One of the world's near-paradises is Tahiti, but the Tahitians are anxious to preserve their paradise and limit residence of foreigners very strictly.

The various countries of Europe hold very great attractions for a lot of people. But where the climate is good, costs are sky-high or getting there. And where the climate is bad, probably only people with ancestral connections could put up with it. In France, Austria, and Switzerland, ski resorts are popular sites for some of the better new condominiums, but the latter two countries have restrictions on foreign ownership. The other area that attracts Americans is the often polluted Mediterranean coast. Here one of the better villas or condominium apartments might run you roughly $50,000, but the term "villa" applies equally to jerry-built concrete boxes at a quarter of that price on Spain's Costa Brava or to the marble-floored units that can cost four times that much at Marina Baie des Anges on the French Riviera. An area you might check into is France's Languedoc-Roussillon, a 100-mile stretch of beach billed as the "New Riviera."

Tonga has an attractive climate and cost-of-living level, but conditions there are still fairly primitive and probably not conducive to long life for a mollycoddled westerner.

Other countries have been omitted on much the same grounds: bad climate, health hazards, high cost of living, lack of welcome for Americans; or because they are forbidden ground for a U. S. national.

**THE CARIBBEAN**   For about 2500 miles, thousands of islands spread in a northwest-southeast curve across the Caribbean Sea. Just over 50 of them are inhabited and only about 30 are developed sufficiently for what you might call civilized comfort.

Of the developed islands, Puerto Rico and three of the Virgin Islands belong to the United States and have been discussed in Chapter 12. Some of the smaller Virgin Islands, four of the Windward Islands (Grenada, St. Vincent, St. Lucia, Dominica), the Cayman Islands, and several of the Leeward Islands (Montserrat, Antigua, and St. Kitts) are British-connected. Martinique and Guadeloupe are French. And the Netherland Antilles (Aruba, Curaçao, Bonaire in the south; St. Eustatius and Saba in the north) belong, as you might expect, to Holland. St. Martin is half French and half Dutch. Jamaica, Cuba, Haiti, the Dominican Republic, Barbados, and the Bahamas are independent.

Some of the other islands are in line for development; still others are very happy to continue as they are and do not welcome bulldozers. The way of life is thoroughly American or European (depending on the island) and facilities of all sorts are available. The population, not counting the tourists, is predominantly black with some European blood in its ancestry.

**Climate and Topography**   Judged by latitude, the climate throughout the islands is tropical with a temperature difference of only about 10° F. between winter and summer averages; the annual average is in the 70's. However, in the mountainous regions on some of the islands, temperature falls considerably below this norm.

Topography varies with the island. Some are mountainous: Jamaica's Blue Mountains reach about 7400 feet; the Central Mountains of the Dominican Republic hit 10,400 feet. Some are flat: Aruba, Bonaire, the Cayman Islands. Many are a mixture of coastal plain and inland hills. Vegetation is likewise varied. Islands and parts of islands with heavy rainfall may have lush jungle growth; Dominica has tropical rain forests on its mountaintops. Those with the least rainfall are quite arid.

Rainfall, dependent on topography, varies from about 35 inches a year on the flatlands to over 100 inches in the higher mountains. Humidity is highest in the rainy season, which is in the autumn. During the rest of the year the northeast trade winds keep it at a reasonable level.

The climate on the coast of some of the more favored islands—the Virgin Islands, the Bahamas, Jamaica, Puerto Rico, Trinidad, Barbados—is very nearly perfect. The Bahamas and the Virgin Islands (and even Puerto Rico) have the added advantage of being within a hop of the continental United States.

**Disadvantages**   But several flies speckle this soothing ointment. The cost of living is astronomical on the most developed islands, especially in those near the United States. True, if you avoid the most popular tourist places, avoid imported foodstuffs, and build your own house, you may pare down the cost. But since you must first buy the land on which to build and since even local foodstuffs are at mainland prices, you will need capital to lay out and a more than moderate income to get by.

A second fly is the unsettled racial scene. Many of the islands have been released from European political dominion quite recently. With all-black governments for the first time, many black residents are, rather understandably, beginning to flex their long-unused muscles in the face of all-too-obvious tourist (read "white") wealth and the white ownership of much of the islands' capital resources. All of which, however justifiable, makes for a great deal of discomfort. If you do have your eye on a particular place, try to get a realistic estimate of what the next 20 or so years may bring.

**MEXICO**   *The Anglo-American Directory* (at foreign-language newsstands) lists American, British, and Canadian residents in Mexico; you can write or call on them for information on the areas in which they are living and, since they list themselves voluntarily, they will be happy to be contacted for help with your preliminary sortie.

**Topography**   From the U. S. border down to the Yucatán Peninsula and for most of its width (the exceptions are the east and west coastal plains), Mexico is high-mountain country. To the east, the Sierra Madre Oriental Range is a continuation of the Rockies. To the west is the Sierra Madre Occidental. Both mountain systems vary 10,000 to 18,000 feet in height. Between them lies the Mexican Plateau—3000 to 4000 feet high in the north and 7000 to 8000 feet high in the south. The Isthmus of Tehuantepec provides a lowland break; high country then rises again to the Chiapas Mountains to the east. Beyond Chiapas, to its north and east, lie the lowlands of the Yucatán Peninsula.

**Climate**   The lowlands throughout the country up to about a 3000-foot elevation (this includes the coastal plains, the Isthmus, and the Yucatán Peninsula) are tropical and subtropical in climate with average temperatures in the high 70's; the minimum temperature recorded has been 60° F. but the maximum has been almost 120° F.

Elevations between 3000 and 6000 feet are in the temperate-to-warm zone with average temperatures of 75° F. Areas above 6000 feet are in the cool zone, averaging 63° at the lower levels; it is in this zone that the major population centers have been built. The highest mountains are perpetually snow-covered.

Rain falls mainly in summer. In the interiors, rainfall averages under 10 inches a year in the north, from 20 inches to 40 inches in the center, 40 inches to 60 inches in the Isthmus and over the northern part of Yucatán. Along the coasts it averages from 20 inches to 60 inches in the north; from 60 inches to 80 inches along the coast of the Gulf from Tampico to Yucatán and along the southeast coast of Yucatán. In parts of Tabasco it exceeds 80 inches.

The coastal plains are tropical rain forest; this becomes temperate forest in the higher altitudes. In the north is steppe and desert vegetation. In Yucatán is thorn scrub (mesquite).

**Population** The populace is about 30% Indian, 60% mestizo (mixed Spanish and Indian), 9% white, and 1% black. The chief language is Spanish but many Indians speak their native language as well; English is spoken all along the beaten track.

The latest estimates of the number of Americans living in Mexico puts the total at about 100,000; some 6000 of these are drawing Social Security checks from the U. S. government.

Up to now, most foreigners have settled within reach of Mexico City, which is the hub of commerce and travel; usually they settle in one of the smaller towns on the Plateau, most of which are at altitudes above 5000 feet, in the cool zone. This altitude can be hard on people with respiratory or heart trouble, and you should certainly check with your doctor before moving to these heights.

Recently the Mexican government has begun development of the Yucatán Peninsula, which is ringed with beaches. Its chief city is Mérida, which has a modern airport just a short hop from Miami. The island of Cozumel off the southern coast of the Peninsula is already a thriving resort. Yucatán is still primitive and its development will probably entail some restrictions on ownership of property—particularly beachfront property—by foreigners (i.e., you). However, these restrictions will not prevent such investments as condominium ownership. Prices are still low on the Peninsula, so this might be a good area to explore for a bargain.

Baja California is another area worth exploring for low-priced real estate. It too is scheduled for development. A healthy ocean-desert climate prevails here, with winter temperatures in the 60's, summer ones in the 70's and 80's. Scenically the peninsula is mountainous, wild, and beautiful. It has good beaches (3000 miles of them) and many bays and inlets, and its offshore waters offer very good fishing. Water is a problem here but plans for irrigation are in the offing.

**Cost of Living**   Prices are still lower in Mexico than in the United States except in the large cities and fashionable resorts. In well-developed resorts like Guadalajara, new apartment developments cater to people of moderate incomes and provide modern conveniences not often to be found in older buildings. In the smaller towns and older buildings you will find no appliances to speak of and will have to hire a maid. But rates of pay are quite low.

**Foreign Centers**   Guadalajara, the second-largest city in Mexico, has a large colony of retired people from the United States and Canada. It has good hospitals, daily flights to Mexico City, plenty of sports and amusements. Other towns with foreign colonies smaller and less well-developed, and sometimes with a housing shortage, are: Acapulco (expensive resort town), Puerto Vallarta (resort town), San Miguel, Morelia, Cuernavaca (expensive), Chapala on Lake Chapala, and a few pocket communities on the Pacific Coast. In fact, there are few sizable towns in Mexico without some residents from north of the border.

**Visas**   The *Visitante Rentista* is the visa specifically designed for people over 55. To get it you must have a certain minimum income. With it you can bring in your car duty-free but not your household goods. You can renew the visa every six months, but at the end of two years you must make another application. The *Non-Immigrante Rentista* is much the same but has no age limit.

The other applicable type of visa is the *Immigrante Rentista,* which requires a larger minimum income and has no age limit. With it you can bring in both your car and your household goods duty-free for one time. For the first three years of residence you can leave Mexico only for a maximum of three months out of any one calendar year. After five years you are eligible to work (if you can find work).

**CANADA**   Although Canada is second only to the USSR in land area, most of its population lives within a couple of hundred miles of the U.S. border. The rest of the country is sparsely populated—for rather good reasons! The greater part is coniferous forest and tundra. Temperate forests and grasslands exist only in the southeast and south, respectively.

The only part of Canada with a winter climate mild enough to make it worth considering for retirement is the southwestern part of British Columbia—Vancouver Island and the facing coast of the mainland. The west side of the island, facing onto the Pacific, is very wet. The east side and facing coast more or less continue the climate and living conditions of the Puget Sound–San Juan Island district of the United States Northwest (see Chapter 12).

Mortgages and home rentals are higher-priced in Canada than in the United States but home-purchase prices are a bit less, as are most other essential goods and services.

Being short of population, Canada welcomes immigrants who will be self-supporting.

**GUATEMALA**  Hot and humid in the northern lowlands and along the coast, Guatemala is cool and comfortable (except at the highest altitudes) in the southern highlands. It is beautiful everywhere.

Most of the population is in the highlands at elevations between 5000 and 8000 feet, and since this is the only really comfortable part of the country, people with heart and respiratory troubles should discount this nation as a retirement possibility. Guatemala City, the capital, at an altitude of 5000 feet, has a year-round springlike climate with warm days and cool nights. Inland, rainfall is heaviest in the summer and fall; along the coasts it extends into the winter.

The population is half Indian, 5% Spanish, 9% non-Spanish white, and the rest mixed Indian and Spanish ancestry. Although Spanish is the main language, many Indian tongues are also spoken.

Housing in Guatemala City costs somewhat less than in the United States; in rural areas it costs a lot less. Clothing is more expensive than in the United States; locally produced food is cheaper. Medical facilities are fine in the larger cities; in rural areas they are not; you should in any case be sure to get inoculations for all tropical diseases.

The country is rich in folk crafts, history, and archaeological sites. A growing population of retired Americans testifies to the fact that living in Guatemala is comfortable enough and cheaper than in most places. Jobs and small-business opportunities are good, and taxes are reasonable.

**COSTA RICA**  Costa Rica has a chain of central highlands in which the *meseta central*—about 800 square miles of fertile plateau between 3000 and 4000 feet high—contains the four main cities and half the population of the country. The plains to the north and on the Gulf of Mexico are tropical rain forest. To the south, on the Pacific, rainfall is lower but temperatures are still high. At heights above 6000 feet rainfall is lighter, temperatures lower. The central plateau, with temperature ranges between 60° and about 80° throughout the year, is the most livable part of the country. Rainfall is regular from April to November, and humidity is always high although not particularly oppressive.

The population, mostly white and of Spanish descent, speaks Spanish, although English is widely spoken in the cities. Many members of the fair-size American colony living on the plateau are retired people.

Housing costs are moderate except in the center of San José, the capital city. Clothing, too, is reasonably priced, and local food is abundant and inexpensive. Medical facilities are good in San José.

**THE AZORES**  Lying 800 miles out from Portugal, in the Atlantic, these nine islands are politically a part of Portugal. Their climate is mild, with temperatures ranging only between 42° and 86°. Humidity is quite high; wind and rain are frequent in the winter. Among their attractions are luxuriant vegetation, beautiful scenery, and fine beaches. The island of São Miguel is the most populated and developed.

Because of the U.S. Air Force base on the island of Terceira, prices are higher there than elsewhere in the islands. On Corvo, Flores, Faial, Pico, São Jorge, Graciosa, São Miguel, and Santa Maria, housing is cheap. Locally produced food and drinks (including wine) are cheap also; imported food is expensive. Although imported ready-made clothes are expensive, you can get outer clothing made quite cheaply on the island. Medical facilities and supplies are good.

Portuguese is the official language and you will need to learn it. The people are hospitable, and the naval base assures a standing American colony of sorts. You can get to the Azores by freighter or by air from the United States and by liner and air from Portugal.

**MADEIRA**  Another group of Portuguese islands, also in the Atlantic, lies off the African coast and yet is only an hour by jet from Lisbon. The two inhabited islands of the group are Madeira and Porto Santo. Madeira Island is where most foreigners take up residence. It is 34 miles long by 12 miles wide and is very mountainous, with rolling green hills descending to flower-covered plains. Its capital city, Funchal, built on a mountainside, is thought to be one of the most beautiful anywhere. With spectacular scenery and an easy pace, Madeira has long been a popular resort (especially with the British), despite its lack of good beaches.

The climate is mild year-round, with winter temperature lows about 60° and average summer temperature about 70°.

Although Portuguese is the official language, English is spoken in the resort areas.

Despite the building boom, which here takes the form of condominiums and villas mostly situated around Funchal and some of the smaller resort towns, housing costs are low compared with the mainland. The large foreign colony (mostly European) ensures that most amenities are available, including adequate medical services. The general cost of living remains low, and Madeira is well away from the problems besetting most of the rest of the world.

**THE CANARIES**   These seven mountainous islands, about 80 miles west of Morocco, are Spanish territory. La Palma and Tenerife to the west, and Grand Canary and Lanzarote to the east, are the most developed of the islands, although Hierro, Gomera, and beautiful Fuerteventura are following quickly along. Being warmed by the Gulf Stream in winter and cooled by the trade winds in summer, the climate is mild. Up to about 1200 feet the temperatures are good and hot; from 1200 feet to 2500 feet they are temperate; above 2500 feet they are cool. The islands are very beautiful: snow-capped mountains, luxuriant vegetation, hot beaches.

The population is mostly Spanish, but rapid growth of the tourist trade ensures that you can get by in several other languages. The locally produced food is plentiful, varied, and cheap. Housing is very reasonably priced, and building development is booming. Ready-made clothing is imported and therefore expensive; tailor-made clothes are much cheaper. Medical and dental services are excellent and low in price.

A large American/English colony lives at Las Palmas, the capital city of Grand Canary, and a smaller one in Maspalomas Beach (also on Grand Canary). Other smaller foreign colonies live on the islands of Tenerife and La Palma. On Lanzarote, the Oasis de Nazaret villas and apartments go for pretty hefty prices. But on Fuerteventura, the condominium hotels and homes at Costa Ventura Village are more moderately priced.

**MOROCCO**   Running the length of Morocco from southwest to northeast are the three parallel ranges of the Atlas Mountains, rising some 13,500 feet. Along the Atlantic and Mediterranean is a fertile coastal plain from which, on the Mediterranean, the Er Rif Mountains rise to about 8000 feet. The mountains and the Atlantic Ocean moderate what would otherwise be a tropical climate. As a result, temperatures on the west coast range from about 60° to 75° on an annual average. The northwest gets the most rain, mainly in the fall and spring, and averaging 30 to 40 inches annually. Winters are short, with average temperatures in the 50's, and nights are cool year-round. Summer days can be hot in the interiors.

Housing and food prices are low, and the bazaars will teach you a whole new way of shopping. Social Security and pensions are not taxed, though property is. Work is impossible to get even for a large percentage of the nationals (you may find the pullulating poverty distressing). Work permits are therefore not given to foreigners in any but exceptional circumstances.

The people are mostly Berber stock in the north and the interior, Arab along the Atlantic coast, with a sprinkling of Jews and Europeans in the cities. Foreigners just do not live in rural areas, where existence is on a subsistence level and where Western ways are little known and less tolerated. But the larger cities, thanks to the long French occupation, have a European section. The Arab section is known as the *medina;* many cities also have a Jewish section, the *mellah.*

The two cities with the largest foreign colonies are Tangier and Casablanca. Tangier, on the northwest coast and within sight of Spain, is the more popular with retired Europeans and Americans. It has a daily ferry to Gibraltar and to Algeciras in Spain. Tangier used to be a free port and it still retains a lot of the atmosphere of those freewheeling days. It is cosmopolitan and, rising on hills above the Mediterranean, very attractive. Young adventurers live—for relatively short periods—in the Arab houses of the *medina,* which, if you are clever, can be had for a song along with no amenities whatsoever. Older adventurers stick to the European section, where modern apartments are available at reasonable prices and where the social life is conducted mainly in French, English, and Spanish.

Casablanca, on the Atlantic coast, also has a large foreign colony. Much of the city is comparatively new, with buildings of the skyscraper variety. The colony tends to be more business-oriented. Temperatures are rather more extreme than in Tangier, as are prices.

Medical facilities are quite good and inexpensive in both cities, particularly if you speak French. For special treatment, Europe is within very easy reach.

**PORTUGAL**　Most of Portugal is mountainous, between 1300 and 2300 feet high, with a fairly narrow coastal belt which widens and runs farther inland at the mouths of the Douro, Tagus, and Sado rivers on the west coast and at the mouth of the Guadiana River on the south coast. The largest foreign colonies are centered around Lisbon and on the south coast in Algarve province. More recently, foreigners have begun to settle on the Atlantic coast north of Lisbon.

The northern coast of the Tagus River mouth, to the west of Lisbon, is known as the Costa do Sol. Its chief beach centers are Estoril and Cascais, which are within 15 miles of Lisbon, but development has spread along the Atlantic coastal road, and inland to Sintra. This is one of Portugal's most fashionable resort areas, famous as the home of deposed and exiled European royalty. The climate is very mild with low humidity, sunny temperate winters and summers, moderate rainfall even in the rainy (winter) season, and cool summer evenings. Housing costs both in Lisbon and along the nearby coast are moderate considering their metropolitan and resort character. So are food, clothing, and medical facilities; and the latter are good, especially in Lisbon.

In the beautiful Algarve province the climate is even milder, with a short winter, lots of sun, and constantly warm water for swimming. To the west of the town of Faro the coast is rocky with beaches nestling at the foot of cliffs; to the east it is flatter. The Portuguese government has taken a hand to stop overdevelopment, and most of the coastal villages remain relatively unspoiled while new building is concentrated along the main road which runs along the coast a few miles inland. This also leaves the agricultural hinterlands largely unspoiled and fairly primitive. Villas, bungalows, condominiums, and hotels now abound along the coastal road and, even with the many huge luxury developments (Quinta do Lago, Cerro Grande, Vale do Lobo), prices remain moderate. Food, clothing (tailor-made, not ready-made), and medical facilities and supplies are also moderate in cost and of good standards.

You can live in Portugal for a lot less money if you choose a small town, a rural setting, or one of the less developed stretches of the western coastline. The countryside is beautiful, the climate kindly, and the people friendly, although you would have to pick up Portuguese fairly rapidly (it is not a difficult language). You should settle within easy reach of a larger city for shopping and medical facilities, although local doctors are competent for normal purposes.

**SPAIN**   The northern coastal region of Spain is fertile, cool, and humid with an annual rainfall of about 40 inches. The dry central plateau, where Madrid is situated, averages about 2200 feet in elevation, and has cold winters, hot summers, and an annual rainfall of 16 inches. The south and southwest regions and southern coastal belt have mild winters, hot summers, and an annual rainfall of about 25 inches. Except for the narrow coastal plains, the central plateau, and the wide valley of the Guadalquivir to the southwest, Spain is mountainous.

Madrid has a large foreign colony, and smaller ones are dotted along the coast of the Mediterranean and the Balearic Islands of Mallorca, Minorca, and Ibiza. Along the coasts, many of the condominiums, villas, and other developments, as well as many local businesses, are run by British and northern Europeans. Thus your neighbors and tradesmen are just as apt to be Swedish, Scottish, German, or Dutch as they are to be Spanish. Rural Spain is not, on the whole, very prosperous, and amenities such as Americans expect in their everyday lives are just not available.

Spain has been swamped with tourism, particularly along the Mediterranean coasts, which has led to a building boom. Whole sections of the coastline have been transformed in just a few years. High-rise apartments and low villas line the beaches, which are jammed in summer. Food, clothing, and entertainment are no longer the bargain they once were. Nevertheless, housing costs are still a little lower than in most of the rest of Europe. You can no longer rent an old Spanish house plus maid for next to nothing, but you can now buy or rent a condominium apartment for less than you would have to pay in the United States, and basic modern appliances obviate the need for a maid if you choose an area with reliable electric current and modern shopping conveniences.

Medical supplies and services are good and cost less than in the United States.

The Costa de la Luz is the new tourist-getter name for the stretch of coast between the Straits of Gibraltar and Portugal. Less advanced in its development, it is still dotted with small fishing villages. However, it is possible to buy a modern home in the vicinity of Algeciras and Tarifa at the eastern end of the stretch even now.

The southern and eastern coastline is divided into several other districts, each about 100 miles long, as follows: The Costa del Sol is that stretch from La Línea, opposite Gibraltar, northeast to Alicante. One of the most highly developed parts of the coast, it has long been very much geared to the tourist trade. On the Costa Blanca, from Alicante to Valencia, and the Costa del Azahor or Costa Dorada, from Valencia to Barcelona, construction of new villas and other facilities is proceeding rapidly. North from Barcelona to the French border is the Costa Brava, another coastal area which was highly developed at an early date. The shoreline is mountainous, with cliffs and deep-carved bays.

The beautiful Balearic Islands have also undergone rapid development in recent years; land values are rising and beach-front property is virtually unobtainable. Although developers have been moving in lately, most villas have been built individually. This has meant that they are apt to be more isolated than those in the conglomerate developments, but also more expensive. On Mallorca, the beautiful Pueblo Mediterraneo condominium apartments cluster about pools overlooking Andraix; the Sol de Mallorca development is ultra-chic.

To live on the islands you would probably need household help and the money to make occasional trips to the mainland for items scarce or unavailable on the islands. If you are willing to do without modern amenities, life can still be cheap in the island villages, although inflation and the tourist boom make this a short-term likelihood. Except in winter, when it is chilly and damp, the climate of the Balearics is balmy.

**GREECE** The northern part of Greece has a less hospitable climate than the southern part and the islands. It gets the most rain and the severest winters, although along the coast winters are somewhat milder. The climate of the southern part and of the Aegean and Ionian islands is the most inviting, with high summer temperatures moderated by sea and mountain breezes and with winter temperatures that seldom fall below freezing.

Prices in the mainland cities, though still moderate compared with those of many other European countries, are higher than on all but the most developed islands. Since the islands are also beautiful, easily accessible from the mainland, and well away from most social disturbance, these are the best bet for tranquil retirement living.

The islands have hot, dry summers, warm, dry spring and autumn months, and short winters, with fairly frequent storms and the annual 25 inches of rainfall. The 40° temperature of these two months feels chilly because of the pervasive damp.

Some islands are no more than a bare, if rather large, rock and many have no electricity or water. These, naturally, are the cheapest, and if you are very rugged and like isolation you can probably make a go of living on them; but lack of medical services and facilities is a major problem. At the other extreme are the large islands (Crete, Rhodes), which are quite self-contained so far as goods and services are concerned; prices here are still somewhat lower than on the mainland, particularly away from the main tourist centers. In between are the smaller islands that have been developed for tourism (Náxos, Andros, Tēnos, Mýkonos, Kéa, for instance) and which therefore can offer most amenities and services yet peace and isolation just outside the resort areas.

The high tourist season is from June to mid-September, when these islands are flooded with people, many of them visiting for only a few hours off the cruise ships. After the tourist season the islands sink back into tranquillity with a small permanent foreign colony (mostly European and English though with increasing numbers of Americans, often of Greek lineage).

You can rent or buy an old house and put in running water, electricity, and (if you have cold bones) central heating for not too high a cost. Or you can buy a piece of land just outside one of the villages and have the island's builder put a house on it for you with the conveniences built in; this, too, can be done for a very moderate sum.

Medical supplies and services are usually adequate, although you may have to go into Athens to deal with complications; there are daily ferries to and from most of the islands to Piraeus, the Athens seaport. Clothing is cheaper if you have it made. Food is cheap, although supplies of fresh vegetables and fruit are limited out of season and variety is never great.

The people are marvelous and you will end up learning Greek with great delight, although English, French, and German are spoken in most areas that cater to tourists.

**IRELAND**  It's a far cry from the blue Aegean to the Emerald Isle, particularly when you consider the source of all that greenery. In fact, you would think that retirement in Ireland would only be thinkable by ultra-loyal people of Irish ancestry. If that is true, an awful lot of retired Americans seem to have a touch of the green brush. How otherwise to explain the affinity for Ireland which seems to transcend rain, damp, winter (and summer) chills, and even some restrictions imposed on foreign ownership of property, for so many otherwise sane people?

The country is ringed with hills and mountains. They surround a central plain of about 300-feet elevation which is full of lakes and peat bogs; the western part of this plain, beyond the River Shannon, is only sparsely settled. Off the west coast are many small islands, and the whole north, west, and south coastline is very rocky and indented.

The climate is damp, not good for rheumaticky ailments. Rainfall is highest—an average of 50 inches per annum—in the southwest, where the warm offshore Gulf Stream keeps the winters at a mild 55° average. The east and north are drier, with about 35 inches of rainfall, but here winter temperatures average about 40°. Rainfall is fairly evenly distributed throughout the year—often taking the form of a constant drizzle. Summers average about 60° in most places.

In recent years the districts around Galway Bay, Limerick, Killarney, Cork, and other traditional resorts in southwestern Ireland (as well as Dublin, of course) have become a sort of thoroughfare for tourists, and prices have gone up accordingly. The tourist season is fairly short, from June to mid-September, so the crowding may not bother you too much. In the rest of Ireland, the limited circuit of the tourists leaves a lot of very beautiful, incredibly green (the island earns its nickname) rural areas and small towns quite untouched.

Housing is inexpensive, especially in the rural or coastal villages. It is cheap enough, in fact, to make the installation of central heating (and you'll need it!) perfectly feasible. Food is also low-priced, except for fruit and most vegetables. Clothing is not expensive, although you will need a lot of the warmer variety. Medical services and facilities are good and much less expensive than in the United States.

**FIJI ISLANDS** Not many Americans think of the Fiji Islands at all; much less do they think of them as a possible place for retirement. However, 10,000 Europeans are permanently settled there and, from all accounts, very happily. Out of the 322 islands which comprise the group, some 106 are inhabited. They are scattered over about 100,000 square miles of the Pacific Ocean, about 2300 miles east of Australia. The two largest islands, Viti Levu and Vanua Levu, hold 85% of the total population and are quite close together. There is also good access to the main islands from most of the smaller inhabited ones. Viti Levu and Vanua Levu are both mountainous, volcanic (not live) islands with fertile lowlands around the coasts and in the river deltas. Coral reefs, palm-shaded beaches, luxuriant tropical vegetation, and mountaintops up to about 4300 feet characterize the scenery.

The climate is tropical. Temperatures are moderate year-round, however, and range between lows of about 68° in winter and highs of about 85° in summer. Rainfall is heavy, from about 70 inches on the leeward sides of the islands to about 140 inches on the windward sides. It falls in quick showers at all seasons, so the humidity is high although not bothersome. There are perhaps one or two tropical hurricanes over some of the islands during the first few months of most years.

The majority of the population is Indian, with Fijians running a close second, and Europeans and Chinese poor runners-up.

The capital city, Suva, is on Viti Levu, which holds the largest population; the city is the business and social center for the islands.

Housing costs remarkably little, although you will probably need to own an air conditioner. Locally grown food is plentiful and inexpensive; imported items, except for some alcohols, cost more. Clothes can be made locally at very little cost, and the way of life is so casual and easygoing that you do not need a large wardrobe. Medical services and facilities are excellent and the islands are very healthful, despite a sizable insect population.

**AUSTRALIA** Most of the population of Australia is concentrated around its east and southeast edges and on the eastern side of Tasmania. Other areas get very little rainfall, or get it after long dry seasons, or get far too much all the time. The northeast coast of Queensland, facing the Great Barrier Reef, is the resort area for the eastern half of the country. Warm winters and hot dry summers characterize the climate. Prices here are quite high.

**Tasmania**    About 200 miles off the southern tip of the continent, to the east, lies the island of Tasmania. It is mountainous and green with many lakes held in the central valleys and a wealth of rivers. Its temperatures are cooler than those of the mainland and it has no long dry season. The western side of the island, which faces the prevailing trade winds, gets a lot of rain; the eastern, leeward side, gets about 30 inches per annum. Like the rest of Australia it has a high percentage of sunny days.

Housing is inexpensive out of the capital city of Hobart, but clothes and furniture are fairly high in price. Food is almost as varied and plentiful as in the United States and mostly a little less expensive. Medical care, facilities, and supplies are excellent and cost less than in the United States.

**NEW ZEALAND**    Twelve hundred miles southeast of Australia lies New Zealand: two large islands plus several smaller ones. Both islands are mountainous. On North Island the only mountains rising above 6000 feet are its four volcanoes, three of which are still active and give rise to numerous hot springs and geysers. South Island's mountains are much higher, with 17 peaks above 10,000 feet; it is a popular winter resort area.

The northwest side of South Island gets heavy rainfall and the northern half of North Island gets moderately heavy rainfall; otherwise rainfall is moderate and fairly evenly distributed throughout the year. Coastal temperatures on North Island range from a summer high of 80° to winter lows at about freezing level; South Island is cooler. Humidity, fairly high throughout the year on both islands, tends to aggravate both heat and cold, though not excessively.

The scenery in New Zealand is beautiful and varied. South Island is alpine, with lovely mountain lakes, swift-flowing rivers, and a fjord-indented southwest coastline. North Island has volcanoes, hot springs, and caves, and the northern part grows tropical fruit and vegetables. Both islands have large forests and sheep-grazing lands. North Island is more heavily populated and on it are New Zealand's two largest cities, Auckland and Wellington, the capital.

Housing is moderately priced throughout the islands, price levels being slightly lower on South Island and slightly higher in the cities where housing is scarce. Clothing costs about the same as in the

United States. Food is a little cheaper and is plentiful and varied. Medical care is excellent and a lot less expensive than in the United States. There are several mineral springs on North Island which have a reputation for easing certain ailments.

Most of the population is of British stock, with a scattering of smaller ethnic groups (Chinese, Indian, Dutch, Yugoslav, Greek, Pole). Maoris, the indigenous people, constitute 7% of the population and are (at least nominally) fully integrated, although a high percentage of them are very poor.

The way of life in New Zealand is easygoing and somewhat conservative.

# III.
# USING
# YOUR
# TIME

For many people their job is the central fact of their life, around which all other activities—from whom they see for lunch to how much time they spend at home—are organized. If you are one of these, your job has been an emotional and intellectual investment beyond financial rewards. Mandatory retirement is like amputation. Your reaction will be to find, posthaste, voluntary work or another job.

Even if your commitment is not total, your job still may confer on you a certain status, even identity, in both your own eyes and in those of your community. This kind of identification can be limiting. If you are, or were, a dockworker or a fireman, for example, your community image may have been one of physical prowess and you may have tried to hide or repress a love of music or poetry as an embarrassment. Once your job and its image no longer distract you, your other needs may become keener, leaving you dissatisfied and incomplete.

On the other hand, the predefined behavior also gives you a comfortable niche in which to rest without too much exertion. Thus you may have used your job as a laborer or clerk to justify a lack of intellectual pursuits; as a doctor you may have been "too busy" for any interests outside medicine. Retirement may then bring on an acute sense of loss.

Your job can also dictate your mode of operation in social situations. Very often the company executive is automatically elected to every important community board by sheer virtue of his job. If this predetermined role ceases with his retirement, he may feel shaken, useless, and resentful.

Retirement yanks the rug out from under established patterns of status, identity, and behavior. People whose jobs have been physical feel decrepit; people who have had executive responsibilities feel ineffectual. A gamut of emotions—rage, self-pity, resentment, depression—accompanies this loss of self-esteem. Some people feel the impact immediately; in others it can be delayed for months. For many the impact manifests itself deviously: physical symptoms, even serious illness, are not at all uncommon.

Even if you are one of the majority with a monotonous job performed mostly to earn money on which to live, you get accustomed to whatever companionship or sociability the job offers.

You have lost something that took up a large part of your life—hence the hollow feeling. This is natural. The important thing is to *recognize* that it is happening, to keep yourself from becoming fixated on the gap, and to find other affairs which will move in to fill the vacuum.

It is quite feasible to find a substitute for the job, particularly if you analyze—preferably before you retire—which of your needs your job fulfills, which of these needs you can learn to do without, and which of them you should attempt to satisfy from a new source. While money is an important consideration, your financial situation is easy to calculate in black and white. The emotional and intellectual losses accompanying retirement are not so easy to express and appraise; for this reason they are too often disregarded and only haphazardly remedied.

For most of us, then, work of some kind is to a greater or lesser degree a necessity. If money earning is not a major consideration, a wider range of interesting employment is open to you. Volunteer work is always available in just about any capacity you can dream up (see Chapter 19). The intellectual needs that work fulfills, as well as those emotional needs satisfied by status, role, and identity, can also be met in the various activities described in Chapters 14 and 15 of this section.

Two general books you might want to check for additional ideas are *Retire to Action* by Julietta K. Arthur (Abingdon Press, 1969) and *101 Ways to Enjoy Your Leisure,* edited and published by The Retirement Council (1 Atlantic Street, Stamford, Conn.). Although some specialized books are listed below, here are a few that might be of wider interest: *Hobbies, An Introduction to Crafts, Collection, Nature Study and Other Life-Long Pursuits* by Alvin Schwartz (Simon & Schuster, 1972); *How to Make Money With Your Crafts* by Leta Clark (William Morrow & Co., 1973); *Retirement Dollars for the Self-Employed* by Steven S. Anreder (Thomas Y. Crowell, 1972);

*Continuing Your Education* by Cyril O. Houle (McGraw-Hill, 1964);
and publications of the U.S. Office of Education, Department of
Health, Education, and Welfare, such as the annually revised *Higher
Education.*

# 14
# In Pursuit of Pleasure

Webster's defines *recreation* as "refreshment in body and mind . . . by some sort of play, amusement, or relaxation used for this purpose, as games, sports, hobbies, reading, walking, etc." It is as well to keep this in mind because most of the activities discussed in this chapter can be undertaken as work—for money, for educational diplomas, for career purposes—as well as for play.

So the stockbroker who looks forward to puttering around his vegetable garden and the commercial artist longing for a round on the golf course are matched by the farmer who loves to dabble in the stock market and the golf pro who can hardly wait to get out oils and canvas. Whether activity is work or play, therefore, depends less on the nature of the activity than it does on your point of view.

A point of view to be recommended for us all is that, like children, we should learn to play at work.

A well-chosen leisure-time pursuit provides continuous opportunities for learning. An activity that you can master with ease and which has a limited scope for skill and exploration will soon pall. One in which every new step mastered leads to another one is much more rewarding and, besides, can lead you into realms of knowledge you would originally have thought totally unconnected. Boredom will not set in and your sense of accomplishment will grow with your knowledge. The very best activities are those that encourage the beginner by having relatively rapid results from the first, and yet remain intriguing in the long term.

Probably any activity undertaken just to keep you busy will leave you less time in which to feel lonely and may give you a chance to meet people who will also help to keep you busy. However, busy-busy activities are essentially boring and few people can keep them up for very long. But it can happen that you start something just to fill in time and then find yourself caught up and involved in the best kind of way.

Age segregation can create in older people the very limitations upon which the segregation is supposed to be based: everyone keeps telling you that only people between 25 and 30 can do a certain thing and you are apt to end up believing it, even though you did it yourself, and did it very well, at the age of 59.

Hobbies, arts, crafts, sports, travel, collecting, and a myriad of other skills and activities counteract such prejudices very well—there is nothing more democratic than a writer's conference, a golf match, a concert, a craft fair, or a state park camping ground. It is at places and activities like these that you learn how much greater can be the differences between people in the same age group than those between people of different ages.

**THE NEED FOR VARIETY**   Your leisure-time pursuits should provide change from your nonleisure activities and also be diverse in themselves. For instance, if you do volunteer work at the hospital gift store and a lot of social visiting, your most valuable recreation might lie in a solitary pursuit such as reading plus a physical activity like bicycling. Or you may have a time-consuming interest in antiques, which takes you to many places and introduces you to many people. You might then find your best recreation in gardening, which gives you time to yourself in one place; you might add a regular game of badminton, say, to give your body a good workout.

Really, it all sounds like planning a balanced meal and, indeed, what you are planning is a balanced program for your whole self, body and mind.

The first step is to appraise your present leisure-time activities. Do they, or will they, provide needed variety? Do they still interest you? Do you see enough people to satisfy your need for company? Are you lonely for other people with interests similar to your own? Can you express yourself fully in your present round of activities or do you feel trammeled by the need to adapt constantly to other people and their requirements?

**THERE ARE LIMITS**   The range of activities available is enormous, but it can be narrowed down right away by certain obvious considerations. Whatever you decide to do should not strain your budget; perhaps the best tactic is to decide on the most money you will be able to spare and choose among things that will not take you over that limit.

Physical capabilities should be considered carefully. A session with your doctor will give you a good idea of your present state of health, and the doctor will be quite happy to define broad physical limits to your activities. However, unless you are already in tiptop condition, it is possible to improve your state of health considerably; so if you want to pursue some particular sport badly enough, you might be able to do so with a careful program of health building (see Section IV).

**INTEREST GROUPS** For every activity—art, craft, sport, study, collection—there is an association, society, or other kind of group that can be the source of useful information and encouragement.

If nationwide, the group is likely to have headquarters in one or more major cities (Washington, D.C., is a favorite) as well as local branches. The headquarters will supply branch addresses which can often put you in touch with members in your area. Directories of incorporated groups can be consulted at your local public library. *The Encyclopedia of Associations* is especially handy because it lists associations by the key word in their names rather than alphabetically; thus you can find all the various golf associations listed under *G*. Many popular activities have their own periodicals and journals, listed by subject in directories such as *Ulrich's International Periodicals Directory*.

## SPORTS

At least one form of sport should be included in your schedule. It should be one you can practice daily, if possible, since it is easier to keep in trim on a close schedule than it is on a once- or twice-a-week schedule. An hour or so a day is better than eight hours in one day and nothing for the other six. Try to find a year-round sport; otherwise you will have to find a substitute for the off season.

The sport should be one that you positively enjoy rather than one that you do just for the sake of the exercise, and it should be geared to increasing your physical strength and endurance—watching every game of the season on television does *not* count as a sport!

If it involves skill, as it should if it is to hold your interest, you should start your training gradually. When you first start you will have to determine how long you should practice by the way you feel. If it is a reasonably strenuous activity, do warm-up exercises first, starting slowly.

Sports that are particularly useful as exercise and which need no fellow players are discussed in Chapter 20: walking, hiking, bicycling, jogging, swimming, and various forms of calisthenics are among them. Here are a few which require at least one partner or which cannot be regarded as pure exercise.

**GAMES**   Golf is the sport most frequently recommended for older people. Certainly, it has many advantages: it keeps you out in the open air doing moderate exercise for good long periods. It is practiced in company and therefore fulfills some social needs. It involves skill of eye and arm which can be very satisfying, while never absolutely perfectible. If you need competition you can get some good contests going.

However, it can be expensive, particularly if you have to join a private club. You will need your own equipment, too, and (although it will last for years) it's not cheap. Sometimes it is difficult to find partners during the least crowded hours; if you run into this problem, mention it to the club manager—since it is in his interests to have the course fully used, he might help you organize a weekday group.

Tennis, unless you are stronghearted, is to be approached cautiously. A doubles game is not so strenuous as a singles. In some retirement communities a modified version has been invented, with smaller courts and rules that cut out the long mad dashes and leaps. If you are up to playing tennis, you'll find it excellent exercise because it involves just about every muscle and joint.

A great number of other sports involve goodly amounts of bodily exercise: archery, fencing, karate, canoeing, rowing, running, squash, deck tennis, badminton, and croquet. Horseshoe pitching, quoits, lawn bowling, boccie, and skittle bowling are not so active but do require a strong lower back!

**BOATING**   Your dream boat may be a 15-foot sailboat with a small outboard motor or a 35-foot inboard cruiser with cabin room to sleep seven. The latter dream is quite expensive to realize, but if you are willing to trim your sights a little you may get to cruise down the Intracoastal Waterway in a 22-foot stern-drive (inboard-outboard engine) cruiser with room to sleep a crowded four.

Sailboats are usually fiber glass. Cruisers are likely to be fiber glass or, less often, aluminum or steel. Fiber glass is hardy, resilient, corrosion- and marine-life resistant, needing little upkeep, and easy to repair yourself. Aluminum is very lightweight, strong, corrosion- and marine-life resistant, and if properly coated, low in upkeep, but you will have to get professional help for repairs. A steel hull is strong, durable, and corrosion-resistant, in need of more upkeep and also more expensive than the other two.

If you don't have a permanent berth on a nearby stretch of water, the most convenient kind of boat for day cruising or land camping is the kind that can be carried on top of your car. This means a boat light enough for you to load and unload. The next most convenient type is that which can be carried on a trailer. Your car will have to be fairly powerful, but a trailer gives you leeway to choose a boat up to 30 feet in length. The boat can be launched straight from the trailer and reloaded by the winch that is part of the trailer's gear.

If you would use the boat for day trips only, you can make do with a fairly small one—although it is pleasant to have at least an awning under which to sit, and some room to move around. For staying out overnight or for camping trips, a larger boat is more convenient, although some hardy souls manage quite well with a small boat and a tent. The larger boat should be able to sleep two people in comparative comfort and three or four with a bit of crowding. Convertible bunks come in handy here but are a nuisance on long trips with a full boat. A small galley (kitchen) and head (toilet) are necessary for anything longer than day trips.

Guides and charts to inland and coastal waterways are available from the appropriate state government or Coast Guard office and from the Army Corps of Engineers. The Government Printing Office (Washington, D.C. 20402) can send you a list of publications, including the Department of Transportation Coast Guard Official Recreational *Boating Guide*. Motor Boating (224 West 57th Street, New York, N.Y. 10022) is another source; they publish *Piloting, Seamanship, and Small Boat Handling* by Charles F. Chapman. (See also the section on houseboats in Chapter 11.)

**FISHING AND HUNTING**   Possibly no other sports offer such a wealth of reading material for neophyte or expert. Consult Bowker's *Subject Guide to Books in Print* at a library or bookshop for a list of books; directories in the library will put you on to associations and specialized publications. Many sporting-goods shops carry useful paperbacks.

## TRAVEL

Traveling can be very expensive, and this puts a lot of people off. But with a little thought and some clever manipulation, many people of moderate income manage considerable travel. Wherever you go, be sure to inquire whether any bargains are offered for older or retired people; many places (Washington, D.C., is one) give discounts on admissions to various sights, on transportation, and on other tourist activities.

Travel agents charge little or nothing for booking flights but if you want an itinerary and hotel reservations, the agent will, naturally, charge for the service. Since agents work on commission it is rarely worth their while to deal with the cheaper hotels; if you are traveling on a tight budget, therefore, you should make your own arrangements. If you decide to use a travel agent, be sure that the firm you choose is reputable. Membership in the American Society of Travel Agents (ASTA), while no guarantee, is a good indication of integrity. With a non-ASTA agent you should check first with friends who have used him or with local authorities.

**THE REGULAR VACATION**   Vacations taken in a holiday season at a well-known resort in a standard hotel are probably the most expensive mode of travel. Some costs can be cut by eating your main meal in the middle of the day; the food is usually the same, though sometimes the menu is more limited, but prices go up for the evening dinner hour. Theaters and often cinemas, too, charge less for matinee performances. For day trips or cross-country trips, it is cheaper to pack your own meals for the day—cheese, bread, and a bottle of wine can taste a whole lot better, too, than many a restaurant meal at roadside and railroad stops.

There is often a "shoulder" period between the in and off seasons during which prices are midway. Don't forget that the in season in, say, Arizona, is an off season for northern Europe, and vice versa.

Another way to cut costs is to choose a resort where you can use the facilities of a national or state recreation area: your sports and amusements will be either free or much cheaper than comparable facilities run for profit.

**Package Tours**   Many airline, bus, and rail companies offer package tours both within the United States and abroad. Prices include transportation, hotels, food, sometimes entertainment, and sometimes tips. You will need pocket money for extra food, shopping, and other activities on your own. The cost of these trips can be much lower than if you were to make the same arrangements for yourself, but be sure to check prices and itinerary carefully: you might be satisfied with cheaper hotels and restaurants on your own; sometimes certain tour features (a nightclub every night, say) that make the trip more expensive don't really appeal to you. Of course, you may dislike the idea of having your program prearranged for you. However, this can be a boon, saving you the worry of the many details involved. Pleasant companionship is often to be found on these tours, and if you are lucky with your guide, the trip can be very rewarding.

**Airline Travel**   Buying a regular airline ticket is the most expensive way to book airline travel, but it offers the advantage of greatest flexibility in choosing your departure times and destinations.

On domestic flights, it pays to investigate possible special fares, since carriers often try to encourage travel at slack times by offering bargains.

On international flights, the fares have long been fixed by international agreement, so it does no good to shop around. The only exceptions are Icelandic Airlines-Loftleidir (IAL) and International Air Bahama; because both offer cheaper fares, they are banned from most major European airports and land only in the British Isles, Scandinavia, and Luxembourg. Occasionally a new airline will propose cheaper flights, so watch the newspapers in case one of these should succeed.

You should consider first class only if you are flush, if you have special needs you feel can be better handled by the more numerous first-class stewardesses, or if you are flying such a short distance that the difference in fares is negligible.

*Charters:* If at all possible, you should try to avoid paying regular airline fares—particularly if you are going a long distance—by finding a charter. A good source for finding these is *Air Travel and Charter Handbook,* available from Travel Information Bureau, P.O. Box 105a, Kings Park, N.Y. 11754. Various types of charters are offered by private organizations, airlines, and travel agents—but for all of them the basic requirement is that you must sign up two or three months in advance and put down a nonreturnable deposit. Sometimes the charter organizer offers transportation only; sometimes it will arrange the whole trip, much like the package tours described above.

Write to Office of Consumer Affairs, Civil Aeronautics Board, Washington, D.C. 20428 for their free pamphlet "Air Travelers' Fly-Rights," describing charter regulations and your rights should your flight be delayed or canceled, your baggage lost, or an airline bump you from a flight.

**Sea Travel**  Oceangoing travel has declined considerably with the development of air travel, and is more expensive. Cruises also tend to be expensive unless you have access to a group-chartered one. Even freighter travel is no longer so cheap; fares to Europe, for instance, may be higher than charter flights. Several directories of freighter lines and their charges can be consulted at your local public library. Or you can write to Harian Publications (Green Lawn, N.Y. 11740) for a list of paperback publications on this type of travel.

**Foreign Vacations**  If your idea of good traveling is to stay in one place in a foreign land, you will find it much less expensive to forgo hotel living and find an apartment or house to rent or a family willing to charge you for room and board in their own house. House or apartment rental works much better, of course, if you can spend several months. If you can also rent out your own home for the period you are away, this will cut costs.

You can make your arrangements before you go by writing to the Chamber of Commerce or the tourist bureau. Sometimes the state or municipality can supply you with a list of families who accept paying guests. In any case it can supply names of reputable renting agents.

Many international magazines and newspapers (the *International Herald Tribune,* 21 rue de Berri, 75380 Paris, France; the London *Times* and London *Observer,* for three) advertise villa rentals in Europe and the Near East. There are also agencies for this purpose: European Villa Vacations, 136 East 57th Street, New York, N.Y.; Villas International, 28 Highwood Avenue, Tenafly, N.J.; and At Home Abroad, 136 East 57th Street, New York, N.Y., are a few of them.

Agencies also exist for arranging home exchanges for longer or shorter periods: Vacation Exchange Club, 663 Fifth Avenue, New York, N.Y.; Vacation Home Exchange, Inc., Box 46, Old Greenwich, Conn.; Home Interchange Ltd., 10 Bolton Street, London W. 1, England; and Holiday Exchange Bureau, P.O. Box 555, Grants, N.M. You will also find ads for home exchanges in certain national and international newspapers and magazines (the ones named above plus such magazines as *New York Review of Books* and *New Statesman and Nation,* London); if you get names from these sources, be sure to check references carefully before you go ahead.

**Farm and Ranch Vacations**   Another low-cost form of vacation within the United States is one spent on a ranch or farm. The genuine western ranches (as opposed to the play ranches set up solely for vacationers) continue their ranch work and fit guests in as best they can; they may be less expensive than the play ranches but will charge extra for such things as long hunting trips, which take the men from their work. The U. S. Department of Agriculture publishes a list of organizations and state directories of farms offering such accommodations, as does the Dude Ranchers' Association, Route South Laramie, Tie Siding, Wyo. 82084. *Farm, Ranch, and Countryside Guide,* 36 East 57th Street, New York, N.Y. 10022, also lists farms, ranches, cabins, and rural inns throughout the country. Farm vacations are also popular in Europe; you can get information from the various countries' tourist bureaus.

**CAMPING**   Camping can cut vacation costs radically: transportation is reduced to the cost of fuel; accommodations are carried along with you; food can be cooked at your site. Being retired, you are in the privileged position of being able to camp during the week, when the kids are in school and Daddy's at work, though in the busy season the crowding at campsites is week-long.

Information on campers, trailers, and mobile homes is given in Chapter 11 as well as below. Rand McNally publishes several handy paperback references, such as *Camping Today,* a general description, by S. Blackwell Duncan, and the annually revised *Rand McNally Campground and Trailer Park Guide,* which lists both public and private campsites (rating the private ones) together with details of facilities, prices, and location. The Mobile Homes Manufacturing Association (20 North Wacker Drive, Chicago, Ill.) publishes *Travel and Vacation Trailer Park Guide;* still another source is *Woodall's Trailering Parks and Campgrounds.*

**Campsites** Many of America's campsites are in national and state parks and forests, and you can drive right in to most of them. However, some facilities have been closed to trailers, a policy which may be extended to more and more public areas. Certain campsites rent cabins by the week.

A time limit, often of two weeks, is imposed at many sites, especially in the busy season. However, many retired people live in them for months on end by moving to another every two weeks. In the busy season, you must often book ahead with the warden of the park or forest; sites with cabins should be booked ahead in any season.

Private campsites abound, usually (depending on the facilities and the state) at somewhat higher rentals than the public ones. Some are very plush, with pools and golf courses and such. Many of these have advance-reservations systems and many offer long-term rentals. Retired people often look for long rentals in a beautiful area where good fishing and local farms help cut food costs—examples are the Ozarks or on the islands off the Carolinas, Georgia, and Florida.

Camping demands good organization if you are to avoid the miseries of unopenable cans, saltless meals, and cold nights. Many books, pamphlets, and periodicals are available on the subject.

**Campers** There are many kinds of recreational vehicles for camping, and the cross-fertilization of types makes them very difficult to categorize. Essentially, though, they are either hauled as trailers or all of a piece with the driven vehicle.

Before you buy, be sure to get full information on safety factors, because anything you haul or build on top of a vehicle is apt to present some hazards. Be sure, too, that you investigate costs thoroughly: often the quoted price does not include the heavier tires, wider rear-view mirrors, or other hidden expenses that may prove unavoidable. The most common types are described here, but you should remember that each kind blends into the next.

*Pickup Covers:* The most rudimentary form of camper is the pickup cover, a shell with windows and door which fits over the back of a pickup truck and provides sleeping accommodations plus whatever other amenities you can fit into the small space. Since the cover is usually about the same height as the truck cabin, standing inside is at a half crouch. Some come with fold-out tent tops to give more head-room at the campsite. Mobility and maneuverability are high, and you can negotiate rough ground and small roads in them.

*Camping Trailers:* That small box you see being pulled around behind an ordinary car is the expandable camping trailer. The simpler ones are basically a fold-out tent which extends beyond both ends of the trailer bed to give sleeping room. They are lightweight and easily hauled by a small car. More elaborate ones have fold-out canvas walls and a fiber-glass top which gives a rigid cover for the road as well as in camp. They are usually larger, and the most expensive ones feature a lot more built-in amenities: cabinets, oven, refrigerator, shower. A third type has fold-out metal walls, but these verge on the truck camper and are quite expensive for a fold-away trailer.

*Truck Campers:* These are a more elaborate form of pickup cover, built longer and higher than the truck so that they extend over the top of the truck cabin and out beyond the truck bed at the back. They come in many sizes. Some have pop-up roofs and extendable backs. The largest have full, if compact, living quarters, including kitchen and toilet. The highest truck campers are apt to be top-heavy, requiring some care on turns and in high winds.

*Travel Trailers:* Much amplified versions of the camping trailer, these require a pickup truck or a high-powered car for haulage. They contain all the amenities of an efficiency apartment—rather like a cabin cruiser on wheels, in fact. They are detachable at the campsite, thus freeing your hauling vehicle for local trips and errands. On the negative side, they are a good deal more awkward to maneuver on some roads; are not even allowed on others. They also require a different kind of driving than even a truck since they are wider as a rule and are slow to accelerate. Thus more isolated areas remain inaccessible to a travel trailer.

*Motor Homes:* These are the most elaborate and, in their largest developments, the least mobile of all the camping vehicles. A mobile home is all of a piece with the driver's cabin (like driving in the front window of a studio apartment!). This is definitely the vehicle for people whose main object is to get to one or maybe two places and then stay there for some time. The larger ones are banned from some roads and highways and cannot negotiate many others. But they are strong enough to haul a compact car or a boat and some have external storage space for motor or pedal bikes.

*Van Campers:* Sometimes known as mini-homes, these are a simpler version of the motor home. The smallest (eight or nine feet long) are as maneuverable as a pickup truck; they usually provide some storage room, folding beds/seats, sink, and a stove. Larger ones, based on a commercial truck chassis instead of a van's, have more living space. Some have expandable tops as well. If they have toilet and water supply too, these can be completely self-sufficient. But, of course, the larger they get, the less easily they handle.

*Conversions:* Many a truck and bus has been converted for camping by its owner. Having the work done professionally by specialists is fairly costly, but your initial cost can be lower if you buy a used delivery truck or school bus. Amenities and mobility depend on size and on the amount of work or money you can put into the conversion.

**Equipment**   If you have a truck, trailer, or van camper, you will need more or less what you would for the same period in a holiday cottage, depending on the elaborateness of your camper fittings.

If you are using a station wagon, you might invest in a tent or tarpaulin that can be attached to the open back of the wagon, thus extending your covered space for camping. If you have an ordinary car and are sufficiently rugged for ground sleeping, a small tent with room enough to sit up inside can be sufficient, although a tent in which you can stand is naturally more comfortable. Most people prefer to sleep on an air mattress or foam-rubber pad rather than directly on the ground.

For any vehicle lacking built-in equipment, you will need an ice chest, a portable stove, a water container, utensils, food, flashlight, sleeping bags, perhaps a saw. Other paraphernalia such as folding chairs or camp lanterns depend on your particular definition of a well-equipped camping trip.

**Boat Camping**   With a small boat and a tent, you can choose a shore point inaccessible from land so that your competition for a site is limited to fellow boating campers.

**BOAT VACATIONS**   Boating vacations are rapidly increasing in popularity. Houseboats and cruisers are available for rent along the large inland waterways, especially in the South. Cruisers can also be rented at coastal marinas around the country. It costs several hundred dollars a week to rent these boats, but they accommodate from two to seven people and are fully equipped with galley and head.

If you buy a houseboat or cruiser you need not be troubled by lack of berthing facilities within easy reach of your home: large trailers are available that will take boats up to 30 feet in length. Some of the houseboats that come on their own trailers are designed so that you can use them for land camping, much as you would use a conventional camping trailer.

If you plan to take vacations of longer than a week, the boat—rented or your own—should have a comfortable amount of room to live in plus a well-equipped galley and a bathroom with a chemical toilet and shower. You would do well to plan ahead for longer trips—a few hours spent poring over navigational maps and tour guides will save you many a headache later on. A boat can travel a fair distance in a day but it is better not to plan mileages near the maximum unless all you want to do is drive. Plan to spend an occasional night ashore to get properly cleaned up, enjoy a restaurant meal, and feel a steady mattress under your back.

## GARDENING

Gardening is not what you would call a sport, but it does involve outdoor activity and exercise. It has some of the hallmarks of an art since it includes the use of design (in both space and time) as well as the nurturing of life. You can be a gardener with no land except that which you put into pots and window boxes. Except for a few months during the depths of winter in cold climates, outdoor gardening is hard year-round work. You should be careful not to get too ambitious —it can be heartbreaking trying to keep up a dozen flower beds, a good-sized lawn, several fruit trees, and a vegetable garden.

**Labor Saving**   If you have a large area and can't keep it all up, you can let part of it "return to nature" and have a wild forest area. You can replace that hard-to-manage lawn with a fragrant ground cover like creeping thyme or chamomile, or with an ivy such as myrtle; low-growing junipers or heathers are attractive in small areas also. All are perennials and evergreen and they are a lot tougher than most weeds. For flower beds you can choose perennials that need little day-to-day care. You can perhaps employ a local teen-ager to cut your lawn, rake leaves, and do other backbreaking tasks for you.

But however you minimize the work, a certain amount of bending and lifting is inevitable. You should learn how to do it to impose the least possible strain in the most vulnerable area—the lower back. Learn proper lifting techniques and space out the work.

If you can splurge on a greenhouse, your gardening will reach posi-lively professional standards, but cold frames in an outbuilding with a water supply can give very satisfactory results.

Local flower and produce shows are a joy to keen gardeners. If you're the competitive type or feel that the world should know of the wonders you grow, by all means enter the shows.

**Growing Edibles**　Vegetable gardens can eke out a modest budget, as well as provide a gastronomic pleasure no store-bought vegetable can equal. Seeds for specially miniaturized vegetables are available for growing indoors or on very small areas of land.

It is wise to start out with easily grown vegetables that give a good yield, such as onions, radishes, peppers, lettuce, potatoes. You can time your planting or choose different varieties so that you get a long yield season; peppers, eggplants, and tomatoes will keep on bearing for the whole summer once they have matured. Most vegetables can be started from seed but many people prefer to buy already sprouted seedlings from local nurseries.

Fruit growing is somewhat more complicated (with the exception of strawberries) because bushes and trees take longer to cultivate and are fussier about types of soil and climate.

Herbs, once started, are very little trouble and can be grown in planters. Many of them are evergreens and most are delightful to use in cooking, being a lot tastier fresh than dried.

## COOKING

The art of cooking is often looked upon as a mere chore. If you have never done so, try taking classes in a foreign cuisine. French cookery is the all-time gourmet favorite. Indian dishes will introduce you to another world of spices. Chinese meals are much less hard on the arteries than most European and American cookery. You could start out cautiously with a couple of paperback books and see where your interest is roused. If you become or are already a whiz, you might consider giving lessons, either privately or at a local institute or adult-education course.

## THE ARTS

**THE GRAPHIC ARTS**　**Drawing**　For this you need decent paper, charcoal and drawing pencil, pastels if you want color, good erasers, and drawing pen and inks. You can try learning from one of the many instruction books, but it is usually quicker and more encouraging to go to a teacher, at least at the very beginning. Once you have the rudiments you can carry a sketchbook and pencils wherever you go. You may be surprised at how much more there is to see than the nonartist suspects.

**Painting**    Watercolors can give a variety of delicate finishes. Oil colors are heavier and a lot messier than watercolors; oils have many textures, available to the painter through different mixes and applicators.

Gouache is a kind of opaque watercolor medium, heavier in effect than watercolors. Regular gouache is mixed with a special gum, but poster paints, tempera, and casein also qualify, being water-soluble and fast-drying. Acrylic paints are water-soluble but cannot be redissolved once they are dry; they are much easier to handle than oils and will give many of the same effects.

The costs of drawing and painting can, by and large, be adjusted to your budget. Canvas, paints, brushes, easels, and other tools come in all grades and prices. Work can be done alone or in groups. You can teach yourself à la Grandma Moses, learn from a book, take correspondence courses, attend classes at your local adult-education center or university extension, or enroll full-time at art school—for a price, of course.

**Sculpture**    If you keep the work small and use low-cost materials like clay, it is easy to stay on a low budget. Once you start getting into larger work and materials such as metal, costs start mounting—and so does the amount of exercise needed to get the work done! Smaller pieces also need less studio space.

Classes in sculpture usually start with clay modeling and are to be found in almost the same profusion as painting classes.

**Photography**    The big problem with photography as a pastime is the expense: you must have a camera and film, and you must pay for the development of the film. As you get more skillful, you find the need for different lenses and a more complex camera. Film development is the costliest part of the process, especially if you use a laboratory; as you become more initiated, you usually have a hard time getting the effects you want until you start developing the film yourself—and there you are into setting up a darkroom. You could use your bathroom, which is fine if you live alone or have two bathrooms, but it's apt to cause ructions if you don't.

All in all, photography doesn't come on the highly recommended list for those on an only average income unless you have access to equipment and processing at a particularly low cost.

**Showing**    Art shows are burgeoning, and if you have a modicum of talent your work can probably be hung at a show by a group of which you are a member. Showing art is easy on the body and refreshing for the mind, not to mention good for the ego.

**Art Appreciation**   Many people who don't paint or sculpt or take photographs themselves find great pleasure in looking at artwork—and a good thing, too, or where would audiences come from? As usual, the more you know of a subject, the more able you are to appreciate its expressions. Art history and art appreciation are frequently taught in adult-education and university-extension courses. As well as learning techniques, the basics of design, and so forth, you'll learn to formulate and to articulate your own opinions. A good teacher will show you how to "take apart" the structure of a work of art and then to synthesize it so that your pleasure is akin to that of the artist in making the work.

**MUSIC**   Many teach-yourself instruction books are available, particularly for such popular instruments as the guitar and the recorder. But personal instruction is unbeatable.

In learning to play, you will find yourself listening to music differently and appreciating it in a quite new way. Once you have learned to play decently, look around for a local group to join for musical evenings, public performance, or both. Many groups are formed specifically by and for older people who can meet at times not possible for those still working.

## THE CRAFTS

The line between an art and a craft is hard to draw: the work of some weavers, for instance, can be treated only as art, while the instrumental work of some musicians is craftsmanlike. And is jewelry-making a branch of sculpture or a handicraft?

**HOW YOU LEARN**   The popularity of handicrafts is increasing rapidly, and hobby and handicraft specialty stores are opening all across the country, which means that materials and tools for most crafts are readily available.

There are two ways to approach a handicraft. You can take it from scratch, finding your own materials and tools and making your own designs. This method is definitely the cheaper in terms of supplies; if you can teach yourself from a book or from sheer experimentation, it is the cheapest method from all aspects. However, you may find it necessary to take classes, at least at the very beginning.

The second approach is to buy a kit. In it you will find ready-made designs, prepared materials, and, sometimes, tools. Detailed instructions are also included—and as you follow them you do, in effect, teach yourself the rudiments of the craft. Kits are expensive, however, and since design and materials are pre-set, they leave little latitude for your own imagination. You can, of course, use such kits to get yourself started and then branch out on your own; but you may need more instruction anyway as you encounter problems that the kit instructions never touch upon.

Whichever approach you choose, be careful not to plunge in over your financial head before you're sure you like the work. And don't think that you're above such indiscretions—some of the materials and tools of the handicrafts are enormously attractive. You should also consider the amount of space you will need for work: a printing press or a full-size handweaver's loom are bulky items, to say nothing of storage space for paper and type and inks or for fibers and shuttles and design samples.

Even if you have always been a fumble-thumb, there are still several possibilities open to you—many kinds of rug making require no fine work, for instance—and you may even end up with a certain degree of dexterity.

Many books on handicrafts are available. Some give a brief introduction to a whole range of hobbies so that you can map your possibilities in terms of cost, energy, space, and availability of supplies. Some, devoted to a specific craft, can be used for instruction or to get new ideas for design and technique. Several of the more general books list craft groups, or you can hunt the Yellow Pages or ask at local schools giving instruction in your particular craft.

When you start, choose a simple, small project on which to learn; increase size and complexity as you grow more assured. Large, involved projects can be very discouraging to a beginner—you spend half your time correcting mistakes and have far too long to wait for a completed work.

**NEEDLEWORK    Tailoring and Dressmaking**    These, the most familiar types of needlework, are also the most practical since you can save money and dress rather well by making your own clothes. Tailoring is usually considered the finer craft of the two, with its particular emphasis on line, cut, and finish of clothes; you should probably take classes if tailoring is your aim.

**Embroidery**    Including needlepoint, this is a purely decorative craft. For it you need special needles, threads, canvas or other broadwoven fabric to hold the design, and a hoop. You need a good eye for color and for detail as well as skillful fingers.

**Knitting and Crocheting**    For many women, who have been taught these crafts, they are usually a matter of reawakening old skills. But men are taking up knitting in particular in increasing numbers—this soothing, rhythmic work can be done at odd times: while traveling, talking, listening to the radio. For both knitting and crocheting you need wool, cotton, or synthetic-fiber yarns, and needles of various sizes. Supplies need cost very little and enable you to make anything from doilies to pants suits.

**WEAVING** Like knitting and crocheting, weaving involves the creation (rather than decoration) of a fabric as you work. But weaving demands a loom and shuttles and is not really portable—although at the start, you can knock together a simple wooden frame of 2 x 4's. Almost any yarn or fiber can be used for weaving, particularly on a frame loom.

Beyond the frame loom come the table loom, which will allow you to work fabric widths up to about 26 inches, and then the floor-model looms which can weave fabric up to 60 inches wide. But by this time you are into a very advanced stage of weaving and expenses are mounting, the biggest single item being the floor loom. However, a search through junk stores may unearth an old one that is not too difficult to repair. Yarns can be picked up at factory outlets or at sales.

Color, texture, and pattern are all-important. An experienced weaver with a floor loom can weave fabrics for clothes or furnishings as well as make sizable rugs. With a table loom you can make scarves, ties, belts, wall hangings, cushion covers, and the like. Tapestries can be made on special tapestry looms, which are frame looms with a harness, or on a simple frame loom.

**RUG MAKING** Rugs can be made by hooking and braiding as well as by weaving, crocheting, and knitting. Almost any odds and ends of yarn and fabric (cut into narrow strips) can be used. The backing for hooked rugs is usually some tough, wide-meshed weave; through this the yarn or fabric is hooked or pushed and then knotted into place. Braiding is exactly what its name implies, and the braided length is then curled around itself in a spiral and sewn together. As with weaving, color, texture, and pattern are very important; if the rug is for the floor, durability is equally significant.

**WOODWORKING** Wood carving can be used to produce sculpture, toys, model ships and airplanes, architectural replicas, and decorative effects on furniture and structures. *Cabinetwork* is a term usually applied to handmade wooden furniture, shelving, and other fixtures and fittings. Furniture repair and refurbishing, antique or modern, is a field unto itself.

Woodworking does need a space entirely its own, plus, at the beginning, a workbench with a vise bolted on, and various hand tools.

Both hardwood (from deciduous trees) and softwood (from evergreens) are available. For the beginner, softwoods are preferable—easier to work and cheaper than hardwoods—but they should not be used where durability is essential.

Classes in woodworking, carpentry, cabinetwork, and furniture repair are numerous, as are instruction books in all phases of the craft.

**CERAMICS AND POTTERY**   If you need an excuse to make mud pies again, this time you can harden your pie and decorate it as you wish. Some clays harden at room temperature, others with baking in a kitchen oven; however, these are not the easiest clays to work. The best kind to start with is the type you can buy at most hobby shops, either already moistened or in powder form; it needs firing in a kiln to harden. Your first tools can be simple: spatulas, knives, and a pointed instrument; boards on which to keep the wet clay; and wire for cutting it (like cheese).

After about 24 hours, normal potter's clay hardens to a point at which it is getting firm but can still be worked slightly. After a week or two it is hard and can be decorated in several ways; however, it is brittle. To make it more durable it should be fired in a kiln at very specific temperatures. For kiln firing it is usually possible to rent time in a local potter's or craft school's kiln. (Later you will want to use a potter's wheel; at this point you might invest in a course and learn the techniques of wheel throwing.)

Potter's wheels are not cheap and kilns also cost a hefty sum. Many potters build their own, or go in with several other potters to buy these items, sharing cost and working time.

**PRINTING   Block Printing**   Almost anything carvable or with its own raised or indented pattern can be used for block printing, which is an easy process. Potatoes, linoleum, wood, signet rings—anything with a raised-design surface that will hold ink can be pulled into service. You can transfer the design to paper or fabrics to make patterned cushion covers, curtains, tablecloths, napkins, greeting cards, stationery, and other useful objects.

**Silk-Screen Printing**   Although this is slightly more complicated, it gives a finer print than block-printing. Ink is squeezed through the exposed part (the pattern) of a stretched piece of silk onto the paper or fabric. The silk is stretched on a wooden frame. As you advance, you will probably want several frames in various sizes; these are cheap and easy to construct. More difficult is the application of the pattern to the silk: you can do this by cutting it out of specially prepared film which you then paste onto the screen; or you can brush it on with special preparations. While you should start out with one color, you can begin to use several colors as you acquire skill. After you have screened your cloth or paper you can apply various materials that will stick to the ink as it dries and produce various effects—adding fuzz will flock a picture for, say, a child's room.

Silk-screening is so versatile that it can be used by beginners (you could make posters, for example, to advertise a local rummage sale), and yet in the hands of a creative expert it can produce multicolor prints that look like paintings of museum quality. Neither the inks nor the other materials are expensive, and unless you start making table-top-size projects, the work is not physically tiring.

**Handpress Printing**  Presses are not cheap, but you can start out with a small box press making stationery and greeting cards. If you get further involved, you will be exploring typefaces, papers, paper cutting, larger presses, different inks. You may even end up as the publisher of your block's newsletter, your own poetry, or stories written by your grandchildren. Book printing gets quite complicated and, once into it, you will have to explore bookbinding, which is a craft in its own right.

## NATURE STUDY

**BIRDS**  The way to study birds is in their natural habitat, not caged or stuffed. You can do this by setting up a bird-feeder in your garden or on your windowsill, where the birds will practically pose for you. However, their behavior at the feeders is obviously limited, and the birds that come most often to feed are somewhat domesticated.

Another way to watch birds is to go to wilder parts of the country-side or to bird sanctuaries, where you can observe a wider range of activities. Many sanctuaries have easy trails, benches near feeders or overlooking lakes or meadows, and blinds from which to watch unseen. Becoming ambitious about seeing rarer birds can mean long hours and lots of patience, and a portable canvas stool is handy.

Many inexpensive paperback books illustrate and describe local birds and their habits. Binoculars are almost essential, a telescope is useful, and a camera with a telephoto lens is a luxury if you are watching on a serious level and keeping records. A battery-operated portable tape recorder will let you pick up birdsong at a fair distance; if you set it up with a device triggered by a suitable sound-wave level, you can leave it in place to record in your absence and thus get songs that have not been affected by your presence.

The National Audubon Society can put you in touch with other bird lovers in your area. Depending on how active your local chapter is, you may find conducted walks, competitive bird counts, lectures, and other activities organized.

**INSECTS** It is estimated that insect species number over 60,000, although they are divided into only four main groups (the mosquito and the bumblebee belong to two different ones). As with birds, the simplest way to start is with an identification book in hand. For insects, however, you also need a hand magnifying lens. Insects can be observed in their native habitats, although it is often difficult to follow the complete life cycle this way.

You will find as you go on that your interest begins to center on a limited number or a type. At that point you can consider setting up your own insect habitats for observation: in a glass jar, a terrarium, or an aquarium if you are stuck on water insects. If you prefer to observe them dead, you can collect specimens—a method that butterfly and moth enthusiasts find very rewarding.

**FISH** Since fish must be observed in an aquarium, you should do some research before deciding whether to get involved in this branch of nature study. A session at the library or with an aquarium owner should help you decide just how interesting you would find the subject.

If you are willing to limit yourself to hardy, small fish, you can get a fairly adequate aquarium and its fittings for a not-too-large outlay. But if you get hooked on large or delicate fish you can find yourself investing rather heavily in larger tanks, pumps, filters, lights, and other equipment. Many species of fish need carefully controlled water temperature and composition, so you must be prepared to take some trouble. They must also be fed.

Some of the more common species cost only pennies, but if your interests tend toward the exotic, you will have to pay out some money for specimens. On the other hand, many people find it just as exciting to catch their own specimens in local lakes and rivers—just be careful that you don't introduce a cannibal all unknowingly!

**PLANTS** A walk in the park or through the countryside becomes trebly interesting when you are keeping your eyes peeled for different trees, shrubs, wild flowers, nonflowering plants, fungi, or molds. The enthusiast may find a related field of interest in the lore of plant medicines, wild plant foods, and herbal brews. A patch of ground set aside for transplanted wild flowers and herbs can be the most intriguing part of a garden.

**ROCKS** Rock hunting and collecting is closely allied in method and procedure to mineral, gemstone, and fossil hunting. Rocks are about everywhere except in rich farming country, although even there they are apt to be found in streams and rivers.

Gold panning is popular in California, the Rockies, and other areas, but, despite legends of lost mines, fortune seems to evade the amateur and the work is tiring. Nor should you take up gem and mineral collecting on the assumption it will make you rich: processing is only profitable on a large scale and market value is in any case lower than you might think because of laboratory imitations. Fossils have value for scientists, but these experts find their own, so sales to museums and other institutions are rare. Some collectors can make pin money selling their finds to other collectors at mineral shows.

Minerals are to be found most abundantly in old quarries and mines, many of which are open to mineral hunters. If the mine is private property, you may have to pay a fee. With advance information on the area, however, you can usually find grounds that provide good hunting at no cost. Gemstones are minerals and are therefore most likely to be found in the same areas, with certain stones predominating in certain places. Fossils are remains of ancient life forms, most frequently found in shale, sandstone, and limestone—sedimentary rocks that once were mud or sand.

As any rock, mineral, gemstone, or fossil enthusiast will eagerly tell you, his finds are beautiful and the best of them are well worth prominent display. There are special techniques for hunting, cleaning, and polishing.

Many clubs and societies exist for amateurs. It is necessary to do some reading in the subjects, and you might visit displays at your local museums. The place to start your hunting is your public library, which will tell you the local sources.

Many hobby shops carry minerals and gemstones in the rough, and if you find that your chief interest lies in the finishing of the stones you can buy the cheaper minerals to practice on. However, as you might guess, this is the expensive end of rock hunting; you will have to invest in some fairly pricy equipment to do a really good job of grinding, cutting, and polishing a stone, although much of the equipment can be bought secondhand.

**SHELLS**  People who combine a love of nature with a love of collecting may find shells the perfect hobby. Apart from the expense of your ticket to the beach, shells need cost you nothing. Of course, shell collecting can run into money if you travel to distant beaches or buy specimens of unusual varieties.

## COLLECTING

You can collect anything—once your collection grows above a certain size, the mere numbers of the collected items begin to be intriguing, as does the variety which begins to be apparent in the assortment. Stamps are probably the best-known collecting hobby, but coins, curios, autographs, toys, glassware, clocks, butterflies, music boxes, paperweights, Victoriana, hats, buttons, playing cards are just a few of the almost infinite number of items upon which you can base a collection. Indian relics and artifacts are a good example of a fascinating collection, as they lead into local and national history, art, and geography.

Almost everyone develops a fondness for certain kinds of things and this is a good reason to start a collection. Or you may have inherited a parent's or grandparent's collection which you would like to continue. Every item you collect will have a history—if only of what you went through to get it!

At the beginning, acquisitions may be easy; as you go on, you will find the hunt getting more difficult as you try to get rare or more specialized versions. You will find yourself doing research on history and design and sources. Side trips to certain districts or special shops will become necessary. You may haggle like a Turk over prices. As your temperature mounts, comfort yourself with the words "collector's fever" and join the aficionados.

## STUDIES

You may feel the need for some completely intellectual pursuit. It is hard to categorize many activities as purely intellectual, although they may usually be regarded as such; geology, archaeology, architecture, and history, for instance, however much brainwork they suggest, may eventually mean fieldwork of a thoroughly physical nature. However, it is probably true that such subjects as mathematics, psychology, and etymology will rarely take you away from your desk. Education is discussed more fully in the next chapter, which deals with methods of serious studying, whether through classes, correspondence courses, or your own reading plan.

**READING**   To the reading addict almost any subject matter can be interesting if the book is well written, but most people discover an affinity for a certain group of subjects. Very often the subject turns out to be literature itself. An initial interest in fiction may give way to a more general interest in literature and eventually in a particular branch of literature—poetry, essays, biography, or French 19th-century literature, for instance.

**WRITING**   Many people who study literature discover in themselves a great desire to write. You may find lines for a poem forming unbidden as you drive to the supermarket. You may wake up one morning with an idea for a story full-blown from nowhere. You may realize that you want to use a very personal approach to a subject that most essayists have long dismissed as done to death.

Not a few famous writers have developed in late middle-age; however, anyone with the urge to write had better just write, regardless of the possibilities of fame and fortune. It is one of those creative urges which, unreleased, can sour everything.

**Getting Published** This is such a complex subject that your library probably has an entire shelf of books analyzing the writing market. Such references are indispensable if you are a beginner who might otherwise waste time and postage sending articles and stories to publications that are entirely staff-written, or which are not interested in your subject matter, or which have strict requirements as to length and other factors.

In general, nonfiction is easier to sell than stories, poems, or plays. If you have specialized knowledge in a particular field you may have luck, even as a rank beginner, by writing on your subject for a general magazine or for a publication devoted to your subject.

Another good way to start might be to submit essays to local magazines and newspapers. If you have a talent for being on the spot when newsworthy things happen, you might find work as a free-lance reporter on a local paper.

One's genealogy can be the subject of an interesting monograph. Many people, once launched into discovering their own ancestry, find themselves with a startling family history and a very good perspective on changing times and mores. Nor does it have to be one's own family; perhaps some figure, famous or obscure, attracts you strongly. Research into that person's background can often yield fascinating information on his or her life and times—and thus a biography is born.

If you are dedicated to fiction, you should study not only the reference guides in your library but also the publications you are thinking of submitting to. Many magazines publish fiction of a particular genre (love stories, science fiction, adventure stories), and to have your work accepted you'll have to learn the knack of writing to their format.

Book publication is harder to achieve. Publishers take very few books that they do not judge to have immediate sales possibilities. Here again, references to the writing market are indispensable if you are to save yourself the wasted time and cost of mailing, say, a cookbook to a house which does not publish cookbooks.

"Vanity publishers" are those houses which advertise to get authors; they do not pay you for your work—on the contrary, you pay *them* for the costs of paper, printing, binding, jacket copy and illustration, and often other expenses as well. They do not have the nationwide distribution system of regular publishers, nor should you count on reviews. Though this is a costly way of getting your work into print it can be rewarding if you can afford it and if you understand fully in advance what you must pay for. Before signing anything, you should compare prices with what local printers would charge to print your work; this might be considerably cheaper.

**AGENTS**   Unfortunately, because there are so few good agents and because it is so hard for a beginning writer to get a good agent, this is an area in which unscrupulous people see a chance for a quick buck. To avoid being gypped, write to the Society of Authors' Representatives, Inc., 101 Park Avenue, New York, N.Y. 10017, for their booklet on how to know the reputable agents.

# 15
# A Life for Your Mind

Most people approaching the age of 65 have had an education in experience—sometimes known as the school of hard knocks—such as no other kind of schooling can instill. And, until recently, it was considered eccentric, if not downright outlandish, for anyone of this age to attend formal school. Indeed, many older people felt it demeaning to kowtow (as they saw it) to a teacher younger than themselves. Others, believing the myth that mental capacity declined with age, felt incapable of performing the work required.

In fact, the faculties of the mind decline mostly because of disuse, and this can happen at *any* age. It is also true that no one of any age is without some limitation on his learning abilities.

Given reasonable health, you can maintain most skills and abilities at a high level of performance no matter what your age. Nor do you lose the ability to learn new skills. You may feel that your mental responses are slowing somewhat, but such decline as occurs is usually insignificant. As an older person you actually have an advantage in being able to apply a wider range of knowledge and experience than younger people can. And, of course, speed is rarely essential in any but test situations.

An effective way to mental activity is to maintain a broad reading spectrum. Besides local newspapers, read national ones; besides daily newspapers, read weekly ones; add topical magazines and journals of specific subject fields. Newspapers and magazines are available at the public library, which usually maintains a reading room.

You may become interested in a particular subject. If so, you can pursue it through books at the public library, through courses at a local adult-education center, even at college; many universities are starting special courses for older people, others are opening their undergraduate courses (free or at reduced rates) to those over 64.

## EDUCATIONAL FACILITIES

**ADULT-EDUCATION COURSES**   These, set up in public schools, are intended primarily to enrich the lives of the adults in the local communities. Some courses are in a specific business, profession, or trade (for example, computer programming, typing, printing) and are intended to provide training for increased earning power. Other courses are in arts and crafts and in sports (for example, tailoring, painting, woodworking, aviation, golf) and may be used to develop a hobby for recreational or economic purposes. Still others are in subjects of wide interest (philosophy, history, politics) for purely cultural purposes.

**Diploma Courses**   In some area schools, certain elementary-level and high-school-equivalency courses with diplomas are offered. These are handy, since people over 65 constitute, on the average, the most poorly educated segment of the population. In 1960, one fifth of people aged over 64 were regarded as functionally illiterate and only one third had continued beyond eighth grade at school. Although the situation is improving, as of 1970 the number of years of formal schooling for people over 64 averaged 9.6; this compared with an average of 11.8 years for the 55–64 age group and of 12.7 years for people aged 20–24. To compound the problem, this formal education almost always took place early in life; not only were school facilities and teacher training in those days not as good as they are now, but a lot of the subject matter taught then, particularly in the sciences, is out of date.

All told, if you have a lively mind and went short of formal schooling in your younger days, you may feel a need for a good basic education. For you the courses up to college level would be a door opening onto a world of vast horizons.

These adult-education courses are usually financed by contributions from local civic-minded businesses and institutions. They are often coordinated at the county or other area level through an adult-education committee or council or its equivalent. As most of the courses are intended for the whole adult community, they are taught outside working hours (evenings or, occasionally, on Saturdays). However, some, aimed specifically at retired people, take place during the day. The cost of these courses is generally quite low, and many allow a discount for retired people.

**Special Courses**   Some adult-education courses in area schools, in senior-citizen centers, and in a few other institutions are specially designed to inform older people about practical issues: health (nutrition, exercise), income management, legal matters, housing, and, occasionally, preretirement courses (financial and emotional preparation).

**Community-Agency Courses**   Many community agencies organize adult education in the form of lectures, symposia, classes, and special interest clubs. The Y's, a well-developed example, hold extensive courses throughout the country and the world. Settlement houses, centers of worship, and community centers are other agencies typically involved in adult education. Costs vary greatly, but are usually discounted for retired people.

Museums and art galleries hold frequent lectures, guided tours, films, and other educational programs. The subject matter can extend to such things as art history, art appreciation, and crafts instruction. The programs are usually free except for the museum entrance fees (and the latter are often lower for retired people).

In large cities the city-recreation department or park authority often has adult sports-education programs (tennis, swimming, golf, and dance).

**UNIVERSITY COURSES**   In addition to information given below, you might want to consult *The New York Times Guide to Continuing Education in America* (Quadrangle Books, 1973), or *A Directory of U. S. College and University Degrees For Part-time Students,* available from the National University Extension Association (1 Dupont Circle, Suite 360, Washington, D.C. 20036).

**Extension Courses**   Also known as continuing-education courses, these are run by university departments devoted to adult education. Courses may be held on campus or in outlying towns and community colleges in the university's area. Most take place in the evening and are not degree-credit courses. No formal educational requirements are set for admission to most courses, although the more advanced or technical ones will assume you have a certain level of knowledge.

The range of courses is often even greater than that of the adult-education courses in the public school system, with more academic and scientific courses and more advanced courses in specific subjects. Costs are unfortunately quite high, at least as compared to local adult-education courses. However, reduced prices are sometimes available to older people.

**Summer Programs**   Many university extension departments have summer programs, some of them sponsored by adult-education groups, trade unions, credit unions, and other such agencies. They may be set up in much the same way as the fall–winter–spring courses; or they may be daytime courses once or twice a week; or they may be intensive, full-time courses for a weekend on up to six or eight weeks, sometimes requiring residence on the premises for the duration of the course. Here, again, costs are relatively high.

If you are interested and think you may be able to afford either evening or summer university extension courses, get in touch with the Director of Adult Education at the nearest university (or universities) and see what he has to offer. You might also inquire whether the university has special low rates for older people or for the particular subject or set of courses you want to take.

**Full-time Courses**   A few years ago the University of Kentucky experimented with the idea of opening its regular courses to people over 64. Enrollment had to be in credit courses, though not necessarily for credits. If you took courses for credits you were expected to meet the same requirements and assignments as any other student. Physical and emotional stamina as well as good sensory perception was the only requirement, and places were awarded on a scholarship basis.

The experiment proved so successful that the University of Kentucky has expanded its program. Older students take part in extracurricular activities, live both on and off campus, and use all the university's facilities as freely as other students. Their rate of academic success is equal to that of any other age group.

Success at Kentucky has encouraged several others, including Fairleigh Dickinson University in New Jersey and City University of New York, to embark on similar plans. You do not have to work toward a college degree, although you can if you wish. Tuition is usually either free or 50% of the regular fees; but you have to pay registration fees and for course materials, transportation, lodging, and other expenses.

Some universities require the usual educational qualifications (high-school diploma or its equivalent if you want to take a bachelor's degree); others require none and assume that you are the best judge of your own capabilities. In most of the programs you may not register for a class until after enrollment of regular paying students.

**Junior Colleges**   These offer two-year courses in a wide variety of subjects. If you complete a full program of study you may earn an associate in arts degree, and can then transfer to a four-year college or a university and get credits toward a bachelor's degree. The usual academic subjects—language, arts, mathematics, sciences—are given, plus many technical, business, domestic, and sports courses. At many junior colleges local residents pay no tuition and have no special requirements to fulfill before entry to the courses.

To find out about such programs, get in touch with the Admissions Officer or the Dean of Older Students at the college or university you would like to attend and see if it has free or low-priced courses available. You will also need information on accommodations if you do not live within commuting distance. Some universities arrange on-campus or nearby lodging; others are not yet so well organized.

**OTHER PROGRAMS**   **Institute of Lifetime Learning**   The American Association of Retired Persons and the National Retired Teachers Association, which are sister organizations, have initiated this institute, designed to provide educational courses of various types to older people. The courses are sponsored by the Associations' chapters in many communities. For information on what might be available to you, write to either their eastern headquarters (1225 Connecticut Avenue, N.W., Washington, D.C. 20036) or their western headquarters (Times Building, Long Beach, Calif. 90802).

**Oliver Wendell Holmes Association**   Lectures and seminars on a variety of subjects, from two to six weeks, are given by older people for older people. The community in which the courses are given must provide space, transport, maintenance, and fees for the faculty. If you think your community might be interested, you can get detailed information from the Association at 660 Madison Avenue, New York, N.Y. 10022.

**Institute of Retired Professionals**   This has been set up in New York City for a maximum membership of 500 retired and semiretired people over 40 who have careers of at least 20 years as professionals or business executives behind them. The institute organizes learning groups led by volunteer members and one daytime course each semester at regular classes at the New School.

Similar groups have been organized in other cities. You can get more information by writing to the Director, Institute of Retired Professionals, New School for Social Research, 66 West 12th Street, New York, N.Y. 10011.

**CORRESPONDENCE COURSES**   A number of universities offer correspondence instruction in high-school and college level courses.

**High-school courses**   If you want to take high-school courses for credit, make arrangements with a local high school or with the state board of education before you start the course.

**Credit Courses**   Many correspondence courses for credit toward a college degree are available; a few institutions also offer work for graduate credit, although many graduate schools will not accept credits earned in this way. Undergraduate credits are usually transferable to other colleges and universities. You should check acceptability if you plan to take your degree from a college other than the one giving the correspondence course. Such a situation might arise, for instance, if you have started studying full-time toward a degree and then find that you can no longer afford full-scale college fees.

You need not work for a degree or diploma to enroll in credit courses; most institutions accept correspondence students on a noncredit basis.

**Noncredit Courses**   In addition to credit courses, many noncredit courses are available from colleges and universities, and they embrace a wider variety of subjects than do credit courses. Sometimes a certificate of achievement is issued on successful course completion.

Most institutions accept correspondence students without entrance examinations or preliminary educational requirements, although some courses presuppose a certain level of prior knowledge. The National University Extension Association (1 Dupont Circle, Suite 360, Washington, D.C. 20036) publishes a *Guide to Independent Study,* which lists colleges, universities, state education systems, and home-study institutions that are members of the independent-study division of the NUEA. Many other institutions of learning besides those listed in the directory offer correspondence courses, details of which you can obtain from the individual institution. (The NUEA also publishes a comprehensive guide to college and university degrees for part-time students.)

**OTHER SOURCES   Television and Radio**   Educational channels carry general-educational programs and university-study programs. In the Northeast, the Sunrise Semester is a degree course starting at 6 every weekday morning. You can enroll in these courses and receive course material and classes in addition to the broadcast television program. Your work is then monitored.

All by yourself you can convert the boob tube into an intelligent informant by choosing your programs carefully. Radio is not all cream soap or hard rock, either. Write to your local television and radio stations for listings of their educational programs and broadcasts, and keep an eye on regular schedules for interesting programs.

**County Extension Courses**   Most states have a land-grant university, set up originally to provide practical training in agriculture and home economics to the rural population. Now that the latter has decreased in number and increased in sophistication, the educational services have been broadened. Ask the County Extension Office about courses offered in your area.

**Special-interest Groups**   The armed services, labor unions, businesses and industries, and other groups with a common interest frequently offer special educational programs for their members and employees. They may also offer counseling, books, films, and other services.

**The Public Library**   In many ways this is the most accessible and certainly the cheapest source of information and knowledge. If your local library is small, you may be able to use the larger county or central city library. Alternatively, if you know what you want (often the hardest part of using a library) your local library will usually be able to get it for you.

Besides the lending section, a good public library will have a decent-sized reading room and a well-stocked reference library for use on the premises. Nor are libraries confined to books these days; most now stock records, tapes, films, pictures, magazines, and newspapers for reference and lending. Learning to use the card index to search out what you're looking for is quite simple, and the librarian is only too happy to help. Many large libraries put out newsletters about local educational and cultural events, about their own services, and list educational opportunities in your area.

**Periodicals**   Newspapers and magazines of the less lurid type will keep you informed of current events and ideas in greater depth than is possible on television or radio. Some are more objective than others in their approach to news. If you favor one of the less objective ones you should make a point of reading the same news items in a paper or magazine biased in the opposite direction. If you find subscription too expensive, a regular session at your local public library's reading room will mend the gap.

**Bookstores**   If you are lucky enough to have a bookstore in your district, by all means use it. You may not be able to buy very much from it, but bookstores usually welcome browsers. The proprietor of a good bookstore knows books and will usually be glad enough to talk about them to an interested customer.

## *LEARNING TECHNIQUES*

Now, with the wealth of educational matter available to your avid brain, it's time to take a look at just how your brain is going to be able to use it.

If you have been taking classes, or teaching yourself new skills, or have kept an inquiring mind all your life, you will have little difficulty in continuing. But if you've been too busy working at an exhausting job or for other reasons have let yourself slip into a passive state of mind, you have some self-prodding and self-discipline (oh, nasty words!) to undertake.

Certainly, it's of little use after 20 years of watching "Perry Mason" to fling yourself into a course on logic or "Great Books of Our Time." You may have all the enthusiasm in the world, but after the first few sessions you'll probably be floundering—and by the halfway mark you'll have dropped out. Your brain will have to be put into good condition with a slowly increasing amount of work. And you must learn how to learn.

If you have chosen a new subject for study, approach it gradually. Read up about it, talk about it, explore its ramifications; find out whether you really want to go on with it and, if so, to what extent. If it is a subject you have had your eye on for years, you will already have covered this stage.

**HOME STUDY** **Time** Once you start classes, you will need time not only for the classes themselves but also for work at home. Until you get accustomed to studying, allow more time than you might think usual for the work to be done at home. Be realistic about how much time you want to or will be able to spend on the subject: your work will be better if you lead a well-rounded life of social intercourse and physical exercise as well as intellectual exercise.

**Place** If you can, set aside a special place for home study; don't rely on a quiet period in your favorite armchair with that new novel at your elbow and that blank television eye right in front of you. And don't count on using the kitchen table—it will have to be cleared for meals, and packing and unpacking your work materials will be a hurdle you don't need.

A separate room is ideal, of course, but, failing that, a desk in a quiet corner of the living room (unless you lead a rip-roaring social life, of course) or in the bedroom is good enough.

Make sure that the desk lighting is good and that all the material—dictionaries, reference books, writing utensils—are within easy reach. Unless you are super-disciplined, avoid distracting views or noises. You should also prevent interruptions by firm notice of your "do not disturb" status. The temperature of the room where you work should be comfortable, and you should eliminate drafts.

**Scheduling** Once you have retired you are more or less free to follow your own body rhythms for working and resting. Notice the parts of the day or night in which you feel most alert and try to schedule your study times to coincide with them.

Don't try to finish all your home study at one time; if you space it out between classes you will have more time for reviewing what you have already learned and a better chance of retaining it. Set aside definite times and dates for studying, and vary them only for emergencies; if you start getting too many emergencies, something may be wrong with your schedule (if not your discipline!) and it should perhaps be revised.

Don't try to work if you are very tired; it's a waste of time. Instead, schedule an extra period later and forget about this one.

If you are taking classes, schedule a study period for as soon after the class as possible so you can go over the material covered while it is still fresh in your mind. You can also get started, at least, on any assignments you have been given. Another study session shortly before the next class will prepare you to work well when you get there.

If you are working on more than one subject, allow time for each within one study session: the variety will aid concentration.

**Procedure** Everyone has a highly individualized pattern, amounting to ritual with some people, for getting work done; you may find, after experimenting, that yours differs altogether from those suggested here. This is fine. But beware the bindings of habit: because you feel comfortable with a particular procedure does not make it the most efficient, even for you.

The way that seems most effective for most people is to make first a quick survey of the material to be covered. This can be done by first scanning chapter heads of the material, then scanning subheads within the first section and the summary paragraphs usually found at the ends of chapters.

Then, if you feel the need, skim-read the section and summarize in your own mind and words what topics were covered and from what points of view.

Third, read the material at your normal study speed to get detailed meanings.

Then restate the essence of the section in your own words: brief written notes are a great help in doing this. Repeat your restatement until you are sure you have grasped the matter.

This procedure should be followed section by section until you have covered all the material. Then you should review all you have learned. Whatever notes you have taken will prove useful not only in clarifying your understanding and anchoring your learning but also in reviewing for the next class and for examinations. The notes should be brief, in your own words, and very much to the point. If a particular phrase catches your imagination, jot it down in full; later it will serve to trigger your memory as you review.

**Study Periods** Particularly at the beginning, it's hard to concentrate for long periods. Starting out on each session is pure murder for many people and is deferred by sharpening of pencils, rearrangement of desks, cleaning of typewriters. One way out of this is to establish a short ritual to be completed *before* your set starting time. Or make sure that you will be starting with something you find easy to do.

Once you start, other dangers rear their distracting heads: boredom sets in after the first fine flush; you remember that you should have called the dentist and the thought keeps nagging at you; you find yourself straining to hear the dialogue in that play your spouse is watching on television (sound turned down low for your benefit); you realize that if you popped out to the bakery right now you could get hot bread straight from their ovens; the telephone rings and you wait irritably for someone else to answer it, hoping it is or is not for you. And so it goes . . . for everyone but the most experienced and disciplined among us. But gradually you learn how to avoid or deal with it all.

You start out with short periods of study and lengthen them as you get accustomed to working again. Once you are settled in to several hours at a time, you give yourself periodic breaks, say 15 minutes out of every hour or half an hour out of every few hours. During the breaks, you do something you want to do and that will get you out of the chair and keep your body moving. You make a note to call the dentist later and thus remove the fear of forgetting which is often the root of the nagging. You remind yourself of your reasons for studying, of your initial excitement about the work, and dismiss that play on television as one that you wouldn't have watched if you were free to do so. You tell yourself—firmly—that the bakery has hot bread every day, and that tomorrow you can get there and back before the time scheduled for your study period.

You may need a carrot—so promise yourself a cup of coffee or ten minutes in the garden when you've finished the section you're working on. Before you stop working, either for a ten-minute break or until your next scheduled period, decide exactly where you want to start next time and how you are going to go about it. If you get completely bogged down, drop it and move on to another part of the subject or to another subject altogether; or go for a walk around the block.

If you find your home situation too distracting despite all your tricks, go to a public reading room, where hush is prevalent and others are working, too.

**Retention**    As a mature adult you will find yourself able to relate your new subject to your past experience. You will see overall associations much more easily than when you were a young student, and will thus assimilate your subject better, which makes for more permanent retention.

You will also be able to appreciate that the material you are studying from has been compiled by someone with a certain point of view, that there may be other aspects of the matter to be searched out, that you yourself are probably biased in your approach, and that all this must be allowed for in your learning.

Retention is also helped by discussion or even just by telling someone about it (this does not seem to apply to "creative writing" by the way, so beware of pouring it out verbally; you may find nothing left in the jug to write from). In spare moments, go over what you have most recently learned or review the subject as a whole. Once your mind is accustomed to your new regime, keep it alert at all times by trying to be observant; by discussing things with your family and friends instead of chatting idly or arguing immovably. Read things that will keep you asking questions, not give you pat answers.

**Progress**   In no course of study is progress ever constant. Every now and again you will hit a plateau during which you seem to be just marking time. These periods can be very frustrating and discouraging, and it is as well to see them for what they really are: a change in some basic attitude or habit or way of doing things of which you are largely unconscious.

While the change is taking place the rest of you, so to speak, suspends development; once the change is made, progress is usually rapid because the change increases your efficiency. The best thing to do while waiting it out is to review work you have already done, think about it, and work on areas in which your knowledge is defective.

**Reading Techniques**   Read with a dictionary at your elbow and look up every word you don't understand. This may be tiresome at first, but as your vocabulary broadens, your dictionary consultations will grow fewer; and you will probably end up enjoying the dictionary for its own sake (although you must be careful not to add it to the list of your distractions).

Use the same scanning techniques as described under "Procedure," above.

You need to worry about your reading speed only if it is definitely holding you back; if it is, try to determine how many pauses your eye makes in reading a line at normal speed; then try to reduce the number of resting places (thus employing more peripheral vision than usual for you). This is a strain at first, and you will often lose the sense of what you are reading because of this secondary concentration. But a little practice will eliminate that hazard, and soon fewer pauses per line will come naturally. Another frequent impediment to reading speed is the habit of pronouncing every word subvocally—your vocal chords form the words even though you make no sound and your lips are not moving. Try to discover whether you are doing this and, if you are, try to break the habit by making the eye rests per line too few to permit such a technique.

Of course, reading poetry and poetic prose requires exactly this technique. If that is what you are studying, by all means stick to it for the poetry and prose themselves—but drop it for the discussions and critiques you probably also have to read.

**Writing Techniques**   The first step is to jot down all your ideas on the subject as they occur to you. Consult your study notes and relevant sections of textbooks to make sure you have the matter well in mind. Then decide exactly what kind of piece you are writing (fictional, descriptive, explanatory; essay, story, poem, thesis) and for whom you are writing. Except for poems, which have their own discipline and technique, you should then make an outline that presents your information clearly and logically.

Then write a first draft just as if it were the final one; go over it and alter it as necessary. Then sleep on it and go over it again. Then type the final draft.

Many of the pointers given for effective studying above apply here as well. The distractions and blocks will all be here and can be gotten rid of in much the same ways, provided your outline is good enough on consultation to clear your mind.

Should you find your presentation changing as you get into the writing, then change the outline as necessary as you go along—it will keep you from losing your theme in details.

In the final reading make sure that you have the exact words for your meanings; that you have not been repetitive in either words or theme; that your presentation and vocabulary is sufficiently various not to bore the reader; and that you have avoided clichés.

In general, the opening sentence or paragraph presents the theme, the middle portion develops it, and the closing paragraphs summarize your reasoning and conclusions.

**In Class**   If you are attending classes, attend *all* of them and get a good seat for seeing and hearing the instructor. Learn to make brief, pithy notes when necessary and enlarge on them as soon as you get home, if possible.

Get your assignments in on time or you will have a harassed instructor to cope with.

Beware of your reactions to the teacher-pupil relationship—a lot of older people have trouble accepting it, partly because it throws them back into a psychological state they haven't known since leaving school, partly because the teacher is usually younger than they. You may find yourself making comments—loudly and often. You may catch yourself holding frequent conversations in whispers loud enough to distract everyone. You may feel resentment that your wisdom and knowledge are not appreciated. Catch yourself and stop yourself; pay attention and keep quiet until your contribution is wanted.

**Examinations**   Here is one event which sends shivers down the stiffest spines, arthritis notwithstanding. If you have been working well all along, you have little to fear and your review work will be just a matter of refreshing your memory.

Avoid cramming at the last minute, get a good night's sleep before the examination, and don't start drinking gallons of coffee or taking wake-up pills: the examination will doubtless be sufficiently exacting in itself to get your adrenalin moving.

Read all the questions carefully before embarking on any answers, and make sure you understand the nub of any question before you attempt to answer it. Divide the available time according to the number and length of the answers required and leave the hardest until last. Deep breathing for a minute will calm any panic you feel rising.

**NONACADEMIC WORK**   Arts, crafts, and other manual skills can be approached in much the same manner, allowing for the differences in work space, materials, techniques, and practice. However, the type of learning involved in manual and artistic work is special: the conscious brain is used to imprint the initial learning, but the aim is eventually to bypass consciousness so that the body can work in conjunction with another level of the mind.

Thus, a course in oil painting will mean that you must learn quite consciously about canvas, frames, paints, color mixing, brushes, and other tools and their application in much the same manner as you would learn economics, say. But you also learn oil painting by physically doing (nobody will give you a market to manage in a course on economics!), and this involves a form of learning through the body: eventually you will know the feel of a paint mix or a brushstroke and your eyes will register visual data, all with no reference to conscious learning.

Some people come to this quickly and are called talented in the medium; others take longer but may find equal satisfaction in their work.

**WORKING ON YOUR OWN**   To study on your own, you need great motivation. With no outside person or institution to whom you must answer, you must find it enough to have to answer to yourself. And isolation brings attendant difficulties: lack of discussion can leave errors of understanding uncorrected; you may wrestle for weeks with a problem whose solution is already known to someone else; and there are times when the mind simply needs the abrasion of other view-points.

Even with great motivation and self-discipline you will probably run into stretches of blocking and discouragement. During such periods, see if you can find an outside source of encouragement. Perhaps your local adult-education institute has a short course in the subject or a related one. Is there a symposium or lecture series you can attend? Is one of your friends interested in the subject? Perhaps you can get a group together for discussion, either one time or for several occasions. In any case, try to supplement individual study with some form of group work.

## WHY BOTHER?

The purposes of education are various. You may want to explore a subject that has always attracted you. You may want a diploma or a degree simply because you haven't got one and feel the lack. You may want to embark on another full- or part-time career in retirement and need preparation. You may want to broaden the horizons of your mind and get to know what there is to know in the world. Or you may, quite simply, love the process of learning and of feeling your mind working at its top bent—much as an athlete enjoys the strength and skill of his muscles.

One incidental advantage (apart from those of enhanced knowledge and brain power) is a kind of increased autonomy in the personality; knowledge and skill bring a degree of self-sufficiency, and this kind of pride can keep backs erect. Another advantage is the increased self-discipline which spills over into other areas, and at the same time lets you really relax when you are relaxing.

If you are taking classes or are a member of a group, your social intercourse may be broadened—shared interests often make good friends. Also the very fact that you are going out—to a library, a class, or a meeting place—gets you moving and changes what might otherwise be a homebound perspective.

# 16
# Do You Want a Job?

In 1970, some 15% of people over 64 (3 million) were in money-earning jobs, either part-time or full-time, and another 104,000 were looking for jobs. This put the older age group at 2½% of the total labor force.

All other things being equal (that is, barring reforms in working patterns, acute inflation, or Great Depression), these figures have remained and are expected to remain fairly constant for the rest of this century.

Given the attractions of retirement, why do so many older people continue to hold jobs?

**BECAUSE YOU NEED MONEY** Although most people would agree that a retired person should be entitled to a little self-indulgence, statistics show that he or she is lucky just to *survive* on a retirement income. A retired couple on Social Security was getting an average of only $3516 a year starting July, 1974. If the couple was in the lucky 25% of retirees who also got a private pension, they probably received an additional $1350 per annum. Compare this to the 1972 federal estimates that a retired couple needed a minimum budget of $3442 a year—at subsistence level, allowing not the smallest luxury—$4967 for an intermediate budget, and $7689 for a higher level budget.

Perhaps some miracle will slow down inflation, but not to anything like the extent needed for Social Security benefits to keep pace. Since January, 1975, Social Security benefits have been pegged to the cost-of-living index of the Bureau of Labor Statistics. Unfortunately, this index is based on total goods produced, and includes luxury items whose price falls during inflationary periods. Thus Social Security benefits, which realistically should be geared to cost of necessities (food, clothing, shelter)—these being all an older person can afford on such an income—are depressed by connection with the cost-of-living index. Even if you draw an average private pension or have an additional source of income from something such as an annuity, you may only just make ends meet. If not, you may have to get a job for sheer survival.

**BECAUSE OF OTHER NEEDS** The introduction to this section discusses the various emotional and intellectual functions that jobs fulfill for many people—those of status, identity, role playing, and companionship—and the devastating effect that retirement can have on your psyche and even on your physical well-being. Thus, even if you might be able to get by financially without a job, you may need to work for some or all of these other needs. Since frustration of these needs can have serious consequences, it is well to pay sober attention to them, deciding which you can safely forgo, which you cannot deny, and how best the latter can be satisfied.

If money is necessary, either for economic reasons or because you need payment to feel your work is worthwhile, then you will have to find paid employment. This, expectably, is a tough proposition. Usually it entails organization, effort, and rather more time than you have been accustomed to allotting to such matters.

## ABILITY TO WORK

**SOCIAL SECURITY LIMITATIONS** See Chapter 2 for a discussion of these.

**PRIVATE PENSION PLAN LIMITATIONS** The amount the retiree gets ranges from well over $100,000 a year for big bosses to well under $500 per annum for what is politely termed "the less fortunate." The average figure for private pension payments given by the Department of Labor Statistics is $164 a month; this figure includes the well-heeled boys at the top. The largest number of workers get a median payment of between $100 and $125, a less comforting amount.

About 40% of workers on pensions are restricted in the kind of work they may undertake. Most are barred from reemployment in the same industry. Some are barred from working for competitors. A few are barred from any gainful employment whatever. Penalties for infringement of these restrictions range from suspension of pension payments during the period worked to suspension for an indefinite period—which may, of course, mean permanently. Pensioners with postretirement union affiliations may find their membership affected as well.

The purposes of the restrictions are twofold. Management does not want "inside information" getting into the hands of rival firms. Unions try to minimize competition with younger workers in the industry both for better bargaining with management and to keep unemployment down among younger workers.

About 25% of workers covered by private pension plans do not face mandatory retirement until they are either 68 or 70 years old, and for them perhaps the restrictions do not constitute too great a hardship. For the 75% subject to mandatory retirement at an earlier age, however, these restrictions can hit hard. This is particularly true of the skilled worker who has liked his job or who has developed no other skills and is thus faced with comparatively dull alternatives on the job market.

Bearing all this in mind, if you do draw a private pension, check carefully on the conditions attached to your right to the benefit (see Chapter 2 for details). If you wait until after you have violated the restrictions you may find yourself with no remedy against forfeiture.

**PHYSICAL LIMITATIONS** The prospect of retirement is pleasing to many people for purely physical reasons. The eight-hour shift may have become a grind. You may find that as you get older you have to exert more effort just to maintain your output; this is especially true where precision or manual strength is required. Certain movements—bending, for instance, or lifting—are perhaps becoming increasingly difficult. Maybe you can no longer quite hear certain (most often high) tones as well as you once could. Or maybe your eyes don't accommodate as well to sudden changes from dark to light and vice versa or to long stretches of close work.

All of these are fairly common bodily malfunctions which begin to appear in later life. Some of them can be halted or even reversed with exercise and nutrition (see Section IV). But there is little point in undertaking postretirement work that is likely to aggravate the conditions, so take close account of your specific limitations.

A part-time job will avoid the stress of long hours. Other possibilities are to find a job with a less demanding pace; one that will let you avoid particularly painful or straining movements; one that allows you to sit, at least periodically; one whose hours can be adapted to your day-to-day state of health so that if your arthritis, say, is bad one morning you need not do the work until you feel better. Thus you can mitigate your limitations so that they have little effect on your ability to function.

Hearing or eyesight can often be improved by external methods. Hearing aids are scarcely the embarrassment they once were and spectacles are actually popular (especially among those who don't really need them).

Fatigue is likely to lower output, of course, but except in the most arduous work, such as mining, several surveys have found little difference in quantity of output between the ages of 50 and 70. On the other hand, the same surveys have found that the *quality* of output in the older age group is often better than that of younger workers. This seems to be a result of better concentration, conscientiousness, and attention to detail among older people.

Even if your physical condition is superb and you feel none of the circumscriptions outlined above, still it's a good idea to avoid highly strenuous or stressful work. At the age of 65 the body is apt to respond better and more efficiently to a bit of leniency, and work involving steady effort is better than that with sporadic exertion. So take it easy.

**MENTAL AND EMOTIONAL LIMITATIONS**   For no very good reason, older people are generally expected to be less adaptable and energetic, to lack initiative, and to have poor memories. As usual, being stereotyped will often bring on the disabilities expected.

In fact, potential disabilities, mental and physical, can usually be compensated for by skill and experience; patience, self-discipline, method, and close attention to detail are high among older people and can be used to replace any receding powers. Consequently, even if some older people allow themselves to fall into the stereotype, these would not be the ones alert enough to be actively job-seeking.

# 17
# Finding a Job

A postretirement job may call for new knowledge and skill, and—particularly if you found retirement a psychically telling blow—you may be nervous during the initial learning period. This nervousness may increase if you are learning along with people a lot younger than yourself, especially in a competitive situation. Your nervousness can then become a stumbling block—anxiety is one of the primary causes of memory failure, for example. If your new job is related to a field in which you are already versed, you may find it hard to overcome long-held ideas.

Thus it may take longer to learn new skills and ideas when you are older. Knowing that this does not stem from age but from psychological blocks you have set yourself, and that you still learn as thoroughly as ever, may not be much comfort; but this knowledge should forewarn you to allow yourself enough time and repetition, and to be more relaxed.

On the credit side, work habits are usually better among older than among younger people. With age usually come stability and reliability; you are more likely to stay on the job, to be absent less frequently, and to be more punctual than a younger worker. An employer can use older workers as a stabilizing influence on younger workers.

Since unemployment rates are lower among people with more education, you might want to take a course to increase your knowledge in a new field. If you would like a higher level of job but lack the formal education required to get it, consider going back to school, part- or full-time, to take the high-school or college diploma you need. (See Chapter 15)

## AGE LIMITATIONS

The Age Discrimination in Employment Act of 1969 prohibits discrimination against 40- to 65-year-olds because of age alone. If you are among those retired before 65, this may bring you some comfort, since it puts the power of the law behind you and prevents blatant discrimination: you may get job interviews which before the Act would have been closed to you.

Unfortunately, the Act is a failure in practical terms. It has not changed those provisions of private pension plans that put pressure on older workers to retire earlier than the mandatory age. Employment agencies still claim they lack "suitable" openings. Employers still specify, albeit verbally now rather than in writing, their preference for applicants under 40 years of age. And the Act will not help you after the age of 65.

So, Act or no, you are unfortunately on your own against the stereotyped objections that employers raise to taking on older workers—even though these are easily refuted:

Older workers are *not* less productive; they are at least equally productive. Older workers are *not* more frequently absent; surveys show that their attendance records are about 20% better than those of younger workers. They do *not* have more accidents than younger workers; they have somewhat fewer disabling accidents and many fewer nondisabling accidents. Longer experience in acquiring and using skills enhances the older worker's chances of learning new ones; in certain instances it may take him longer but, allowing for that, the learning itself is just as complete as a younger worker's.

Even if you are able to dispose of these objections plus, possibly, a few more bogies, you are next faced with the nitty-gritty: you cannot be accommodated in the firm's pension plan because it would be too expensive for the employer. But, you answer, you have no interest in the pension plan, you are willing to waive any right to it. Ah, no, says the personnel manager of the larger, less flexible firm, company policy prohibits exceptions to rules, or union regulations will be violated. If you cannot maneuver an exemption for yourself, you'll have to confine your job-seeking efforts to smaller, less rigid firms.

In dealing with larger and less flexible companies, a second crunch may appear: your presence on the work force will increase the company's insurance costs. Such is the blighted vision of insurance companies that this may very well be true of certain policies. Again, you must seek a way to bypass the rules or, failing this, look for work in less formal circumstances.

## *LOOKING FOR A JOB*

**PERSONAL CONTACTS**   Undoubtedly, the jobs publicly advertised in magazines, newspapers, and employment agencies are only a fraction of what is actually available. Most jobs, particularly the good ones, get filled long before the need to advertise arises, or before the responses come in. The jobs are filled through personal contacts and recommendations, as word goes out along the grapevine.

With this in mind, do a bit of grapevining of your own, before you retire if possible. Tell colleagues in your own company and in other companies with which you may do business that you will be interested in working after your retirement from your present job. If your employer is having to retire you because of mandatory requirements, tell him too; he may know of another company with no such rules to which he is willing to recommend you. If you belong to a union, ask your local officials for help (but be careful that you are not jeopardizing your pension rights); this might work if yours is a multiemployer union.

Friends are another source, particularly if your skills are readily transferable to several industries. Contacts obtained through friends are apt to travel through a long line of leads, but they are worth pursuing with all the patience you can muster. If you belong to a club or organization such as the Kiwanis or the Masons, send the word out among your fellow members. Some of these organizations are unrivaled for influential contacts. Your church or civic organizations may provide leads, though this is a longer shot when it comes to paid work. A hobby or sports group (golf is the notorious sport for contacts) may also put you in touch with a chance or an idea.

These possibilities are best explored simultaneously rather than consecutively. The wider your net, the likelier a catch, and the worst that can happen—and keep your fingers crossed for such luck—is an embarrassment of riches.

**LETTER CAMPAIGN**   A more direct approach is to select a number of companies in your chosen field and to write directly to them. The letter will explain the type of job or any related ones you want, and ask if the company has, or will have soon, an opening suitable for you. You might also explain that you are not interested in joining any pension plan. You will also enclose a résumé of your working life (see below).

Many firms respond quite favorably, taking the trouble to look for possible openings. Most favorable responses will be received within a month or so.

The Yellow Pages of the telephone directory will yield company names within your area. For other areas you have chosen as possibilities, you can write to their Chambers of Commerce for lists of appropriate firms.

For most purposes it is better to avoid the huge companies whose policies on worker insurance and pension plans are apt to be nonnegotiable. A better bet is the smaller company that is located somewhat out of the central business district and which may, therefore, be having trouble attracting employees.

**ADVERTISEMENTS** The most fruitful nonspecialized advertising sources are the big-city newspapers such as *The New York Times, Chicago Tribune, Washington Post,* and *Los Angeles Sun-Times.* Their Sunday editions usually have a whole section devoted to the job market; jobs in such areas as finance and engineering may also be listed in the financial section; and jobs in education in the educational section. Local newspapers are also worth watching, especially if you would like to avoid the commuting hassle.

If you belong to a trade or profession, search the appropriate journals—not only the one you are accustomed to taking but also the others in the field.

*The New York Times* publishes an annual free list of job agencies that have advertised in its pages plus a separate list of agencies dealing in temporary jobs.

You might also consider running your own advertisement in an appropriate newspaper, magazine, or journal. But try a few spot placements, at most; a full-scale advertising campaign can run into a lot of money and, unless you possess a rare skill, seldom justifies its cost.

**STATE EMPLOYMENT AGENCIES** These, federally funded through the Department of Labor, charge neither the employer nor the applicant for their services.

Many state agencies perform other functions besides straight job placement: job counseling, job development, and, when appropriate, referrals to job-training services. They may also refer applicants to health and social services when necessary. Recognizing the special problems faced by older workers, some of the agencies have special units specifically to deal with them; you can get information on this through your local state agency. The state employment agencies are also useful as a source for a broad picture of industry in their areas.

**PRIVATE EMPLOYMENT AGENCIES** The usual private employment agency is not very satisfactory for older people. Few bother to overcome employers' prejudices against taking on older workers. And, while many comply with the letter of the anti-age-discrimination laws, few protest the constant violations that occur in practice. You should certainly stay away from those agencies that charge the applicant for their services rather than the employer.

If you are in the market for an executive job, you might try an executive-search consultant agency if there is one in your area. But check that you are dealing with a bona fide operation, particularly if you must pay for the services and sign a contract. Beware of those with a glamour-oriented presentation that promise to "groom" you for the business world; many are counting on a temporarily low self-esteem in their clients, whereas you probably know a lot more about your neck of the business woods than they do. On the other hand, a good consultant agency can have invaluable contacts and may well be worth your while.

Some agencies specialize in temporary jobs. To do this at all efficiently they must build up a reliable work force. Some of these, such as Manpower, Inc., and Olsten's, are interested in placing "mature" (that's you) workers, and can be useful if temporary works suits you. The work they offer will be local. It will be of many kinds, from moving furniture to office work, but usually fairly limited in caliber, because of the difficulties inherent in teaching complex work to a short-term employee. Often the jobs are fill-ins for sick or vacationing permanent staff. Or they may be jobs which themselves are temporary.

The usual financial arrangement is for the employer to allot the agency a fixed percentage (decided by the agency) of your pay. If, as sometimes happens, your temporary job turns into a permanent one, the agency usually charges you a fee.

**NONPROFIT PRIVATE AGENCIES** Special job agencies advise and place older, particularly retired, workers. Many of them are run by older and/or retired people who have felt at first hand the difficulties of the job market and the need to keep on working. Thus their interviewers have better understanding of the older worker's difficulties and are better able to estimate his requirements and limitations.

Because it so often takes longer to sort out an older person's possibilities and to find job openings for him, it is not possible to run these special agencies for profit. Most are therefore run on a voluntary basis. Some have qualified for government grants. Others have been set up as a supplementary service of local senior-citizen centers or other civic agencies such as the Y or the Salvation Army. They also may enlist the help of local civic organizations such as Chambers of Commerce to get contacts, publicity, and moral backing.

The agencies are often successful in convincing employers that most of their adverse opinions about older workers are emotionally based and quite unfounded, and that what real problems exist are perfectly solvable.

Many senior-citizen clubs operate counseling services for members, and in some cases this includes job counseling. But job counseling requires a finger on the market, innumerable business and professional contacts, and much other special knowledge. Run as a lateral service it may not be effective for actual job placement.

These specialized nonprofit agencies are scattered throughout the country. Some of them have lasted for years, others become defunct after a short time. When not connected to another community agency, they are generally to be found under such names as Senior Personnel Placement, Senior Citizens' Employment, Over-Sixty Employment, Mature Personnel, and so on. There seems to be no central source of information about them, nor are the agencies themselves able to provide references to those in other parts of the country. If your local county or state office on aging is alert and active, it might be able to give you the names of any such agencies within its purlieus. Otherwise, try your state employment office or the Yellow Pages of the local telephone directory.

One voluntary agency that has locally run offices in many cities (including New York, Philadelphia, Washington, D.C., Chicago, Denver, Cleveland, Oakland, Los Angeles, Houston, Tucson, Honolulu, and Toronto) is the Forty-Plus Club. It is run by and for business executives of all professions over 40 who need jobs. In the better-run branches, contacts in the business world are wide, the counseling operation is very efficient (and human), and the rate of placement is good. If you have belonged to the $15,000+ salary category, they are well worth contacting.

Mature Temps, Inc., places older people in temporary jobs. It is sponsored by the National Retired Teachers Association and the American Association of Retired Persons, and offices are being established in major cities. The kinds of jobs most often available are clerical, accounting and bookkeeping, proofreading, and library work. The service does not charge the job applicants.

**GOVERNMENT JOBS** **Federal Jobs** Unless arduous physical work is involved, the upper age limit on federal-government jobs is 70 and higher for certain temporary work. For most federal jobs you must pass a Civil Service test, although this may not be necessary in jobs calling for specific qualifications which you can prove that you possess. Post offices carry lists of current job openings; you can also write to the U.S. Civil Service Commission in your area, describing your qualifications and experience and asking if they have any suitable openings.

The federal government has outposts across the country and its jobs cover a full spectrum; look through the "U.S. Government" listings in the telephone directory of a large city to get an idea of the scope.

**Outdoor Jobs** If you are in good health and would like an outdoor, perhaps seasonal, job not limited by age restrictions, try the Department of Commerce's Fisheries and Weather Services. Or you can try the National Forest Service through one of its regional offices (the addresses can be obtained from your state employment office).

In the national parks, all services except Ranger services are operated by independent concessions. Summer jobs are available but can only be had directly from the concessionaires. Their names can be traced by getting a list of national parks from the Superintendent of Documents in Washington, choosing the park or parks that interest you, then writing to the Superintendent of each park for a list of his concessionaires. These jobs are so popular that you should apply well in advance of the season.

**State Jobs** For state government jobs, write to the state Civil Service Commission, giving your background, experience, and qualifications, and asking whether it has a suitable job opening for you.

**Local Jobs** In your community, the mayor's office (or its equivalent) is the place to make inquiries. Local Chambers of Commerce do not set themselves up as job agencies, but because they are concerned with local enterprises they are often in a position to pass on word of your availability where it may count, or to give you a lead on a possible opening.

**JOBS ABROAD** Before considering a job overseas, read the general suggestions on moving abroad in Chapter 13. The U. S. Chamber of Commerce (1615 H Street, Washington, D.C. 20006) information in *Employment Abroad—Facts and Fallacies* is particularly helpful.

You'll find advertisements for jobs abroad in some U. S. newspapers and magazines. General lists of jobs abroad, often advertised in American magazines, may provide leads; however, by the time you have seen the ad, sent for the list, picked out a job and sent a résumé to the firm, the job is likely to have been filled. You could also try to get hold of English-language journals of the country in which you are interested. The *International Herald Tribune* and the *Rome Daily American,* for instance, list a number of jobs.

The U. S. Civil Service Commission has a pamphlet called *Federal*

*Jobs Overseas,* which lists federal agencies employing personnel overseas. The U. S. Department of Commerce publishes *Trade Lists of American Firms, Affiliates and Subsidiaries,* which covers most countries. The tourist bureaus and diplomatic offices of some countries will let you have lists of American firms operating in their countries and may be able to give you information on the possibility of getting a job there.

Be warned, however: U. S. firms abroad employ mostly nationals— only a very small percentage of their employees in any country are American. Getting a work permit is very difficult in most countries unless you have a special skill (doctors, nurses, teachers, engineers, for example, stand a good chance); and even then the red tape can be discouraging. If you work for a foreign firm, your wages will gear you to the local standard of living, which you should therefore investigate closely, and you may find yourself in a tax hassle with both your host country and the U. S. Internal Revenue Service.

*How to Get a Job Overseas,* by Curtis W. Casewit (Arco, 1970), covers the field in general. More specific are *A Listing of Sources for Employment Overseas,* available from the National Council of Churches (475 Riverside Drive, Room 656, New York, N.Y. 10027); *U. S. Non-Profit Organizations in Development Assistance Abroad,* available from the American Council of Voluntary Agencies for Foreign Service, Inc. (200 Park Avenue South, New York, N.Y. 10003); and *Social Work Opportunities Abroad,* available from the National Assembly for Social Policy and Development (345 East 46th Street, New York, N.Y. 10017). Additional sources for volunteer service abroad are listed in Chapter 19.

**GOVERNMENT-FUNDED PROGRAMS   Peace Corps   The most** famous international program of all is the Peace Corps. From the point of view of people who could otherwise be working full-time and drawing a good salary, it is a volunteer agency. But for a retired person looking for a supplement to a low income, the Peace Corps is more in the nature of paid, albeit low-paid, work.

During your tour of duty the Peace Corps pays your travel expenses to and from the host country; it pays a settling-in allowance and a living allowance based on the local cost of living. It also pays what it calls a "readjustment allowance" for each month of your tour, paid to you at the end of your tour; this sum is taxable but will not adversely affect your Social Security or private-pension-plan benefits.

The Peace Corps sets no upper age limits, and a goodly percentage of the Corps has been over retirement age. If you are married and both of you wish to go, you must both qualify as Corps members. The Corps serves only in a country that requests volunteers. Technical skills such as printing, forestry, sanitation, and electrical engineering are much in demand, as are teachers, librarians, social workers, truck drivers, farmers, bricklayers, carpenters, and those in the health professions. Nevertheless, people with no such precise skills fill about one third of the jobs.

You must be adventurous, healthy, energetic, and of good stamina, because living conditions in most places where you would be posted are not as comfortable as they are in the United States (you will seldom find central heating or air conditioning, for instance) and you will have to work hard in often alien circumstances. You must be accepting of different values and ways of life, and able to put up with inconveniences. You will be subject to the laws of the country in which you are serving.

A Peace Corps doctor provides health care while you are overseas and will decide on any treatment you may need.

The Peace Corps sends its people to Africa, Latin America, South and East Asia, the Pacific, and the Near East.

Once you have been assigned a post, you will usually get a three-month training and orientation session. During training you will get a certain amount of dental and eye care, immunizations appropriate to your destination, and you will be taught preventive health measures and emergency first aid.

The usual tour of duty is two years, although you can apply for extensions of duty elsewhere for up to a total of five years; the Peace Corps is not a career force.

You can get general literature on the subject from any local office or from the central Washington office of ACTION (at 812 Connecticut Avenue, N.W., Washington, D.C. 20525), the agency that recruits personnel for this and several other government programs. For details pertinent to older people, write to the Senior Citizen's Liaison office of the Peace Corps, Specialized Recruiting, Washington, D.C. 20205.

**International Voluntary Services, Inc. (IVS)** This private organization takes contracts with several American government agencies to provide over half of its funding—not, strictly speaking, government-funded, but included here by a stretched definition.

Volunteers work in agriculture, agronomy, engineering cooperatives, economics, water resources, social work, counseling, public health, nursing, medicine, and education (teacher training, English-language, vocational, and science teachers). Academic qualifications of at least B.A. level are usually required, although sufficient practical experience in your field may suffice, particularly in agriculture. Most IVS programs are in Asia, Africa, and Latin America. Volunteers work under the supervision of a group leader who also acts as liaison with the host government and with IVS headquarters.

Assignments are for at least two years, with round-trip transportation and daily expenses paid. In addition, volunteers are paid a monthly vacation allowance plus a monthly salary which is high if you have had previous volunteer experience. For work in French- or Spanish-speaking countries, prior knowledge of the language is preferred. For others, basic language training is offered in the host country. A briefing is given in Washington before you embark.

IVS is at 1555 Connecticut Avenue, N.W., Washington, D.C. 20036.

**The Volunteers in Service to America (VISTA)** Another AC-TION program, VISTA provides a stipend for its volunteers as well as living expenses. Like the Peace Corps, of which it might be called a domestic variant, VISTA gears its basic living allowance for food and housing to the local standard. An additional allowance per month is made to cover other costs such as transport and laundry. Besides these, a monthly stipend is set aside for you to collect after you complete your service. The stipend and the allowances are taxable but have no effect on Social Security benefits since it is unlikely that they will exceed a volunteer's allowable income limit in a calendar year. Costs of transportation to and from your post are paid, as are food, lodging, and pocket money during training. No allowance is given for spouses who are not covolunteers.

The purpose of VISTA is to try to help break the cycle of poverty in poor American communities ("American" also refers to communities in the Virgin Islands, Guam, Puerto Rico, and American Samoa). The community to be helped must request its services before VISTA will send volunteers. About 40% of its volunteers are, in fact, recruited from the community itself.

The work may be in an urban ghetto, a rural slum, a migrant camp, an Indian reservation. Skills most in demand are in architecture, city planning, business, legal services, health care, and social services. They get used in such concerns as adult basic education, day-care centers, drug-abuse programs, recreation centers for various groups within the community, consumer education, and mental-health programs.

Volunteers live among, and at more or less the same income level as, the people for whom they are working (although not in the squalor so often found) under the auspices of the local community group that requested their services.

If you are over 45 years old you will have to pass a medical examination before your training starts. Volunteers get comprehensive medical-care coverage, including dental care, during their training and service periods.

Once you are offered a post, you get a three- to five-week training and orientation period. One year is the usual length of a tour, but sometimes you can extend this for periods of up to another year.

General information about and application forms for VISTA can be obtained from the ACTION office for your region (there are regional offices in ten major cities). For literature geared to older people's needs you can write to Liaison Programs for Older Workers, VISTA, OEO, Washington, D.C. 20506.

**Foster Grandparents**   The idea behind this program, also administered by ACTION, is breathtakingly simple: that the lonely, underused oldest generation should be linked with their equivalents in the youngest generation, to mutual advantage. The idea has worked beautifully, as many polls among foster grandparents and administrators of children's institutions testify enthusiastically.

To become a foster grandparent you must be at least 60 years old, in good health, and of low income; you must also be able to give attention, sympathy, and, if possible, love to two children (separately) for two hours a day each for five days a week. For this you will be paid by the hour; you will also be paid for transportation and meals. The children served are needy, and most often in institutions of some kind: hospitals, psychiatric or correctional homes for the physically or emotionally handicapped, and orphanages, to name a few.

Training for the job is undertaken by a local nonprofit agency or organization and usually consists of about 40 hours in the institution where you will be working. Sometimes you will give practical help to your "grandchild"; most of the time you will be the only source of personal and intimate care, conversation, attention, and interest for the child. The response of the children is not always immediate— many of them have years of neglect and loneliness, and consequent mistrust to overcome—but it eventually surfaces both directly toward the foster grandparents and throughout all aspects of their lives.

For information write to ACTION headquarters or call in at its offices in your locale.

**Senior Companion Program**   Set up on lines similar to Foster Grandparents, the Senior Companion Program engages older people to serve adults with special needs. Under this program you become a sometime companion to people unable to leave their homes, people in nursing homes and other institutions—anyone who is lonely and in need of a friend. Qualifications are similar to those of the Foster Grandparents program; you will be trained for the job, and your pay will be at about the same rate.

**DEPARTMENT OF LABOR PROGRAMS**  The Department of Labor funds several employment assistance services besides the state employment offices. Most of these services are aimed at the poor population and many consist of education and job-training programs. What is available differs from place to place, and it is not possible to list them all.

**Operation Mainstream**  This fairly widespread program creates jobs and gives work training to chronically unemployed poor adults, with particular emphasis on those over the age of 40. The program, administered by the Forest Service in about 20 states, offers employment to older people for an average of three days a week. You can get information from the USDA Forest Service, Room 3243, South Agriculture Building, 12th & Independence Avenue, S.W., Washington, D.C. 20250.

**Green Thumb**  In this program, funded by the Department of Labor and sponsored in many states by the National Farmers Union, men over 55, who are in reasonable health and are below a certain income level, restore or improve public areas or facilities. They work in crews under the supervision of a foreman on a schedule of about three days per week. For information write to Green Thumb, Inc., 1012 14th Street, N.W., Washington, D.C. 20005.

**Senior Community Service Aide**  Sponsored in 18 urban and rural areas by the National Council on Aging, this program provides part-time employment for older people in Social Security and state employment offices, public housing, libraries, hospitals, schools, food and nutrition programs, escort services, homemaker services, house-repair services, and programs for information and referral. For information write to the National Council on Aging, 1828 L Street, N.W., Washington, D.C. 20036.

**Senior Aides**  This program, sponsored by the National Council of Senior Citizens in 33 urban and rural areas, offers part-time work for older people in a wide variety of local services—child care, adult education, home health, homemaker, to name a few.

The senior-citizens programs are usually administered locally through the county Office on Aging, which contracts the worker out on local projects at a guaranteed hourly rate. Many projects, like Green Thumb, are concerned with improving or beautifying the community—perhaps by helping in the management, conservation, or development of natural resources, historic sites, recreational areas, parks, highways, and other rural and small-town lands. Inquiries at your county or state Office on Aging or its equivalent as set up under Title III of the Older Americans Act will usually elicit information.

Or you can write to the Administration on Aging, U. S. Department of Health, Education, and Welfare, Office of Human Development, Office of State and Community Programs, Washington, D.C. 20201.

Since one of its main functions is to provide a referral service for this and all other types of aid available to older people, the Office on Aging for your county or state should be able to put you onto other funded paying programs in your area.

## GETTING A JOB

**SELF-ASSESSMENT**   Not all jobs require elaborate preparation or self-examination; summer jobs certainly do not, nor do jobs that will involve only a couple of hours a week or into which you fall quite happily and naturally. But jobs that are going to take up a substantial amount of time and are necessary to survival at a decent level of subsistence are worth serious consideration and some trouble.

In assessing your ability to work you will presumably have gained a fairly clear idea of your physical, mental, and emotional capabilities and limitations, and these will provide useful guidelines in looking for the right kind of job. If you are going into a relatively new field, it is also wise to consider matters of temperament. Do you need to work with people, or do you feel and perform better on your own? Are you aggressive, or on the retiring side? Do you value the chance to make your own decisions, or do you prefer some external directive? Are you a lover of order or do you thrive in chaos?

You should also consider other attributes. Do you have a good speaking voice and enunciation, or do you sound like a crow with a sore throat? If the former, you might be able to put them to good use; if the latter, avoid a job which will bring them to the fore. What kind of personal appearance do you present? Would anyone buy a used car from *you?* Are you habitually cheerful? If tact is not your strong point, you should perhaps not bother angling after that public-relations job. You might be totally speechless and a whiz at organization—a behind-the-scenes type.

Honesty, at least with yourself, is the best policy in making these assessments.

**MARKET ASSESSMENTS**  Besides considering yourself, you should assess the local supply and demand in your chosen field. The local state employment agency can be a big help with this because it is in touch with the market from both employers' and workers' sides. If the market is oversupplied, could your knowledge and abilities be applied to other fields? It may even be that your woodworking hobby will prove more lucrative than your 40-year meal ticket.

**CAREER RÉSUMÉ**  You may never have needed a résumé through all your working life, especially if you have stayed with one company or in one locale. Or perhaps you have not needed one for many years. Or perhaps your present one will have to be revamped to emphasize hitherto secondary experience; indeed, if you are applying for different kinds of jobs, you may need a different version of your résumé for each application.

**Purpose**  The primary purpose of a résumé is to give a concise account of your career as it pertains to the job you wish to get. You should also give brief information on such matters as your marital status, hobbies and other interests, and education.

**Contents**  The résumé will start out with such basic data as name, address, and telephone number. Your educational background may then be noted, just briefly unless continuing education has been integral to your career, as it might be in some of the sciences.

You can list the jobs you have held either chronologically or by type. If your career has been in one kind of work, the chronological method is probably most apt: the most recent job is listed first and in the most detail; your earliest job need only be briefly noted. Give most detail about the work pertinent to your current application.

A checkered career might require the functional method of listing. Here you would list the most relevant jobs first and in the greatest detail and give only a brief outline of other work. Your description of relevant work should include the amount of skill it required of you, the degree of your responsibility, and the success of its completion.

Housebound women have particular difficulty in assessing their abilities and in composing convincing résumés. One way to get a bird's-eye view of your functioning is to consider housekeeping as a management job which involves such skills as bookkeeping (if you manage the household finances), purchasing (otherwise known as shopping), maintenance and repair (at least you knew when an electrician, not a plumber, was needed), public relations (neighbors and assorted acquaintances), personnel management, chauffeuring, moving furniture, entertainment and recreation direction, and so on. If you have been involved with the PTA, the school board, or some other volunteer work, these activities can be similarly assessed. They may have entailed such duties as fund raising, organization of business or social functions, or recruitment of other volunteers. Write down each activity as it occurs to you—over several days, if necessary. Then translate the activity into business language. Since all of these functions have taken place more or less coevally, yours had better be the functional type of listing.

**Form** A résumé should be typed or printed, and laid out to achieve maximum clarity. Job descriptions should be terse. Using plenty of active verbs gives a positive tone to the information and makes it livelier to read. You should note in the résumé that references, personal and business, are available; but there is no need to actually give them. Nor is there any need to mention salary at this stage.

Try to get your first draft checked by someone in the business who knows you fairly well; many good suggestions can come from such a source. If you are going to apply for a number of jobs using the same version of the résumé, have copies made by offset printing. Never send out carbon copies.

In sending out the résumé, accompany it with an individually typed letter referring to the advertisement being answered or other source of information about the job. The letter should ask (politely) for consideration of your application and should refer to the résumé as a source of information about your qualifications. The letter should be short, simple, and straightforward.

**THE JOB INTERVIEW** Assuming that all these preparations come to something, you will get a job interview. It is surprising how many otherwise knowledgeable people find themselves totally unprepared for playing the part of the interviewee.

**Before You Go** The first thing to do is to conduct some research into the firm involved. Find out about its products and/or services—what they are and how they are generally rated by consumers. Ask around and search through the *Consumer Reports Index* of the Consumers Union (in your local library). Find out also, if you can, the current reputation of the firm in the industry as a whole. Consulting Dun & Bradstreet will give you a pretty good idea of its financial situation.

Try to find out what sort of jobs the firm has to offer and what its hiring practices and employee policies may be (if you find that they have a quirk about platform soles, don't wear them to the interview, for example). This kind of information is best obtained from current employees if you can find any; if not, a few inquiries at the local Chamber of Commerce (and town bar) may give you enough to work on. You should also know about present problems in the industry at large and, if possible, in this firm in particular. Knowing the local going wage for the job in which you are interested is also useful.

Get your references lined up because you may need to give their names at the interview. For personal references it is good manners to ask their permission ahead of time; for business references this is not so essential unless you want the referee to stress a particular aspect of your capabilities.

**While You Are There**  Dress suitably, arrive punctually, and allow plenty of time if you have later appointments (if the interviewer is interested in you, you may get the three-hour grand tour, so don't bet on finishing quickly). Go alone: do not take your spouse or a friend; even if they are prepared to sit in the waiting room, the impression given is of dependency.

When you go in, be pleasant, friendly, direct, and businesslike. Forget—or at least suppress—any anxiety you may have; this is often (sometimes unexpectedly) brought on by the fact of retirement but is absolutely not useful. Enter as an equal, and avoid any hint of apology or obsequiousness. On the other hand, beware of exaggerating your qualifications or of boasting about what a good bargain you are. Avoid talking about your own problems and needs unless you are asked, in which case you should mention them quite succinctly. Give as much evidence as you can of having a lively mind and of flexible thinking, since lack of these is one of the bugaboos about older employees.

If the interviewer encourages questions, get as much information as you can about the firm and its current situation. Pay close attention to what the interviewer is saying and pick up any cues you can as to the kind of person and abilities the firm is seeking for what particular duties; you can then use them in presenting your own qualifications, although you must, of course, be careful not to contradict your résumé too directly. An interviewer's questions will usually try to elicit more information than you have given in the résumé; you may, by picking up the cues quickly, be able to emphasize what seem to be desirable aspects of your work experience and play down undesirable ones.

If you can avoid having to name a salary, do so. Try to get the ball into the interviewer's court—get him to give a figure. If he does and you consider it too low, say so, giving sufficient reasons to keep the discussion open. Needless to say, the figure he names will never be too high!

An interviewer will often take an applicant around the plant to give him an idea of the physical setup. These tours are usually very confusing, involving a welter of sights and sounds and information at too fast a rate for assimilation. What you can do, though, is keep your feelers out for impressions of the general atmosphere: How do the employees look and sound (indifferent, lively, cheerful, grim)? Is the physical maintenance of the plant good, or is it dingy and rundown? Is it a place in which you would like to work, or one that you would merely have to put up with?

Before you leave the interviewer, get it clear who is to call whom about the job decision.

**After You Leave**   Go over the interview in your mind while it is still fresh. Assess your performance: what mistakes you made, what went over particularly well, how much of the success or failure of the interview was a matter of personality play between you and the interviewer, what jarred on you, what information about yourself you should clarify before undertaking another interview. Then file it all away for use on the next occasion.

Should you be offered the job, make sure that you really want it before accepting. If you feel hesitant, examine your reasons; you may find some very cogent objection under that general feeling of distaste. Perhaps a disability of your own is going to make this particular work insupportable, however willing you may be to try to overcome the problems. Maybe something you saw or heard or just sensed during your interview or tour is bothering you. If so, pin down the discordant note and do some more research into the appropriate aspect of the firm's operation to clear it up.

It is better not to accept a job with a vague idea of leaving before you even start. Not only is it expensive and wasteful to the employer to train you and then have you leave in short order, it is also bad for your own morale, to say nothing of your reputation.

# 18
# Your Own Business

Perhaps the idea of working for somebody else—again—just makes you tired. You have a few ideas of your own that you would like to try. Or perhaps you would prefer to work full-time on an old hobby. If it can be adapted to produce some income, why not?

Well, actually, there may be several reasons why not. You may lack the energy and aggression to run your own business profitably. You may not be able to raise sufficient capital to give the business a fair chance. You may be totally production-oriented and lack interest in and knowledge of finance and marketing.

A new business has a 50–50 chance of surviving its first two years; during the next two years it has a 1-in-3 chance; ten-year survival has a 1-in-5 chance. Nevertheless, the total number of business firms keeps growing, along with population and the discovery of new wants and needs. Given the right auspices, you could be on the small-number side of the statistics.

As a retired person with Social Security benefits to keep you clothed, fed, and sheltered, you can approach the whole question of a business of your own in a more relaxed fashion than can a younger person who is putting his family and fortune on the line. Of course, once started you may find yourself embroiled in far more than a part-time or casual venture, and this is something you should think hard about before wetting your big toe.

**RETURNS**    However much you may like the business you start and however casual you feel, you are not doing it for charity. Even if you run the concern out of your own home with a minimum of investment, you still expect to make money for your time and effort. Profit becomes even more important if you are putting money into the business, money which might otherwise be invested to bring in interest or dividends.

**PERSONAL REQUIREMENTS** Seriously consider your character and personality, which will, in the end, make or break your chances of success. You will need a lot of energy, initiative, and industry; must be able to persevere despite obstacles; must be able to take responsibility, make decisions, know when to stick by them and when to be flexible. You must be able to deal with many kinds of people and, if you will be employing them, you must inspire confidence. You must be good at organizing and at staying organized.

Experience, either with the particular product or with business management in general, is also important; without it, mistakes are unavoidable and can be costly. The greatest cause of business failure is reckoned to be sheer inexperience plus ineptitude in management. If you do lack management experience, think about taking a course in its rudiments—the Small Business Administration (see below) sponsors many free courses through local institutions.

If you greatly lack any of the qualities touched upon, you should think twice about what you are letting yourself in for. Alternatively, you might take on an associate or partner who will make up for your weaker points.

**CAPITAL** It takes time to build a business up to the point at which income will exceed expenditure. It takes months, sometimes years, to establish a clientele large enough to make the business self-supporting. Therefore you should have sufficient money to cover your expenses during this period as well as for initial outlay.

**Raising Capital** If you have the money or can raise enough from friends and relatives, all well and good. If not, perhaps you can arrange credit with your suppliers to tide you over, or buy equipment on the installment plan—many manufacturers are geared to this kind of setup. If you still have insufficient capital, try to find a local creditor (bank, loan, or insurance company) from whom you can get a loan.

Failing this (and loans for new small businesses are hard to swing), approach the Small Business Administration through its local office. The SBA will not only give you counseling at no charge, it may also give you a loan. Since the SBA's policy is to encourage loans by private institutions, they usually either make loans in conjunction with an institution such as a local bank or act as guarantors of an amount lent by the institution. If you cannot get a loan, even on these terms, the SBA will perhaps make a direct loan, though it will be for a smaller amount than you wanted. Whether you are eligible or not can best be found out directly from the SBA. However, gambling, alcohol, and real-estate speculation are all out.

**LOW-INVESTMENT BUSINESSES** **Services** A small service

business run from your own home will require little capital. For a home-repair service, for instance, you need tools, work clothes, and some local advertising; but even if you already own a car, it may be necessary to exchange this for a station wagon or small van. Other businesses that require little capital outlay include home-appliance repair, interior painting and decorating, dressmaking and tailoring, telephone answering, plumbing, and electrical service. Hairdressing and carpentry are examples of businesses which require a slightly greater, though still small, outlay.

**Hobbies and Handicrafts**   To begin with, you will probably get orders for your product by word of mouth so that expenditure on materials will remain small and sales will be guaranteed.

To expand, you might advertise locally. If you get a number of orders simultaneously, your materials expenditure will have to be greater and your working hours longer, and you may need more equipment for quicker production. If your product's popularity grows and you find a good outlet for it through some area retail stores, you will have to think about getting assistance with the work and a bigger work space.

The next step would be national advertising and contacts with store buyers over a larger region, perhaps national; eventually you might want to set up your own retail outlet, although such a step would lead you into another type of work, to which you might not wish to devote the time.

In such expansion, expenditure is backed up fairly well by income; where your expenses run ahead, it is with the fairly sure knowledge of sales to come.

**Retail Businesses**   For a small retail outlet you will need more capital investment. Your rent must be covered, preferably for the first two years so that you will not be forced to meet it out of income. Painting and decorating are almost always necessary. You will need stock to sell; fixtures and fittings for display, wrapping, and sales; insurance; a sign outside; and a dozen other miscellaneous items.

**LOCATION**   If your business is to be part-time and an adjunct to other activities, then your location will be at or near your home, and yours must be a business suitable for your area.

If your ambitions are greater than that, or if you need separate premises for the business, then you have a wider choice. If yours is a service or retail concern, you must consider the type of population to which it is suited; where that population is to be found; the ease with which it can reach you or you it; the amount and kind of competition; the general business trends in the region; the specific business trends in particular locations; space requirements; rents; zoning laws; whole-salers' or manufacturers' deliveries.

If your ideal business location (or the best one you can come up with) means you will have to move, then you must also consider whether you would want to live on or near its site.

**GOING CONCERNS** **Advantages** You can save yourself many of the headaches of those starting phases by buying a business someone else has already started. Equipment, stock, and clientele are already at hand. Costs, prices, and sales figures are already available, and you can use them as a basis for your own operation. You may be lucky enough to get the business for a good price because of factors external to it (some crisis in the present owner's life, for instance).

**Precautions** But you must watch out that the low price is not because of business failure; if it is, get to the root of the failure and judge whether it was a quality of the present owner's or of the business itself. Location may be bad, equipment may be out of date or in bad working order. Stock may be poorly judged or poor in quality. The owner may lack goodwill and you will have his reputation to over-come.

**Finding One** The business-opportunity columns of newspapers carry many advertisements of businesses for sale. There are several directories (the Acquisition Newsletter *"500" Directory,* 300 East 40th Street, New York, N.Y. 10016, for instance) devoted to the sale of businesses. Business brokers who act as go-betweens (much like real-estate brokers) are also a source of information, although, since they charge the seller a percentage of the sale price, you may have to pay more for the business.

**FRANCHISE** A franchise is something of a compromise between starting a new business and buying a going concern. The basic arrange-ment is that you, as owner of the business, operate it as though it were part of a chain enterprise: you use the trademarks, symbols, and equipment of the franchise and you sell his standardized goods or service, usually with an exclusive right for a specific area. In return, you pay a fee or percentage of your sales to the franchiser, and/or you buy equipment or supplies from him.

You get the benefit of the franchiser's sales, management, and promotional experience. Usually the franchiser will give you initial training and continue to act as your management consultant. Your facilities and equipment will most often be designed for you, and the franchiser's name will provide you with immediate customers.

If you value independence, you may be bothered by the Big Brother aspect of the larger franchisers, who have a reputation to uphold through their franchisees and often a direct interest in keeping up sales volume; the franchisee is more like a manager than an owner. But with less supervised franchises there is danger of having to pay for equipment or stock without enough sales income to cover them.

Many larger franchises are expensive to buy into, and require hard work and long hours: drive-in eateries, for instance. Other franchises are smaller and more amenable to shorter hours. All require lots of energy, however, if only because you must keep up payments on equipment, or buy the agreed amount of supplies, or justify your initial fee.

Franchises are to be found in almost every field of business, from home-cleaning services to nightclub operation. You can find ads for them in newspapers, in publications of particular trades, and in special franchise publications and exhibitions. Agencies also exist to help you investigate and select a suitable franchise. Beware of fast-buck artists who promise you a fortune in three months if you buy their equipment and use their name.

As with any venture, check out the market for, and the quality of, the product or service you will be marketing. Also check out the franchiser and the terms of the contract he offers. You can do this through the SBA (see below).

**SMALL BUSINESS ADMINISTRATION**  The SBA, with local offices across the country (consult your phone book for an office near you), is your best friend. In addition to providing free counseling and sometimes loans, it publishes a large number of instructional booklets. Its publication *Starting and Managing a Small Business of Your Own* is probably the best place to start, since it gives an overall picture of what you might be getting into and provides some good specific data (such as a franchise checklist). Other publications are listed in Form SBA-115-A (*Free Management Assistance Publications*), Form SBA-115-B (*For-Sale Booklets*), and *A Survey of Federal Government Publications of Interest to Small Business,* compiled by Elizabeth G. Janazeck; all of these are available from the Superintendent of Documents, Government Printing Office, Washington, D.C. 20402.

**Service Corps of Retired Executives**  This is a volunteer arm of SBA's advisory service. Volunteer executives advise owner/managers of small businesses on any aspect where they are having trouble. They are especially helpful to people thinking of starting their own business; they help you to reach decisions about what business to choose, to analyze personal factors, capital requirements, beginner's problems, factors in buying an existing business; and they can explain the workings of franchises.

# 19
# You Can Be Special

One of the great counterbalances to the idea that our system of values is based on an "only for folding money" criterion is the long and solid history of voluntary service. The desirability of giving what you can is instilled in us during childhood, but for many people it gets lost somewhere in the years when they are supporting themselves and their families. Not for everyone—most community services would be non-existent if that were true—but for a large percentage, certainly. Retirement is a good time for looking back to that early training and perhaps wondering what we have missed. Because undoubtedly there is a very special pride and satisfaction in giving service because you want to, in not being beholden to the task because of contractual obligations, and in feeling committed to another person's need rather than to your own.

**WHAT YOU HAVE TO OFFER**   You have time available during the day when younger volunteers are making a living. Since you are no longer concerned with advancing your career, you can take a more altruistic approach to your voluntary work and will be less concerned with making business or social contacts and looking important. Time and experience will—it is to be hoped—have given you objectivity and judgment lacking in all but the most exceptional younger people.

**WHO NEEDS HELP**   A surprisingly large number of people are in real trouble, and most of them need a hand to help them, if not to get out of it, at least to ameliorate their distress.

By far the greatest number of people in such need are children, the ones least able to help themselves. They are hungry, sick, orphaned, neglected, abused, retarded, deprived—and if you have an affinity for them you can find many opportunities to help them. Adults have plenty of troubles, too, often the same kind as children—if they are poverty-stricken they are usually malnourished, badly (if at all) housed, poorly dressed, ill-educated. Many are sick (some chronically) and injured (some permanently). Many are physically handicapped—blind, deaf, mute, crippled. Some are in prison, or just out of it and with little chance of getting a job and staying off the street. Some are mentally retarded or going through an emotional crisis that makes them unable to function.

And if that roster of pain puts you off, there are still more kinds of help that the community as a whole needs: if what is happening to our planet physically fills you with alarm for its future, you will find many branches of the ecology cause which need help badly. Peace and justice and equality and freedom are very big words but there is much to be done in their behalf, nonetheless.

**HOW CAN YOU HELP?**   You may already have a favorite cause. You may want to stick to something that you can do within walking distance of home. You may want to be a world citizen as part of a large international movement. Or you may want to see betterment in your national and local community.

In many ways looking for volunteer work is like looking for a job— at least when you start thinking about the kind of work you want to do or feel you can best do.

**Your Likes and Dislikes**   Are you the retiring type (no pun intended)? Do you function best in an orderly environment? Are you a fluent and relaxed speaker? Do you work well in groups or are you a loner? Do you take orders well? Do you like children or do you get along better with adults? How about adults younger than yourself, older than yourself?

**Your Skills and Talents**   If you play a musical instrument, carve wood, know about electricity, sew, paint, read well, cook well, know a language, are an archaeologist or a gardener—any of these or of many more technical, artistic, craft, and domestic skills can be passed on to people who need them, either as knowledge which they have no other means of obtaining or as products which would make their lives easier.

Other kinds of talent are just as valuable: a facility for putting people at their ease: a rapport with children; an ability to remain calm and comforting in the face of blood, pain, and death; a gift for extracting practical or financial help from previously unwilling philanthropists; a gift for listening sympathetically, for bringing cheer, for organizing office procedures, for persuading committees, for publicity ideas.

Even if you decide that you are entirely devoid of all such talents, still you are needed. Can you type, answer the telephone intelligently, effectively shove a collecting box at passers-by, drive a car, understand filing, run errands, address envelopes, show people to the right room or to their seats? The list is endless.

**How Much Time?**  What volunteer-service organizers find most valuable is regularity. Perhaps you can only spare two hours every two weeks, but short hours on a regular schedule are more useful than long ones only sporadically available. Volunteer programs can plan ahead with the former; many hours will be wasted with the latter. In deciding how much time you can give, consider not only your other activities, but also your health and energy. If you tire easily, offer short hours—at frequent intervals if you want to put in a good amount of time.

**Your Health**  This decides other things besides time to be given. A bad back will bar you from heavy lifting jobs. Poor eyesight will absolve you from close written work. Varicose veins will make standing impossible for you.

**Expenses**  If you are short of money, mention this to the agency you approach and don't be embarrassed about it: most older people are in the same fix, and the agencies know it. Many will pay for transportation and out-of-pocket expenses if they know that you can ill afford the money. Those volunteer agencies that pay a stipend as well as expenses are discussed in Chapter 17.

**VOLUNTEER PROJECTS**  Now, for whom do you want to work? If you already have a pet cause you are all set; all you have to do is talk with the organizing agency to see how and when they can use you.

**Your Own Projects**  If there is no organizing agency and you still want to do something about a specific community need, think about doing something by yourself. If it needs more time and money than you have, try pulling some of your friends and neighbors into the scheme, or broach the idea with fellow members of your social, civic, or religious groups. If neither of these approaches works, consider forming an organizing agency yourself (you might wind up doing this anyway if you manage to involve a sufficiently large number of friends or fellow members).

**Sources of Funding**  Federal, state, and local governments as well as private nonprofit agencies and foundations are possible sources of funds. Among the federal resources, for instance, are Volunteers in Service to America (see Chapter 17); RSVP (see "National Service Organizations," below); and the Administration on Aging, which is working with the National Center for Volunteer Action, and through local and national organizations, to develop local services, using both public and private resources.

It is possible to drum up enough money within the community itself to get started on a community project. Once the project starts, it is easier to attract financial help from foundations and state agencies. For help in getting started send for a copy of "Operating Manual for a Volunteer Talent Pool" from the Volunteer Talent Pool (620 Lincoln Avenue, Winnetka, Ill. 60093). Winnetka Senior Citizen's Center began by volunteering its members to give talks at a local school. So successful were they that their participation expanded to school programs throughout the district and then to other types of service, until eventually volunteers of all ages were needed and a fully fledged volunteer agency was in operation.

**EXISTING PROJECTS**   You have a plethora of choices. One way to find out what they are in your own locale is by looking through the "Social Service Organizations," "Clubs," and "Associations" entries in the Yellow Pages of your telephone directory. Most large cities have bureaus that act as clearing houses for volunteers and organizations, matching skills to requirements. Many civic and religious organizations, as well as labor unions and professional societies, need volunteers; if they have no openings themselves, they can usually refer you to others that do.

The names of national and international organizations can be obtained from libraries, educational institutions, political organizations, government departments, and the United Nations. The Commission on Voluntary Service and Action (475 Riverside Drive, New York, N.Y. 10027) publishes an annual catalog of volunteer-service opportunities called "Invest Yourself," from which many leads for the information which follows were obtained.

**COORDINATING ORGANIZATIONS**   Several organizations exist to link volunteers with service needs; some of them overlap, in fact. Some of the following are international, some national in scope.

**The National Center for Voluntary Action** (1735 I Street, N.W., Washington, D.C. 20006)   Helps to establish local voluntary-action centers as coordinating agencies of volunteer and community needs. It also cooperates with other private agencies and volunteers to organize specific volunteer programs.

**The International Liaison for Volunteer Service** (39 Lackawanna Place, Room 4–5, Bloomfield, N.J. 07003)   Acts as a regional point of reference for all volunteer service agencies in the United States and abroad. Though sponsored by the Catholic Archdiocese of Newark, it places volunteers on a nonsectarian basis with both church- and non-church-affiliated agencies.

**The International Secretariat for Voluntary Service** (10–12 Chemin de Surville, 1213 Geneva, Petit-Lancy, Switzerland) A clearinghouse for information and assistance to 56 governments, the United Nations, and national and international volunteer-service organizations. Most of the volunteer assistance is technical in nature.

**The Association of Volunteer Bureaus of America, Inc.** (P.O. Box 7258, Kansas City, Mo. 64113) Has local offices in over 200 communities.

**The United Way of America** (801 North Fairfax, Alexandria, Va. 22314) Has local offices in about 2500 communities.

These last two, as well as the National Center for Voluntary Action, channel volunteers into existing local projects. The national offices provide information to people interested in creating or expanding programs for their communities. The National Center for Voluntary Action is particularly concerned with this latter work.

**Ecology Center Communications Council** (2000 P Street, N.W., Washington, D.C. 20036) Acts as a national clearinghouse for ecology centers; also provides training and public-relations services. Work ranges from filing through research, preparation of fact sheets or statements for hearings, and community organization.

**The United States Information Agency** (1750 Pennsylvania Avenue, N.W., Washington, D.C. 20547) is a good source of information on projects designed to improve international understanding, such as the U.S. Book Exchange and Magazines for Friendship.

**INTERNATIONAL ORGANIZATIONS** A few samples of the many volunteer-service organizations that exist in this country follow; the list is not even remotely complete, but it may give you some idea of the range of services and organizations that concern themselves with bettering conditions in society, in both the United States and foreign countries.

**The International Executive Service Corps** (545 Madison Avenue, New York, N.Y. 10022) A nonprofit corporation which sends executives to help small industries and businesses (those employing from 12 to 5000 people) in developing countries. The request for help must come from the overseas company concerned, and weight is given to the company's growth potential and local economic effect as well as to its inability to get help from other sources.

Volunteers are not salaried, but their travel and other expenses (plus those of their spouses) are paid. Assignments are normally for two or three months' duration in Africa, the Near East, Asia, and

Latin America. Every kind of industry and business concern is catered to, from appliances to motion pictures, and every kind of business skill is used—general management, production, marketing, finance, personnel, and so on.

**The Volunteers for International Technical Assistance** (College Campus, Schenectady, N.Y.)    Gives what you might call mail-order help. VITA originated on the college campus and has now enlarged to a volunteer force of over 7000 specialists in technology, education, or business. Requests for help from Africa, Latin America, and Asia are routed to a volunteer or group of volunteers (called a chapter), whose solutions are sent back to the inquirer by mail. Correspondence is often voluminous, most problems not being solvable in one go. To be a successful VITA volunteer you must have an area of specific knowledge and be able to express it in writing or diagrammatically.

**Medico** (CARE/Medico, 660 First Avenue, New York, N.Y. 10016)    A service branch of CARE, Medico specializes in the health field. It sends trained health personnel to needy areas overseas. Long-term workers are salaried and usually below a certain age. But Medico also needs volunteers of any age, similarly trained, to lend their services for a month or so; they must pay their own transportation and living expenses.

**Aesculapean International** (Division of Direct Relief Foundation, 27 East Canon Perdido Street, Santa Barbara, Calif. 93101)    Places medical and paramedical personnel for either fieldwork or teaching. Assignments are to Central and South America, the Far East, South Asia, the Pacific, and Africa, and may be for any period, depending on the volunteer's and the service's needs.

**The Committee of Returned Volunteers** (National Office, 840 West Oakdale Avenue, Chicago, Ill. 60617)    Formed of ex-overseas service volunteers. Its aims are to change the policies of the United States through political and educational programs, and through support for liberation movements at home and abroad. CRV has local groups in Boston, Chicago, Los Angeles, Milwaukee, Minneapolis-St. Paul, New York City, San Francisco, and Washington, D.C.

**Interaction** (1500 Farragut Street, N.W., Washington, D.C. 20011) A coalition of six organizations: LAOS, Inc. (see below); EPICA (Ecumenical Program for Inter-American Communication and Action); Third World Reader Service; CALC (Clergy and Laity Concerned); and CODOC (Coordination and Documentation). Interaction trains volunteers, both religious and lay, for overseas and domestic service, with emphasis on understanding social change.

**LAOS, Inc.** (4920 Piney Branch Road, N.W., Washington, D.C. 20011)    An interdenominational organization, Laymen for Overseas

Service is Christian-oriented, though it welcomes volunteers of all religious persuasions who can work ably and with dedication. The organization has no projects of its own; it fits its volunteers into vacancies reported by other agencies. Once placed, volunteers work under the aegis of the requesting agency. Housing is usually provided, but board and transportation less commonly and stipends rarely. Assignments last for one month or more, and may be in Africa, Asia, South America, or the United States. All kinds of talents, skills, and knowledge can be used.

**The United Church of Christ** (Specialized Ministries, R.D.#2, Pottstown, Pa. 19464) Places some older volunteers abroad, usually for assignments of less than one year. Volunteers must provide round-trip fares; lodgings and expenses are usually provided. Many abilities and talents are needed, and the work is church-related.

**Jesuit Volunteer Corps** (P.O. Box 4408, Portland, Ore. 97208) Welcomes mature men and women, whether Catholic or not, to work with the Jesuits, with Catholic agencies, and with secular agencies. Emphasis is placed on dedication and on Christian community. Many assignments are in the United States but some are in Africa and Micronesia. All sorts of skills and talents are needed, plus guts, stability, and a sense of humor.

**United Presbyterian Church in the United States of America** (Division of Voluntary Service, 475 Riverside Drive, Room 1133, New York, N.Y. 10027) Has many one- and two-year assignments abroad for Christians (of all denominations) with professional and technical skills who can pay at least their own transportation and sometimes their expenses, although housing is usually provided. Much of the work is at medical, religious, or educational institutions.

Many other religious bodies send volunteers abroad; talk to your pastor about the possibilities. The Catholic Church, for instance, has a Medical Mission which accepts non-Catholic volunteers; service, however, is at Catholic-sponsored institutions. The Mennonites send volunteers abroad for all kinds of work; Mennonite volunteers are preferred.

**NATIONAL SERVICE ORGANIZATIONS** The number of overseas volunteer-service organizations is as nothing compared with the multiplicity of such organizations within the United States. The names of some national coordinating organizations have been given above. Several of the international volunteer agencies also place volunteers in service in the United States. Among these are the Committee of Returned Volunteers, the International Liaison for Volunteer

Service, Interaction, LAOS, the Jesuit Volunteer Corps, and Volunteers in Technical Assistance; these, too, are described above.

Federal and state governments either organize or fund many voluntary social services in the United States.

**RSVP** The Retired Senior Volunteer Program is one of the ACTION (see Chapter 17) projects specifically designed for placement of volunteers over age 60. It has federal financing arranged on a shared-cost basis, with the local agency taking part of the financial burden from the start; this share is expected to increase steadily over the following five years until the local agency is entirely supported by nonfederal funds. Each RSVP is locally controlled, planned, and operated and thus geared to local conditions and needs.

Working with other local agencies known as volunteer stations, which provide on-the-job orientation and supervision, RSVP places volunteers in work suited to their interests—in hospitals, nursing homes, schools, libraries, prisons, courts, telephone hot-line and reassurance programs, anywhere help is needed. Volunteers get regular assignments, usually on a once-a-week basis, and transportation expenses are paid. Sometimes lunch is provided.

**SCORE** The Service Corps of Retired Executives is another ACTION (see Chapter 17) volunteer agency, this one in conjunction with the Small Business Administration. ACTION is responsible for recruitment, publicity, and budgetary matters; the Small Business Administration directs and administers the program.

SCORE links retired businessmen who have management expertise with owner/managers of small business and community organizations that need management counseling. The volunteer works in his own or a nearby community and is reimbursed for out-of-pocket expenses by ACTION. The volunteer has the choice of accepting or rejecting each assignment, but he must be careful about conflict of interests—advising a businessman with whose chief rival the volunteer has family connections, for instance, would obviously lead to difficulties. Chapters have been established throughout the country; where there are insufficient volunteers to form chapters, the local Small Business Administration office manages the volunteer's services.

**VAVS** The Veterans Administration has a voluntary service of over 100,000 volunteers. Work is commonly in one's locale and may be at a VA hospital, outpatient clinic, domiciliary, or with a home-care unit which serves veterans in need of help in their own homes. Work ranges from occupational therapy to providing transport, installing aids in a handicapped veteran's home, and housework. You can put in any amount of time so long as it is on a regular basis. To find out if you can help, contact the Director of Volunteer Service at your nearest VA hospital.

**The Red Cross** (Office of Volunteers, National Headquarters, Washington, D.C. 20006)   Chartered by Congress, it operates on private donations. Its chartered aim is to give volunteer aid to sick and wounded members of the armed forces, but its services extend to many nonmilitary causes: local and county medical institutions, rescue work in disaster situations (floods, earthquakes, fires), and educational work. Training courses in various kinds of volunteer work are available, but you wouldn't necessarily need them. You can do fund raising or office work, provide transport, teach first aid or child care, provide food and shelter in a tornado, give help to hospitalized and institutionalized people. The Red Cross also provides volunteers to the Veterans Administration when needed.

**Recording for the Blind** (Public Relations, 215 East 58th Street, New York, N.Y. 10022)   A national organization with recording centers in 14 states, it provides recordings of educational books and materials to the blind. Volunteers are needed to read for the recordings (sessions are at least two hours each) and to work in the libraries and offices of the organization. Write to the headquarters in New York for information on volunteer possibilities in your district.

**The National Welfare Rights Organization** (Poverty Rights Action Center, 1762 Corcoran Street, Washington, D.C. 20044)   Welfare recipients and other poor people are the concern of this agency. Its aims are to achieve adequate incomes, dignity, justice, and participation of the poor in the decision making that concerns them. Volunteers are needed both year-round and in the summer at national, regional, and neighborhood levels.

**Boy Scouts of America**   This agency uses older volunteers in organizational and administrative jobs as well as directly with boys in the Cub and Scout groups. Full-time professional leaders need the assistance of part-time volunteers. You can be Scoutmaster, Cubmaster, Explorer-Advisor, or Merit Badge counselor—this last if you are expert enough in some field to teach it to the boys.

**Girl Scouts of the U.S.A.**   Volunteers can work directly with the girls in any of the four age groups into which they are divided, or they can do organizational work on the committees which plan, train, and fund the local organizations. A program called "Adopted Grandmother" calls on older women (and men as well) to impart their skills and learning to the Scouts.

**Big Brothers, Inc.** (341 Suburban Station Building, Philadelphia, Pa. 19103)   Boys aged six to 18 who are exhibiting troubled or antisocial behavior are helped. The boys might be involved with street gangs, or having problems at home, or failing at school. You are put in touch with a boy who becomes your protégé; you and he are matched for compatibility and your relationship is supervised—unobtrusively. Your job is to give him affection, sympathy, and understanding as well as guidance and a stable relationship upon which he can rely.

Only male volunteers are used in Big Brothers, Inc. Big Sisters uses only female volunteers and performs the same services for disturbed girls. The addresses of local branches can be obtained from the telephone directory or from the central offices.

**Goodwill Industries of America, Inc.** (9200 Wisconsin Avenue, N.W., Washington, D.C. 20014)   Work is done through locally autonomous agencies. Its aims are to get physically, mentally, and socially handicapped people into the labor market so that they can become self-supporting so far as possible. This is done by raising funds and gifts of surplus inventory from business and industry, and to some extent from private households. Goodwill also sets up certified sheltered workshops in which handicapped people can work. Volunteers who can supplement the work of permanent staff members are needed at the agencies and workshops. Work may be in public relations, rehabilitation, physical and occupational therapy, clothing drives, and many other areas.

**National Council of Senior Citizens, Inc.** (1627 E Street, N.W., Washington, D.C. 20004)   One of the more civically oriented membership organizations for older people (see Chapter 24). Its aims are the economic betterment of older people through, for example, low-cost housing, tax relief, and job availability, and it does its best to influence legislation at all levels of government. Local units encourage political discussion and involve themselves with community organizations. Volunteers are needed for both national and local work; the latter often includes volunteer work with community agencies.

**National Council on the Aging** (1828 L Street, N.W., Washington, D.C. 20036)   A private, nonprofit, voluntary agency, which provides what may be described as leadership services to organizations and individuals aiding the aging. A main concern has been the establishment of senior-citizen centers and services. From leisure-time day centers, these have evolved into multiple-purpose, full-time centers whose members may offer as many services to the community at large as they receive. Activities vary from center to center.

**Settlements and Neighborhood Centers**   These are voluntary organizations committed to bettering conditions for the people in their neighborhoods. Volunteer service may be in immediate community needs—day-care centers, home help, adult education—or in broader activity such as agitation for legislation to remedy a problem felt keenly by the neighborhood. Almost all settlements and neighborhood centers are urban. Information can usually be obtained at the local library or from social-service agencies. Or you can write to the National Federation of Settlements and Neighborhood Centers (232 Madison Avenue, New York, N.Y. 10016).

**RURAL SERVICE ORGANIZATIONS**   Almost half of the nation's poor live in rural areas, small towns, and villages, yet far fewer local agencies exist to care for them than exist for the urban poor. Partly this lack is due to the problems presented by low density, a condition that further aggravates the poor's own problems through scarcity of transport and medical and commercial facilities.

It is far easier in rural than in urban areas to see what must be done to help, to give direct help yourself, and to see the results of that help. Contact is much more personal, and you can have more influence.

**Cooperative Extension Service**   This educational branch of the U. S. Department of Agriculture is the largest of the rural agencies, with offices manned by specialists in agriculture, home economics, finance, and many other fields in every rural county. The service, originally designed to give domestic and economic instruction to rural dwellers, has broadened its functions with the times. Today's projects include youth programs like the 4-H clubs, providing transport for isolated people, home help to the aged, and so on.

To see what help is needed, get in touch with your county's cooperative extension service (listed in your telephone directory under the county name or under "Extension Service"). You can get a general picture of the service by writing to its headquarters (Cooperative Extension Service, Human Development and Human Relations Department, U. S. Department of Agriculture, Washington, D.C. 20250).

**County Welfare Offices**   These local governmental agencies are concerned with aiding the poor. They may do this directly by providing services, or they may refer people to organizations that provide them. Either way, they are a good source of information on volunteer work.

**The National Farmers Union** (Senior Member Council, 1012 14th Street, N.W., Washington, D.C. 20005)   Also concerns itself with rural community programs, particularly with bringing help to the sick and isolated and with restoring beauty to ravaged countryside.

Other sources of information on local volunteer opportunities are your Chamber of Commerce or City Hall; your religious organization;

the board of education for your local school district; the local Y's; the League of Women Voters; the PTA; a political party; or any of a number of other agencies.

## TYPES OF WORK

If you like face-to-face contact, you will find much to be done in educational, social, and recreational activities for the needy. If yours is a back-room personality, you will find plenty of jobs in office organizing, fund raising, and publicity work. If you like to be in on the planning stage, a thousand committees need minutes taken, meetings convened, and sometimes new ideas. A lot of lobbying goes on at all government levels, and here, too, a volunteer's help is often invaluable. These last two functions are, of course, more suited to volunteers with lots of experience and training.

**YOUR OWN NEEDS**    Before offering yourself for volunteer work, take inventory of your abilities and consider the kind of work you would feel happiest doing. This last is not the selfish consideration it may seem. If you are happy in your work, you will stay with it longer and do it better than if it nauseates you or bores you to the screaming point.

It is also important that you feel your work to be worthwhile and that you have some sense of having made a difference by your contribution.

The work should be naturally expressive for you and not land you in a situation where you have to suppress yourself completely to be able to function acceptably. If you want stimulation, the work should challenge you and not be entirely routine. There is, of course, a lot of routine work in any agency or program and someone has to do it; but it doesn't have to be you all the time, unless you want it that way.

To keep up your interest in any job, the long view of the project should be familiar to you. It is most alienating to be addressing letters to committee members about a meeting whose purposes are unknown to you.

**TRAINING**    Once you have accepted a job, you will probably go through a period of training. This may be anything from a couple of hours in a small, direct service project with relatively simple tasks, to a couple of weeks in a larger, more complex one. The training should include orientation to the aims of the program, to the policies and methods of approach generally approved, and to the procedures you must follow in certain situations. If you are lucky, this last item will be minimal and you will be left to your own good judgment. However, it is important that you be told where to turn for help in case you need it.

Usually your work will be supervised for an initial period. If you are working with a group you must take time to discover its methods of working and see if you can fit into them by being as flexible as possible. Not all the people you will be working with will be fellow volunteers. Most organizations, at least the larger ones, have a nucleus of paid professional staff to provide certain continuity. Their attitudes may be somewhat different from yours inasmuch as they must consider their jobs and careers. You, on the other hand, are freer at least to express yourself, if not to act exactly as you would wish in a given situation.

If you are working directly with the people at whom the service is aimed, you will generally get a fair amount of latitude in the way you can do things. To some extent, doubtless, you will have to conform to policy, if only in restricting your endeavors to the assigned work.

One of the things that frequently happens to a new volunteer going for the first time into an institution for the mentally or physically handicapped is a dreadful sense of revulsion; dreadful because it seems so inadmissible and ugly in oneself. Partly it stems from fear for oneself in realizing what can happen to the human body and mind. Mostly, though, it is the shock of being surrounded by so much deformity at once.

The best you can do in such a case is to go in prepared, both for your own shock and to cover it efficiently. Handicapped people are ultra-sensitive to this kind of reaction, and you must not hurt them by showing either distaste or pity. For a while, perhaps, you will find their physical aspects blocking your ability to see them as people. But this will soon pass, and you will find you no longer take much account of anything but the person behind the handicap.

# IV.
# KEEPING YOURSELF FIT

Time was when at the age of 65 your only permissible gait was the dodder. But now you're more apt to find yourself being shoved onto charitable committees, pestered into the swimming pool, and expected at the local course on The Modern Novel.

Most gerontologists agree that this is the best thing that could happen to you—keeping brisk, alert, and involved avoids the common complaints of aging. Many of them believe that senility is often the result of inertia, boredom, depression—a concomitant of negation and a form of despair.

Since today we know that life will be comparatively long, and we are also offered good information on how to remain healthy, you yourself should make use of that information so that your body continues to keep you in touch with the world around you rather than becoming a burden whose malfunctioning isolates you from the rest of your life.

An excellent guide to medical products and preparations, crammed with tips on many aspects of health (such as side effects of many drugs), is *The Medicine Show,* a paperback periodically revised by the Consumers Union and available in most bookshops. Good, direct information on ailments and their treatments is to be found in *Feeling Alive After 65: The Complete Medical Guide for Senior Citizens and Their Families* by Robert B. Taylor, M.D. (Arlington House, 1973). Also of interest is *Aging and Mental Health* by Robert N. Butler and Myrna I. Lewis (Mosby, 1973). Under the general title *Aging Around the World,* Columbia University Press has published *Biological Aspects of Aging,* edited by Nathan W. Shock, and *Medical and*

*Clinical Aspects of Aging,* edited by Herman T. Blumenthal, both Proceedings of the International Association of Gerontology, San Francisco, August, 1960.

# 20
# Maintaining a Healthy Body

**THE FIRST STEP**  Get a thorough checkup by a doctor, a dentist, and an eye doctor to determine your present health and likely future problems. You should then keep tabs on yourself with medical and eye checkups at least annually and dental checkups twice a year. If you are over 60 years old, consider transferring to a geriatric specialist if there is one in the area.

Financially speaking, it is wiser to get dental work done before retirement, if possible; it is not covered by Medicare, and on a retirement income you are unlikely to gain much in income-tax deductions. The same is true for hearing aids.

**BODILY CHANGES**  Biological maturity occurs during the mid to late twenties; after that physical capacities decline, at varying rates for different organs of the body, for different genetic endowments, and for different ways of life. Why decline occurs is not really known, though it seems to be true of all living organisms. Theories on the subject abound (cell mutation, accumulation of cellular waste matter, genetic programming are a few of them) but none is proved.

To a greater or lesser degree, sooner or later, we can expect certain physical and mental changes as we grow older. The following summary of common changes is based on those observed in the average 75-year-old man as compared (unless otherwise noted) with averages for a 25- to 30-year-old man. Equivalent data for women are not available, but where female characteristics are known to differ, this is noted.

**Weight**  Overall body weight reduces by about 12%. The proportion of fat in your body increases steadily from your 20's on, until it reaches a total of about 10%; where your total weight has not increased, the fat has replaced lean tissue. In women, fat content levels off by age 69. In men it declines from the ages of 60 to 80. Fat can be kept to a minimum with exercise and with a diet appropriate to metabolism and activity. Metabolism (see below) diminishes somewhat as we get older so that we need fewer calories to perform the same functions. Even with regular exercise, most people's physical activity just naturally lessens as they get older (think of those all-night parties in your early 20's). Estimates are that you need about 22% fewer calories at age 65 than you did at 30.

The water content of the body decreases by about 18%, which accounts for some of the weight loss common in people over 70.

**Height**  Your height decreases by about one inch between rising and going to bed. This is because the soft discs between the vertebrae of the spine compress during a day of erect posture. During sleep the pressure is off and the discs return to almost their previous size. But not, by a hairsbreadth, quite. Hence the compression, repeated day after day for a lifetime, is cumulative; in addition, the disc may lose up to 30% of its water content by age 70; so that eventually your height permanently diminishes—at the rate of one-quarter to one-half inch every ten years after the age of 30.

You can mitigate this reduction with exercises which stretch the spine. You can also help by holding the spine as tall as possible when you are erect, thus keeping the pressure on the intervertebral discs to a minimum.

**Muscles**  The muscular system constitutes 40% of a man's total weight and 32% of a woman's. Muscles are strongest at ages 25 to 30, losing strength steadily thereafter until, at age 75, your gripping strength is about 55% of what it was, and your muscular endurance is somewhat less than that.

Deterioration is best offset by regular exercises—preferably throughout life, although some recovery is possible even with a late start. Some nutritionists believe that Vitamin E helps keep up muscle tone.

**Bones**  Because the calcium content of bones tends to decrease with age, they become more fragile. One possible cause of this calcium loss is that, as the elastic fiber in the body changes with age, the coating around the fiber attracts deposits of calcium phosphates; the deposits are drawn from other calcium sources in the body, including the bones, thus causing shortages there. Women have lighter and softer bones than men, and their calcium requirements are greater throughout life. Maintaining sufficient calcium in your diet to meet these increasing needs, helps counteract the progressive shortage and maintain bone strength.

**Joints**  Bones are attached to each other at the joints by ligaments (bands of fibrous tissue). Between the ends of the bones is cartilage, another tough connective tissue. The movement of the joints is made easier by a lubricating fluid. As we get older the ligaments tend to get shorter and harder, the cartilage tends to get thinner, and the fluid tends to diminish. Thus our joints get stiffer and we complain louder. Fortunately, exercise will keep the joints flexible.

**Skin**   Directly under the surface of the skin is a layer of fat and another of elastic tissue called collagen. The fat layer gradually disappears toward age 75, while the collagen is replaced by nonelastic fibrous tissue. Both events lead to wrinkling; this happens sooner for women because their skin, having less collagen, is thinner than men's. Reduced oil secretion on the skin and less sweat-gland activity can lead to dryness and scaling.

Dryness and scaling can be relieved by external oil applications, by avoiding direct sunlight (ultraviolet rays shrink collagen), and by not taking a bath or a shower every day. Good diet (and hereditary tendency) can maintain elasticity in the collagen.

**Mucous Membranes**   These are really a continuous layer of thin skin which coats our internal passages and orifices and thus forms, with our outer skin, a complete wrap (waterproof, at that) around our flesh. The nasal membrane thins with age, with a slightly detrimental effect on our sense of smell. This loss is greater among habitual smokers.

A young child has taste buds on the roof of the mouth, walls of the throat, and central upper tongue, which doubtless explains those wistful memories of vivid tastes in "the old days." By the age of ten these are gone and we have to make do with what is left, mostly at the tongue's perimeter. As we get older, we undergo still further reductions, until eventually only about 35% of our original taste buds are left. This reduction, plus that of the sense of smell, with which taste is closely linked, means that you will have to use spices and herbs more heavily for gastronomic pleasures.

A diet rich in the B vitamins is believed to help keep the membranes in healthy condition and minimize the shrinkage of lips (not uncommon in old age) and lip cracking. Vitamins A and C may also help prevent lip cracking.

**Hair**   Most people's scalp hair gets thinner and drier as they get older, and almost everyone goes gray or white. Paradoxically, eyebrows get thicker, and hair may develop in the nostrils and ears. The hair on women's chins and upper lips tends to get stronger and thicker, probably because of gradual hormone changes after menopause.

Scalp and head-hair conditions are helped by diet sufficient in protein and generous in the B vitamins and Vitamin A. Massage and the use of mild shampoos also help to keep them in good condition. Nostril and ear hair, if unsightly, is easily plucked, as is eyebrow hair if you dislike the thickness. If you are the wrong sex for that shadow moustache and beard, they can be kept down by depilatory creams or permanently removed by electrolysis. Or, if they are not too coarse, they can be disguised by bleaching.

**Eyes**   Eyesight is at its most efficient when we are infants, decreasing steadily until about age 55, at which point it levels off. By this time color perception has diminished slightly, particularly in the violet end of the spectrum (a result of increased yellowishness in the eye's lens). So has peripheral vision. The depth of the eyeball may shorten, leading to farsightedness and, for some, the cure of nearsightedness. The eye's lens stiffens somewhat, making it more difficult to change focus quickly from near to far and back. The pupil may get smaller and thus admit less light. You may also find it more difficult to adapt to sudden and extreme changes in light levels.

Some of these losses can be moderated by exercises. For instance, if you are losing your ability to change focus quickly, you should spend a few moments each day shifting focus between near and distant objects. More immediate relief of farsightedness can be obtained by using spectacles; sometimes bifocals are needed. It helps to use brighter lighting, particularly for close work, but also in general areas. You may need up to about double the intensity you used when you were younger. Allow more time for adjusting to the dark when coming from a lighted place, and vice versa. Vitamin A in the diet is thought to help develop better night vision.

**Ears**   The sound waves of normal speech usually have a frequency under 1000 vibrations per second. In infancy we hear as many as 40,000 vibrations per second, by the late teens about 20,000, but after age 40 we lose only about 15 vibrations per second each year. These losses are aggravated by loud noise, which damages the hair cells of the inner ear (hence the dire predictions for our rock-and-roll generations). Losses are mostly at the high-pitched sound levels. Since women have thinner eardrums and lighter ear bones than men, their loss tends to be less significant.

Although about one quarter of older people complain of some hearing difficulty, some of the apparent loss may be (perhaps unconscious) lack of attention; one tends to have "heard it all before."

Marginal loss can be combated (so long as it is real!) by using increased volume on radios, television sets, and record players. Sometimes the hearing loss is due to ear-wax accumulations which muffle sound; your doctor may irrigate your ear to remove the wax, but don't do this yourself without his instructions—if the wax has hardened to your eardrums, you risk damaging your ear. For some kinds of hearing loss, your doctor may recommend a hearing aid (these are tiny enough nowadays not to be embarrassing).

**Teeth**  Strictly speaking, there is no reason why we should ever lose our teeth—small comfort if all your teeth are falling out. Complications do arise, however, from long-term wear on the teeth; if they wear unevenly, your bite is affected and previously regular teeth become crooked and sometimes loosen in their sockets; decay can set in from food particles caught in unevenly worn areas. Neglect will also result in tooth decay and often in gum disease. If gum disease is neglected, teeth loosen and eventually fall out.

If he thinks it is not too late to save your teeth, your dentist will prescribe such remedies as gum massage or medication. At the same time, you should make sure that you have a generous amount of calcium and of Vitamins A, C, and D in your diet.

Since you need teeth for chewing food, for speaking clearly, and for enhancing your personal appearance, they are well worth taking trouble over. Pay attention to the state of your teeth, gums, and mouth in general and get a dental examination every six months, even if it means waiting in line at a clinic for it. Avoid sweet foods, and clean your teeth after eating, if possible (especially after those forbidden sugary foods).

**Digestive System**  Although the digestive system is complex, its main organs are the stomach, liver, kidneys, and small and large intestines. With aging these organs tend to lose some efficiency, mostly because of life-long abuse.

As you get older your stomach may secrete less hydrochloric acid and fewer digestive enzymes, and this makes it less easy to digest food. Avoid those foods that cause you obvious difficulty. Chew your food well to give your stomach a head start. Adding lemon juice to the diet helps some people. Your stomach may shrink slightly and you will need smaller helpings at mealtimes.

The digestive-enzyme secretion in the intestines may also lessen, reducing your ability to absorb nutrients from food. Allow for this by increasing your intake of nutritional food and cutting back on "fluff" foods such as candy and cookies.

The muscles of the anus and large intestine may get weaker, which means that you have to allow longer for evacuation. Do not, whatever you do, resort to laxatives, because the strong convulsions forced on the muscles will only weaken them further. The sphincter muscles (those around the anus and bladder) can be strengthened by exercises which consist of contracting and relaxing the buttocks and thighs.

The kidneys filter waste products from the blood; they are usually functioning at a little over two thirds of their maximum by age 75. Since each kidney can function normally with only about one quarter of its tissue in a healthy state, this one third loss is not usually significant. A loss of more than 50% of their blood supply will, however, leave the kidneys functioning poorly.

The liver, the largest organ in the body, secretes bile; modifies, stores, and distributes fat, sugars, and proteins; breaks down waste products; filters out poisons before they reach other organs; produces antibodies to destroy bacteria; and manufactures lecithin and cholesterol. Its role as detoxifier is so essential that the liver should be in good working order at all times. The liver rarely gives much trouble unless it has been badly abused over a long period (alcohol is a prime offender) or is diseased. Obesity can cause fatty deposits in the liver, which impair its functioning.

Such symptoms as heartburn, "sour stomach," frequent urination, and indigestion are not inevitable with aging, as many people think. You should never treat them with patent medicines (which can do harm in themselves as well as leave the symptoms unattended); instead, consult your doctor.

A well-balanced diet and exercise program are the best maintainers of the digestive system and the earlier such a program is undertaken, the more benefit you will feel.

**Circulatory System**   Impairment of the circulatory system centers mainly in the lungs, heart, and blood vessels. By age 75 the normal, fairly sedentary person will find his breathing reduced to less than half of its prime capacity: this reduction is mainly due to the formation of fibrous tissue in the lungs, which cuts down on oxygen/carbon dioxide exchange. The heart gets similarly logged with fibrous, plus some fatty, tissue and may be left with a pumping power only two thirds of prime.

Arterial walls thicken with fibrous tissue and harden accordingly. They also roughen and this causes deposits which stiffen them. The very fine blood vessels in the muscle fibers tend to become inert with the heart's decreased pumping power and with sedentary habits. The amount of oxygen in the blood may decrease slightly.

The best way to support the circulatory and respiratory systems is through exercise and diet. Contrary to a widely held belief, exercise does *not* harm the heart, even an injured one; rather, in careful installments it can be beneficial. Exercise should be tailored to your physical condition but it should be regular and energetic enough to stretch you a bit. Apart from deliberate exercise, move around as much as you can in your daily activities. If you are apt to be sedentary you may have to make a point of this.

To be on the safe side, diet should be low in cholesterol and high in Vitamins E and C, although the role of any of these in relation to the circulatory system is still a matter of fierce debate.

**Endocrine System**  This is the system of ductless glands whose secretions pass directly into the bloodstream. It includes the pituitary gland (tucked right under the brain), thyroid and parathyroid glands (in the neck), adrenal glands (on either side of the kidneys), pancreas (near the stomach), and sex glands (ovaries in women, testes in men). This system is generally responsible for maintaining the body's chemical and physical balance and intellectual activity.

With age, the pancreas loses some ability to produce enzymes for protein and sugar metabolism, the sex glands produce fewer sex hormones, and the thyroids produce slightly fewer of the hormones that control energy levels. Otherwise there is relatively little apparent change in normal functioning.

However, the ability to adapt to stress—a function particularly of the adrenal and pituitary glands—grows less. This will show up as a disadvantage in sudden extreme stress, such as illness. On the plus side, you will stay calmer during certain kinds of crisis.

Estrogen therapy can keep up the hormone production from the ovaries. A generally good state of health will ward off the stress of illness.

**Temperature Regulation**  Because of slowing circulation plus a decrease in the activity of the sweat glands, the body's temperature regulation becomes less efficient. The neatest solution is to avoid very hot or very cold climates, if possible; wear clothing suitable to the climate; and make sure that adequate heating and air conditioning are available when necessary.

**Basal Metabolism**  This is the energy you use when you are resting. It reduces to about 85% of what it was at maturity, the result mainly of lessened thyroid activity, which is just as well for the aging circulatory system. This means that you need less food energy (calories) for fuel in pursuing your regular activities; as long as you are careful to make the right adjustment and thus avoid obesity, little else need worry you.

**Central Nervous System**  Changes in the central nervous system, particularly in the brain, are still the subject of much argument among doctors, scientists, and sociologists. Mental changes are also the subject of much erroneous folklore.

The folds of the brain become somewhat flattened by the age of 75, and this may indicate decreased blood (sometimes down by 20%) circulation. The number of brain cells is also thought to decrease. The nervous system leading from the brain, along the spine, and thence throughout the body shows some replacement of nervous tissue by fibrous tissue and may also suffer a decrease in blood supply.

What all this means to our functioning is not yet clear: differences among test findings are great, which may mean that individual development varies too greatly for researchers to be able to arrive at a norm. Laboratory tests seem to show some slowing of reaction and performance times; however, outside the laboratory situation, any such slowing is very adequately offset by experience, practice, and concentration. It seems also that learning time is longer for older people, perhaps because they approach a new task with accumulated preconceptions and set habits. Both of these factors are certainly avoidable, and in any case the slightly slower process makes little difference in everyday life.

The way to avoid or overcome these effects is to keep your mind stimulated and active, to keep your body's reflexes in good form, and to make every effort to stay out of mental ruts, since it seems to be true that those faculties in constant use suffer no deterioration and may actually improve.

**Sleep**   Our need for sleep remains about the same at all ages after maturity, averaging about seven and one quarter hours per night but with startling variations ranging from three to 12 hours. Sex or physical or mental activity seems to have little bearing on sleep needs, except that extremely low intellectual activity seems to result in longer sleep (as many very bored people can attest). More sleep-aiding drugs are taken by sedentary than by active people and more by women than by men; perhaps because women tend to be more sedentary.

Exercise and the avoidance of boredom are probably the best aids to sound sleep. Calcium is thought to relax nerves and thus aid sleep —hence the custom of a (warm) glass of milk at bedtime.

**Sex**   Sexual activity shows very little falling off up to the age of about 60. By 70 it may have been moderately reduced, possibly because of reduced hormone production. Much seems to depend on lifetime habits: given good health in oneself and in a willing partner, an active sex life will continue; an inactive one rarely picks up.

Sex, however, is good for what ails you and should be indulged in whenever possible (never mind the sideways looks from your Victorian children!). It is certainly invaluable for relaxation, both mental and physical; and there is some evidence that it increases the adrenal gland's output of cortisone, which eases arthritis.

# 21
# Avoiding Common Ailments

Aging brings—inevitably, it seems—a decreased resistance to disease. Once your body is worn down by faulty nutrition or by a prolonged illness, for instance, you are apt to find it harder to get back to normal health again, and in the meantime you may be vulnerable to other illnesses.

Keeping yourself healthy is obviously the most effective guard against disease. You should take precautions against ailments toward which you know you have a tendency. In addition, the following information will help you keep a sharp lookout for symptoms of those diseases to which older people seem most prone.

## CIRCULATORY AILMENTS

The highest mortality rate in the general population is from heart and blood-vessel diseases. The percentage is decreasing now that effective means of coping with these diseases are being discovered, although the mortality rate from arteriosclerosis specifically is still increasing.

**HYPERTENSION** This is characterized by blood circulating through the system at greater pressure than normal. The result is that the heart must work harder and the blood vessels must withstand the pressure. Many people have this condition and seem none the worse for it. In some cases, though, the prolonged pressure on the vessel walls eventually breaks them at a particular point, resulting in hemorrhage. In other cases the heart is eventually strained beyond its ability to keep pumping and fails. A third possible effect is deficient blood circulation to the kidneys and consequent damage to their functioning.

**Causes**   Stress, both from personal and from external causes (high noise levels are coming under increasing scrutiny in this respect), is thought to be a major factor. Heredity may also play a part in predisposing you toward the condition. Salt intake is also thought to be a factor, although this seems to be true only for some people. As you can see, the full range of causes is not yet known.

**Prevention**   The first rule is not to worry about getting it. You should avoid stressful situations whenever possible. Take care of your general health by making sure that your diet is nutritious, your weight is kept at a proper level, and you get regular exercise, sleep, and relaxation. A medical checkup every year is important.

**Recovery**   A salt-free diet is occasionally recommended by the doctor if he detects either hypertension or a tendency toward it. In some cases he may judge drugs to be effective.

**ARTERIOSCLEROSIS**   Here the arteries leading to the heart become hardened or narrowed by deposits on the interior walls of the vessels. If the condition becomes severe, the artery may block completely, shutting off blood supplies to a part of the heart. The heart can sometimes manage for a while, but eventually either the shock or the extra hard work for the undamaged part may stop the heart's beating.

**Causes**   Why the blood vessels become blocked is not known. Part of the deposits are known to be a fatty substance called cholesterol. One theory has it that too much cholesterol in the diet causes the deposits. Another says that the body, for unknown reasons, fails to metabolize the cholesterol in the diet properly. Still other theories hold that the cholesterol itself has nothing to do with the matter, that the stress and pollution of modern—particularly urban—life are the basic causes.

**Prevention**   Obesity is anathema because it causes extra work for the heart. Regular exercise without sudden or violent exertion is advisable to keep circulation good. Emotional stress should be avoided because of its shock effects on the heart. Many doctors will advise a diet low in animal fat and organ meats (the prime sources of diet cholesterol) to be on the safe side.

**Recovery**   Two thirds of the people suffering this kind of heart attack survive, some for many years, and lead normal lives. When the heartbeat remains unsteady or weak, a cardiac pacemaker may be implanted for either constant or periodic stimulation. The implant is not uncomfortable and existence can return to normal with it.

**STROKE**   This is damage to the blood vessels of the brain and is a third, statistically less important, form of cardiovascular disease.

**Causes** The damage may be from a blocked blood vessel cutting off circulation to a part of the brain. The blockage may be a blood clot or a foreign body in the vessel, or it may be a swelling in the brain (such as a tumor) pressing on the vessel. Or the damage may result from blood leaking from a ruptured vessel.

**Recovery** Most victims live through the stroke but suffer such effects as partial paralysis (usually down one side of the body), numbness, loss of organ control, or slurring of speech. The particular result depends on the extent and whereabouts of brain damage. The effects wear off in time or are reversible through special training in about 90% of cases.

The National Heart Association (44 East 23rd Street, New York, N.Y. 10010) publishes and recommends literature on circulatory ailments.

## RHEUMATIC AILMENTS

Some fifty forms of rheumatism and arthritis have been distinguished, of which the most common are rheumatoid arthritis and osteoarthritis.

**RHEUMATOID ARTHRITIS** Its symptoms are pain, redness, heat, soft swelling of joints, general weakness, and general body stiffness, especially in the mornings. It can fluctuate in severity from time to time.

**Causes** None are known but rheumatoid arthritis is often observed to set in after mental or physical strain or shock.

**Recovery** If your condition is severe, your doctor will prescribe rest, exercise, and perhaps heat treatments. Drugs can be used in certain cases. Weight reduction is prescribed when necessary.

**OSTEOARTHRITIS** On the whole this is a less serious type of rheumatism than rheumatoid arthritis. Here, too, pain and swelling affect the joints, but with little accompanying heat and redness. Apart from the middle and end joints of the fingers, the weight-bearing joints are the most frequently affected. Where there is joint enlargement it is hard and bony. Osteoarthritis, while it can be a great nuisance, does not cripple; the only deformity likely is permanent swelling of the joints of the fingers which eventually becomes painless.

**Causes** Although the causes are not known, heredity, obesity, and prior injury are thought sometimes to play a part.

**Recovery** The doctor will prescribe special rest and exercise procedures. Drugs are seldom used except for aspirin or, in severe cases, injections into the rheumatic joint to kill pain. Body weight must be kept down to take some load off weight-bearing joints.

**LOWER-BACK PROBLEMS**    Pain in the lower back is usually described as the penalty we pay for walking on our hind legs. It is a common ailment with disabling effects: as a chronic ache it can spoil everything you do just as a headache can; in its worst manifestations it can immobilize you for weeks at a time.

**Causes**    For a few sufferers the cause lies in spinal injury, mostly in the form of ruptured discs between the bottom two vertebrae and/or between the bottommost vertebra and the sacrum. But by far the larger percentage are suffering from tired, strained, or torn ligaments, tendons, or muscles in the lower back. Apart from tears caused by sudden overuse or by accident, the main reason for this weakness is lack of exercise. The trouble may be compounded if you take the physical brunt of tension in the lower back (others take it in the head and in neck and shoulder muscles, to name common areas).

**Recovery**    In cases of severe spinal or disc injury, surgery with possible spinal fusion may be necessary. However, this is an extreme procedure suitable only for a very small number of people.

In cases of milder spinal or disc injury, manipulation by an orthopedist or chiropractor may serve to put your back in place again. In order to maintain the improvement, though, you must exercise your back regularly and correct the poor posture which is almost always a contributing factor.

Sometimes supporting muscles go into spasm and movement is consequently painful. Tranquilizers will ease muscle tension, and a day or two of partial rest will usually straighten it out.

Exercises aimed at flexibility and slow gaining of strength (see Chapter 23) plus a daily dose of walking or swimming will keep your lower back muscles strong and thus avoid the weariness and strain that causes so much lower-back pain and injury.

The Arthritis Foundation (1212 Sixth Avenue, New York, N.Y. 10036) provides information on latest research and treatments for these ailments.

## CANCER

Cancer frightens people of any age, not only because little is known of its causes but also because so many people believe, erroneously, that cancer is untreatable and invariably fatal. Many forms of it, however, can be arrested—often apparently for good—if caught early enough. This is particularly true of cancers of the uterus, cervix, breast, prostate, rectum, and colon.

**Danger Signals**    Seven danger signals are usually cited for cancer in general. Most often they turn out to be symptoms of something else altogether; nevertheless they should be reported to the doctor for examination and treatment, if only for one's own reassurance. These signals are: unusual bleeding or discharge; a lump or thickening in the breast or elsewhere; a sore that doesn't heal; persistent change in elimination habits of either bowel or bladder; persistent hoarseness or cough; persistent indigestion or difficulty in swallowing; change in a wart or mole. Low back pain accompanied by difficulty in urinating are warning signs for prostate cancer.

**Avoidance**    A routine annual medical checkup should include an examination of your mouth, a chest X ray, the Pap test for uterine and cervical forms of cancer in women, and the rectal examination for both sexes. A second Pap test halfway between the annual checkups is also wise. These tests often detect early cancers before you have any symptoms—the best time to catch them for curative treatment.

Women should examine their breasts once a month; only by familiarity with them can you detect lumps that were not there before or which feel larger. Tobacco smoking has been definitely linked to lung cancer and should not be indulged in. Constant exposure to strong sunlight increases the risk of skin cancer and should be avoided.

**Recovery**    Treatments are many and varied; new ones are being introduced all the time; and often more than one is used in a particular case. The best source of up-to-date information is the American Cancer Society, whose national office is at 219 East 42nd Street, New York, N.Y. 10017, and which has local offices in most states and larger cities. The Society will send you descriptions of symptoms and treatments of the various types of cancer and can also advise you on any unorthodox treatments you may hear about.

## RESPIRATORY AILMENTS

These are among the commonest ailments of modern city-dwellers of all ages. The common cold grows less frequent with age but bronchitis, emphysema, and asthma do not.

**EMPHYSEMA**    This is overinflation of the lungs in which the elastic tissue is replaced by inelastic scar tissue, with irreversible damage to the air sacs. The people most subject to it are those whose lungs have been long subject to abuse or overuse, such as wind-instrument players, asthma sufferers, heavy tobacco smokers, and workers exposed to occupational lung diseases. Living where air is polluted can aggravate the disease or a tendency toward it.

**Danger Signals**    A chronic cough and breathlessness, particularly in the mornings, are early signs of the disease. You should attend to them the moment you notice them and not wait until the breathlessness occurs during your ordinary day's activity. If your head colds tend to develop into chest infections, this may be another warning sign.

**Recovery**   If you smoke, you must stop. You should move to an area where the air is cleaner. Your doctor may prescribe special breathing exercises and physical exercises in more severe cases. In the most severe, administration of oxygen often proves helpful.

**BRONCHITIS**   Chronic bronchitis is very closely linked to emphysema and, like it, affects the whole lung and air passages to the lung. In addition, bronchitis involves thickening of the walls of the air passages, increased production of mucus, and difficulty in expelling the mucus. Acute bronchitis is an infection which brings on these effects. The danger signals and recovery for bronchitis are substantially the same as those for emphysema.

**TUBERCULOSIS**   Though not the killer it once was, at least in the United States, tuberculosis can prove a long, debilitating illness if not caught early. It is an infection by a specific bacterium and is cured by antibiotics.

The disease can lie dormant in an infected person for years before it breaks loose—usually because of lowered bodily resistance. As it shows no symptoms until it is well under way, it is important to have a periodic tuberculin test (a simple skin injection of dead tuberculin bacteria). If you get a positive reaction you will need further tests to find out whether the disease is active or dormant in you.

**PNEUMONIA**   Any inflammation of lung tissue is, strictly speaking, pneumonia. But the type usually referred to is caused by certain bacteria which most of us carry and which, under certain conditions, infect the lungs very rapidly. Fatigue, temperature extremes, dampness, and general physical debility are the conditions which most often leave you open to pneumonia. Fortunately, it is almost always curable by antibiotics.

**ASTHMA**   Originally, this is an allergy disease, but long-standing irritation of the lungs and bronchial tubes can extend their sensitivity beyond the original irritant. If possible, you should avoid your particular irritants (often things like animal dander or specific foods). Anti-allergy injections may ease the reaction to such unavoidable irritants as pollens or molds. Adrenalin-type drugs are available for immediate relief of bad attacks. For severe and chronic asthma, inhalations are available which, taken daily, ward off attacks in all but the most provoking circumstances. Those whose asthma is brought on by cold spells or by chronic bronchitis may be helped by a warm, dry climate.

The National Tuberculosis and Respiratory Diseases Foundation (1740 Broadway, New York, N.Y. 10019) is a good source of the latest information on these diseases.

## OTHER AILMENTS

**DIABETES** In this condition the pancreas fails, for reasons as yet unknown, to manufacture enough of the hormone called insulin; as a result, the body cells are unable to make use of sugar in the blood. Insulin is also necessary for the metabolism of proteins and fats, although this metabolic failure shows up only in extreme conditions.

The tendency to diabetes increases after the age of 40 and seems to be hereditary in some cases. Obese people are also prone to it, and it is more frequent in women than in men. In older people it has no recognizable early symptoms, and the best guard against it is a test for sugar in your urine at your periodic medical checkup. Symptoms of intermediate-stage diabetes are: excessive hunger, thirst, and urination; fatigue, blurred vision, and loss of weight.

In mild cases a diet low in carbohydrates and somewhat higher in fats may control the disease. In more advanced cases, insulin injections may be necessary. Untreated diabetes is fatal because of the accumulation of acids (acidosis) arising from the body's inability to burn fats. Many people, especially women, who do not have diabetes nevertheless develop low tolerance for glucose. They must then cut down on carbohydrates in their diets until they reach a tolerable level.

The American Diabetes Association (18 East 48th Street, New York, N.Y. 10017) will provide up-to-date information on request.

**DIGESTIVE PROBLEMS** These are often the accumulated results of nervous stress, bad eating and drinking habits, or lack of exercise. Reduced secretion of digestive juices makes some foods difficult to deal with; these foods must be avoided. Correcting most of the abuses brings relief too.

**VARICOSE VEINS** When the valves of a vein break down, the vessel wall swells with the pressure of blood that is not circulating properly; the vein becomes what is known as varicose. Swelling occurs at the weakest points, and is thus irregular. Varicose veins frequently afflict people (especially women) who have stood for long periods over many years.

Not only are they cosmetically undesirable, they also make your legs feel heavy, and your whole body tires easily with the effort of moving around with them. If varicose veins are left untreated, varicose ulcers may form, and this will mean long periods in bed. Minor surgery, in which the affected veins are "stripped" and circulation restored, may be necessary in some cases. In others, support stockings or elastic bandages may suffice.

**ACCIDENTS**   As you grow older, it's not uncommon to feel that you are becoming accident prone. Sometimes it is simply that your accidents cause more injury than they used to: if you have osteoporosis (a frequent condition among older people caused by the body's withdrawal of calcium from the bones) a fall is more likely to result in a fracture.

Or you may actually be having more accidents because of failing faculties. Poor eyesight, defective ears, diminished sense of smell, slowed reaction time, and failing strength can lead to accidents. Impaired eye-ear coordination can lead to imbalance, or sometimes the very fear of falling can bring a fall on slippery surfaces. Occasional memory lapses, particularly during the night, make it all too easy to take medicine overdoses.

**Avoidance**   Fluoride (usually in the water supply) and higher calcium in the diet are thought by some researchers to combat osteoporosis, although both theories are controversial.

Sensory losses can usually be remedied with devices—spectacles, hearing aids, and the like. A night light will guard against the results of uncoordinated movement in the dark. Keeping medicine in the bathroom and not on the bedside table will give you the chance to wake up properly before taking it.

You can consciously correct your way of walking so that you do not shuffle, and you can forgo floppy footwear. Floor space clear of small furniture, doodads, and discards will forestall bruising and tripping. Give yourself a few minutes extra in which to get things done and thus make hurrying unnecessary. Cross the street at the crosswalks instead of darting out between cars. Take extra care to turn off gas fixtures and to keep electric wiring in good shape. If you must smoke, make sure your cigarette or pipe is not left burning; and don't smoke in bed. Keep doors and drawers closed to avoid bruises.

Do not wear clothes that can trail into open heaters, gas burners, or around tippable objects. Portable heaters are dangerous; if you have one, keep it well away from your normal areas of movement; radiators should be shielded.

If your night vision is defective, try not to drive in the dark; also, your diet should be adequate in Vitamins A and D.

**EYE CONDITIONS**   Apart from the marginal deterioration of eyesight which is common, glaucoma and cataract are sometimes encountered with aging. Both cause blindness if they are left untreated for too long.

**Glaucoma** Here blocked drainage channels from the eye cause increased fluid retention in the eyeball; the fluid presses on the optic nerve and on blood vessels in the eye. Sometimes pain around the eyes is sharp, sometimes there is no pain before vision has been affected; often the affected eye sees colored halos around light sources.

A yearly eye test will detect onset of glaucoma. Treatment may involve decreased liquids in the diet, eye drops to help remove excess fluid from the eyeball, or sometimes an operation for the same purpose. Eye exercises and several two-minute sessions a day with sun or lamp on closed eyes (with head moving from side to side) are sometimes beneficial.

**Cataract** The lens of the eye develops a milky clouding right behind the pupil; it eventually reduces vision to detection of only light and dark. In early stages nearsightedness may develop, enabling previously long-sighted people to discard their spectacles. As with glaucoma, the cause is not known, but cataract has been observed to set in after an injury to the eye or after an emotional shock.

The clouded lens can be removed by a relatively simple surgical operation, although from then on you will have to wear bifocals or contact lenses since the affected eye will not be able to focus alone. Fatigue, particularly of the eyes, must be avoided since it aggravates visual difficulties caused by cataract. Relaxation exercises for the eyes and gentle practice of proper visual techniques might be helpful. The National Society for Prevention of Blindness (79 Madison Avenue, New York, N.Y. 10016) disseminates information on this subject.

**EARS** Significant hearing loss among older people is not so common as you might think: only somewhere between 5% and 13% of women and 7% and 17% of men are affected. If the loss is simply one of lower threshold, hearing aids will usually correct it. Other conditions, such as loss of discrimination between tones, are not helped by hearing aids. For certain conditions, surgery on the bony structures behind the ears can bring permanent improvement.

If your doctor proposes a hearing aid, do not fail to use it. Modern hearing aids, tiny and unnoticeable, are no embarrassment. Loss of background noise and inability to hear normal conversation, on the other hand, make you feel isolated and can be very depressing. You might get your doctor to steer you to a nonprofit hearing-aid clinic where you can be tested fully before buying from a retailer.

Contact the National Association of Hearing and Speech Agencies

(919 18th Street, N.W., Washington, D.C. 20006) for further information.

**FEET**   What happens to your feet as you get older is the result of accumulated neglect and abuse—ill-fitting shoes, high heels, long periods of standing with your weight badly distributed, corns or bunions ignored. The more your feet hurt, the more sedentary your habits become, with bad consequences for your general health. Therefore it is important that you take good care of your feet.

If you have a persistent condition such as an ingrowing toenail or a bunion, if you injure your foot or if it gets infected, go to your doctor or to a competent chiropodist for advice and treatment. Make sure that your socks or stockings fit properly (badly fitting ones are surprisingly irritating) and allow your feet to "breathe"—cotton and wool are probably best for this. Your shoes should be a pleasure to put on—comfortable and pliable while supporting your feet well. Footwear should always be clean, soft, and dry. The exercises described in Chapter 23 will help to keep your feet flexible and strong.

**FATIGUE**   Chronic fatigue can usually be solved provided it does not stem from illness that would itself have to be cured first. If your fatigue is the result of constant overexertion, your activities will have to be curtailed. Sometimes underexertion causes a surprising amount of lethargy and apathy; in this case you will have to add more exercises and activities. Or your fatigue may stem from boredom with routine—here change is the obvious cure.

Lack of sleep, either in length of time or in depth of sleep, is another possible cause of weariness. A well-exercised body and mind sleep better. Relaxing for an hour or two before bedtime will make it easier to get to sleep, as long as full-time relaxation is not the cause of the problem in the first place. A good firm mattress, lightweight covers, the correct pillow height for you, and a well-ventilated bedroom will all help counter insomnia. Sleeping pills, a last resort, are better avoided unless your doctor advises to the contrary.

Another cause of fatigue may be obesity—it becomes increasingly hard on the bones, muscles, heart, and respiratory system to carry around all those extra pounds; all too obviously the cure will involve diet and exercise.

When depression is at the root of chronic fatigue, the only cure is to get to the bottom of the depression. This may take some doing, and even when you get there you may not be able to remove the cause of the depression. But you will probably cure the fatigue just by laying bare the depression.

**DEPRESSION**  Depression has any number of sources. Sometimes you can find and remove the source. But when the cause cannot be changed, the only solution lies in changing your attitude or reaction to it.

The very fact of aging is monumentally depressing to some people. Since aging is unavoidable, the best you can do is to minimize its disadvantages (both in practical terms, by taking care of yourself, and in your mind, by letting go of the idea of youthfulness as the *sine qua non*), and to recognize and welcome its advantages.

The depression brought on by the onset of retirement or by the consequent reduction in income is also of this type. You may be able to ameliorate your situation (by undertaking an interesting project, say, or by earning extra income) but it is placing less value on the work ethic and a materialistic outlook that will be the lasting cure.

At the bottom of some depressions lie unacknowledged anger or frustration. Facing these emotions can relieve the depression, since you will then have recovered the real emotion and no longer need its substitute, the depression. Express your anger and work around your frustration, or you may slip back into the depression again.

Unless the depression is of long standing, it can usually be shaken off by directing your attention away from yourself toward external activities that you *know* to be worthwhile, even if you are too depressed at the moment to *feel* them so. Interest in the activities is almost always aroused once you get started.

A long-established depression, or one of the (fortunately) rare ones which has a chronic physical cause, may call for medication. Nothing on the open market is equal to coping with this kind of depression, and you'll have to consult your doctor. He may prescribe tranquilizers which work immediately and temporarily; or he may put you onto antidepressants which may take a week or more to build up their effect but which are longer lasting in their elevation of mood.

For information on the latest research and treatment of depressions, write to the National Association for Mental Health (1800 N. Kent Street, Arlington, Va. 22209).

## MEDICATIONS

Our society has been accused by many observers of being pill-happy. Certainly advertising and the availability of so many new drugs contribute to the trend. And the overuse of medications does have dangers since so many are aimed at removing symptoms rather than diseases, and symptoms—the body's warning signals of trouble—should be investigated.

Some observers question what happens to character (sometimes known as moral fiber) if pain is avoided at all times; it might be that we become less and less able to withstand pain, frustration, and, in the end, any adversity.

If you have ever had the chance to browse through a *Physicians' Desk Reference* or the descriptive pamphlets packaged with some drugs, you must have been startled to see how many effects can occur besides the intended one when you take a prescribed drug. True, side effects are minor for most people; but then so little is known about body chemistry that some consequences may go unnoticed.

Antibiotics, for instance, destroy disease microorganisms; but they don't stop there—they go on to kill a lot of benevolent (and some essential) microorganisms, too. Thus they deplete the body's resources at the same time as they cure the disease. If you know this and use antibiotics discriminatingly, while doing your best to replace the loss by stepped-up nutrition, all is well.

Again, some tranquilizers and antidepressants tend, among their other side effects, to curtail sexual drive and to retard orgasm. This is true at any age, but it can be upsetting for the older person who mistakenly sees it as just one more irreversible loss entailed in growing older instead of for what it really is—a drug-induced state.

Another aspect of drug taking of which little is yet known is the different effect that the same dosage can have at different times of the day or night. The body has many types of rhythms. If you take medication regularly and have some choice as to when, try to discover the most effective times for you.

As we get older, we tend to take medications more frequently. The largest number are taken for cardiovascular problems (about 40%) with arthritis and rheumatism running close behind (at 33%). Nervous and mental disorders are the other notable reasons (10½%).

It might be worth remembering that, of the 20 most frequently used medications, 12 have sedative effects on the brain, mostly as a side effect.

## HEALTH-CARE FACILITIES

Chances are about 5 to 1 in your favor that you will never be so seriously ill as to require extensive medical care. But you should, to be on the safe side, learn what facilities are available. (The financial aspects are discussed in Chapter 7.)

If you need a new doctor, you should look first for the best hospital in your area and ask there for a list of its staff internists and general practitioners. This is because a good hospital monitors its staff physicians to insure their work meets high standards. (Or you could compile your own list at the public library by consulting the *Directory of Medical Specialists* or directories published by the county or state medical society, listing doctors' addresses, hospital affiliations, and board certifications.)

Finding the best hospital in your area is a bit trickier. At the very minimum it should be accredited by the Joint Commission on Accreditation of Hospitals (the certificate is usually posted in the lobby). Best of all is a hospital affiliated with a medical school or approved for residency training (you can find out which of your local hospitals has this approval by writing to the Council on Medical Education and Hospitals, American Medical Association, 535 N. Dearborn St., Chicago 60610). Failing this, a hospital that has a nursing school or is approved for intern training is probably a good choice. And finally, you might consider whether you prefer a voluntary nonprofit community hospital or a private hospital looking to make a profit.

For a fuller explanation of what to look for in a doctor or hospital, an excellent source is *The Medicine Show* (see the introduction to this section).

A recent adjunct to health services are extended-care facilities for patients who need full-time nursing or other health services but who do not require hospitalization. Your doctor will decide whether an extended-care facility is available and suitable for your needs.

Nursing homes, which once provided services similar to those of today's extended-care facilities, now have become mostly permanent homes for aging people. For more information on them, consult *Choosing a Nursing Home* by Jean Baron Nassau (Crowell, 1975).

Local health departments run by state, county, or city government often provide free services such as detection programs for cancer or for communicable diseases such as tuberculosis; some also run dental, mental-health, and public-health education programs, hospitals, and other services. They work closely with welfare departments and other health agencies in arranging for necessary care for people who cannot afford to pay.

Voluntary health agencies usually deal with a specific disease— such as The Allergy Foundation of America or The National Association for Mental Health. These agencies research causes and cures and educate specialists, but they are also an excellent source of up-to-date information for the layman; often they run diagnostic centers or clinics, and sometimes help financially needy sick people. Some of their addresses are given above; others can be found at your public library in the *Encyclopedia of Associations.*

Voluntary and government health agencies will also advise and help you should you need home care. Nursing (and sometimes also physical, occupational, or speech therapy) is available from your local Visiting Nurses Association or public-health department, with fees adjusted to your income. Meals on Wheels (financed by the federal government, with service charges adjusted to your ability to pay) delivers prepared meals if you are homebound and unable to prepare your own food. Hospital-type beds, wheelchairs, walkers, oxygen supplies, and other equipment—available from private suppliers and from voluntary agencies—can be rented or purchased, usually under Medicare coverage.

# 22
# Food for Vitality

You can eat better, and often more cheaply, if you know something about nutrition. A pioneer in popularizing nutrition was Adelle Davis, whose *Let's Eat Right to Keep Fit* is available in paperback; but today you'll find dozens of sources, from basic books such as *Nutrition* by Margaret S. Chaney and Margaret L. Ross (Houghton Mifflin, 1971) to practical guides such as *The New York Times Natural Foods Cookbook* by Jean Hewitt, available in paperback. Among the many excellent publications from the U. S. Department of Agriculture are the Home and Garden Bulletins, including *Food Guide for Older Folks* (Bulletin 17), *Your Money's Worth in Foods* (Bulletin 183), *Money-Saving Main Dishes* (Bulletin 43), *Nutritive Value of Foods* (Bulletin 72), and *Conserving the Nutritive Values in Foods* (Bulletin 90), all available from the Superintendent of Documents (Government Printing Office, Washington, D.C. 20402).

## TYPES OF FOOD

**PROTEIN**   An essential part of every living cell, animal and plant, it builds new body tissues and replaces old ones, helps form antibodies to fight infection, helps form enzymes and hormones, and gives up to 25% of body energy.

Many different forms of protein exist, each built up of various combinations of amino acids. All but eight of the 22 known amino acids can be manufactured by the body from fat or sugar plus nitrogen. The eight that the body cannot make (isoleucine, leucine, lysine, methionine, phenylalanine, threonine, tryptophane, and valine) must be obtained from food. Foods containing all eight of them have come to be called "complete" proteins; the greater the amounts of these eight amino acids in a food, the higher its protein value.

The very highest amounts are found in organ meats, fresh milk and buttermilk, and egg yolks. The next highest group are the muscle meats (beef, veal, lamb, pork), fowl, fish, dried milk, yogurt, cheeses, wheat germ, soybeans, cottonseed flour, and brewers' yeast.

Many foods contain partially complete proteins which are lacking in just one or two of the eight essential amino acids. A meal containing two or more of these proteins may, if chosen carefully, make up a complete protein meal between them. If the two proteins are eaten more than one hour apart, however, the body cannot utilize them to form the complete protein.

Examples of these partially complete proteins are whole-grain cereals and flours with the germ removed, peas, beans, split peas, lentils, and certain nuts such as peanuts and walnuts. Other vegetables, fruit, and gelatin lack more than just one or two of the amino acids and are therefore low in protein value and could not, alone, sustain life.

If you're inclined toward a vegetarian diet, you can use eggs and cheese; or you can substitute legumes and certain vegetable combinations to get adequate protein. However, since the right combination is important in getting the complete protein, get hold of a cookbook that gives you this information very specifically (Frances Moore Lappé's *Diet for a Small Planet,* published by Ballantine Books in paperback, is one such cookbook).

**CARBOHYDRATES**   These various forms of sugar and starches are converted by the body into glucose (blood sugar) and used for energy. What is not immediately needed is stored as animal starch and fat.

The sugars are the more quickly absorbed and used. No one sugar is essential in the diet in the way that amino acids are, but some source of glucose is needed for normal life processes. Sources of sugar are fruit and fruit juices, extracted sugars (from beet and cane, mostly), honey, syrup, and molasses.

The starches are present in grains and grain products, potatoes, sweet potatoes, and legumes; other vegetables contain varying small amounts. Grains are also fair secondary sources of protein and good sources of several vitamins and minerals.

Cellulose, whose chief function is to provide roughage to aid in elimination, is another carbohydrate contained in fruits, vegetables, and whole grains.

**FAT**   Digestion breaks fat down into fatty acids and glycerol. The body can manufacture all but three of the fatty acids; these three— linoleic, arachidonic, and linolenic—must be obtained from food.

Linoleic acid is the one most essential to life (the other two act as somewhat inadequate substitutes for it) and is used to form sex and adrenal hormones, intestinal bacteria, and cell structures. Fatty acids in general are used for replacement of cell structures.

Fat stored around internal organs helps support them; the layer of fat under the skin helps to regulate body temperature and to protect muscles and nerves. The rest is stored in the liver and elsewhere in the body (usually just where you don't want it) against times of hunger or illness.

To minimize the risk of arteriosclerosis, many doctors think, it is best to avoid overuse of saturated fats—the animal fats—and to use, whenever possible, the polyunsaturated fats. The best sources of polyunsaturated fats are certain liquid vegetable oils; these are also good sources of linoleic acid and are low in cholesterol. You can use vegetable oils for cooking and for salad dressing; olive oil, the most popular for this purpose, is fairly low in polyunsaturated fat, so you might try another flavor (sunflower seed, walnut, and almond oils are delicious) or mix the olive oil with 50% of another vegetable oil. You can substitute vegetable-oil margarine for butter if you can stand the taste. In the process of hardening the oil for margarine, however, much of the unsaturated fat becomes saturated, so try to find "soft" margarines, which have a higher proportion of unsaturated fat.

**VITAMINS** These are organic chemical compounds which are essential to good health and growth. The fat-soluble vitamins (A, D, E, and K) are not easily destroyed and can be stored by the body. The water-soluble vitamins (B-complex and C) are easily lost in soaking, cooking, and refining processes; they cannot be stored by the body and must be ingested daily in the diet.

**Vitamin A**  Fat-soluble; it helps keep the skin smooth and clear, helps mucous membranes resist infections, helps the eye adapt to different light levels, and helps in bone and tooth-enamel growth. Its best food sources are liver, eggs, dark-green and leafy vegetables, and deep-yellow vegetables and fruit.

**Vitamin D**  Fat-soluble; it is important in the formation of strong bones and teeth, its presence being necessary for calcium to do its work properly. It is formed in the oils on the skin by exposure to sunlight, and then absorbed by the body (one good reason not to shower immediately before or after sunbathing). In food, the only good sources are fish-liver oils and milk that has been fortified with the vitamin. A little is present in egg yolks and organ meats.

**Vitamin E**  Fat-soluble; it is the most abundant vitamin in the body, being especially concentrated in the pituitary, adrenal, and sex glands. Its best-known function is to prevent unsaturated fats in the body from being destroyed by oxygen.

It helps other vitamins (particularly Vitamin A) do their work and helps maintain healthy cell structure. Improved muscle tone, reduced amount of scar tissue on wounds, lower oxygen requirements (a help to aging lungs), prevention of "liver spots" and yellow pigmentation of the tissues, and improved fertility are among the many claims made for Vitamin E. Indications are that the body's need for Vitamin E increases with age, either because of heightened demand or because of reduced ability to metabolize the vitamin. Its best sources are unrefined vegetable oils and wheat germ.

**Vitamin K**   Fat-soluble; it is really a group of vitamins and is necessary for the proper coagulation of blood—important in stopping bleeding from wounds. It is formed in the intestines and is also present in many foods, including milk, vegetable oils, wheat germ, and green vegetables.

**The B-complex Vitamins**   Water-soluble; this is a group of vitamins which depend on one another's presence, in a certain balance, to be used effectively by the body. If one or a few of them are taken in any quantity, the need for the rest of them is increased accordingly. The whole grains (including brown—unpolished—rice), liver, wheat germ, and brewers' yeast are the best sources for the whole complex.

*Vitamin B₁ (Thiamine)*   Used by the body to help convert food, particularly the carbohydrates, to energy; to maintain a healthy nervous system; and to keep the appetite and digestion good. It is found in greatest abundance in wheat germ, whole (not pearl) barley, blackstrap molasses, soy beans, brewers' yeast, brown rice, and wholegrain cereals.

*Vitamin B₂ (Riboflavin)*   Used by the body in the conversion of all food. Also helps maintain healthy eyes, keeps lips from shrinking, and keeps lips and corners of the mouth from cracking. Riboflavin is found mostly in milk and milk products, organ meats, and brewers' yeast. It is easily destroyed by sunlight: foods will lose about 50% of their riboflavin in two hours of exposure.

*Niacin*   Necessary for food metabolism and for the enzyme system. The greater the food intake, the more niacin the body needs. It is found mostly in brewers' yeast, organ meats, wheat germ, fish, peanuts, chicken, tuna, lean beef, whole wheat, lamb, peas, and mushrooms.

*Vitamin B₆*   A group in itself, consisting of pyridoxine, pyridoxal, and pyridoxamine. It is necessary for the metabolism of all foods and is found mostly in lamb, veal, legumes, potatoes, wheat germ, and brewers' yeast.

*Pantothenic Acid*   Essential for metabolism of food. Found in rice polish, wheat germ, organ meats, soy beans, peanuts, egg yolks, and whole grains.

*Biotin*   Also necessary for food metabolism. Found in most foods but can be destroyed in the intestine by too much raw egg white in the diet.

*Vitamin B$_{12}$*   Helps form red blood cells and is used to treat certain anemias. It is mostly found in the organ meats, muscle meats, fish, milk and milk products, green leafy vegetables, wheat germ, and brewers' yeast.

*Folic Acid*   Also used in the formation of red blood cells. Helps too in the formation of body protein and in the metabolism of body fat. It is most abundant in the organ meats, wheat germ, brewers' yeast, and is also found in beef, fish, nuts, dark-green vegetables, and whole-grain cereals. It is easily destroyed in vegetable sources by cooking.

*Cholin and Betaine*   Two B vitamins used in the metabolism of fat, particularly important in the prevention of fat deposits in the liver. They are also believed to help absorb cholesterol in the blood stream. They are found most abundantly in brains and kidneys and to some extent in all plant and animal tissue.

*Inositol*   Possibly involved in maintaining normal vision and in heart action. Also promotes hair growth and proper elimination processes. From recent research, it seems that inositol might be synthesized in the body; in any case, it is found mostly in blackstrap molasses (an effective laxative), liver, brewers' yeast, wheat germ, whole-wheat bread, oatmeal, and corn.

As can be seen from this summary, one of the best and cheapest sources of the B-complex vitamins is whole-grain products. Refined bread, cereals, and pastas have had most of these vitamins removed, and the enrichment processes do not return all the nutrients.

**Vitamin C**   Water-soluble; it has many functions in the body. It helps produce the connective tissue between cells (collagen), which is important in healing and in elasticity and strength of blood vessels. It is necessary for strong bones and teeth and for healthy gums. It helps cells use oxygen, is used in the enzyme system, and assists the body's use of iron, other vitamins, and the amino acids. It helps fight infections. Although found most abundantly in citrus fruits (oranges, grapefruits, lemons) and juices, a goodly amount is also in other fresh fruits (berries, watermelon), in green vegetables, tomatoes, sweet red peppers, and potatoes (when cooked in their skins). It is lost from vegetables if their cooking water is thrown out; there is even some loss when they are washed.

**MINERALS**   Minerals are inorganic substances composing some 4% of the body's weight. New ones, usually in minute quantities, are discovered in the body all the time. To date, the following minerals have been established as essential to good nutrition: calcium, phosphorus, iron, chlorine, iodine, fluorine, sodium, potassium, magnesium, sulfur, copper, zinc, cobalt, manganese, molybdenum, selenium, and chromium. Most of them are present only as traces in the body.

The amount the body needs of each varies greatly since they have a variety of functions. Usually a diet generous in meat, cereals, leaf vegetables, and fruits will supply an adequate balance of minerals. Special care, however, should be taken in getting enough calcium and iron; the body seems to need more of these as it gets older.

**Calcium**   Found in milk and milk products, it is used throughout life to maintain bone structure and keep teeth healthy. It helps carry nerve impulses, and its lack can result in tense nerves and muscle cramps. Excess calcium is stored in the end of the bones and not, as was long feared, in the joints; it does not, therefore, cause arthritic conditions.

**Phosphorus**   This mineral combines with calcium to do the latter's work on bones and teeth. It is found in high quantities in liver, brewers' yeast, and wheat germ and in some quantity in all food.

**Iron**   This is important in the manufacture of hemoglobin (the part of the red blood cells that transports oxygen) and in energy production. Iron is found in the nucleus, or center, of all body cells. It is present in greatest and most easily absorbed quantities in organ meats, apricots, and eggs; it is also present in red meats, whole-grain breads and cereals, blackstrap molasses, green leafy vegetables, wheat germ, raisins, prunes, and other dried fruits. Hydrochloric acid in the stomach is necessary for proper absorption.

**Iodine**   Necessary for the proper working of the thyroid gland, iodine can be obtained from iodized table salt.

**Fluorine**   Fluoridated water supplies all necessary fluorine, an element which is thought to minimize tooth decay and promote bone strength.

**Others**   The rest of the minerals are usually obtained from the foods containing calcium and iron. In hot weather, particularly after perspiring a lot, you should take a little extra salt (sodium) to ward off heat exhaustion.

Many vitamins and minerals are available in pill form (and, less often, in powder or liquid form), some from natural sources, some from chemical equivalents of the natural substance; the first type is generally supposed to be the best one. Although doctors sometimes prescribe vitamin or mineral pills as a supplement, and many people take them on their own initiative, controversy exists about whether a normal American diet is adequate and whether your body can absorb the pill form of vitamin or mineral: absorption efficiency differs from person to person and from time to time in the same person. So it is hard to know when you are getting as much as the pill's potency implies.

You should be particularly careful about how you take B-vitamin pills. Large quantities of one or several B vitamins will increase the need for all of them in a specific balance. Many of the B-complex pills have a badly balanced formula, and taking them regularly could make you sick. Your doctor can probably give you information on whether and how you should take them.

## NUTRITION IN FOOD

Fruits and vegetables grown out-of-doors in sunlight are likely to have higher nutritional content than those grown in greenhouses; in-season produce, is, therefore, more valuable. The same is true of freshly harvested produce—the longer the storage, the greater the loss of vitamin content.

In buying produce, watch for nutritional indications: bright-orange, mature carrots have more Vitamin A than young, pale ones. Deep-orange sweet potatoes have the greatest amount of Vitamin A. Darker green leaves are richer in Vitamin A, calcium, and iron than are lighter green ones—and this goes for those on the same plant as well as for those on different plants. Vegetables should have no signs of wilting, withering, or shriveling to indicate long storage.

If you're worried about weight or cholesterol, whole milk contains about 3.5% fat and partly skimmed milk about 2%; totally skimmed milk contains only a trace. Buttermilk, contrary to its name, is skimmed milk; it can be bought in dried form.

Dried, powdered skim milk can be shaken up with whole milk for a high-calcium drink. Dried milk can also be added to cereals, mashed white and yellow vegetables, and meat dishes for additional protein. Making instant beverages (coffee, coffee substitutes, cocoa) with dried or fresh milk (whole or skim) instead of water gives extra calcium and protein.

Wheat germ is the embryo of the wheat kernel from which the plant sprouts. Rich in B-complex vitamins and Vitamin E, it is also high in protein. Toasted wheat germ is available at most supermarkets (raw wheat germ, which some people have trouble digesting, at health-food stores) and can be substituted for part of the flour in most baking recipes (for all of it in cookies). It is a good thickener in stews and can be substituted for bread-crumb coatings.

In any recipe calling for refined white flour, it is possible to substitute whole-grain flour by using about two tablespoons less per cup. The grain foods, though, are high in calories and should be used sparingly, unless you are one of the world's blessed for whom overweight is no problem.

Brewers' yeast is available in tablet form, but you have to swallow an awful lot of tablets to get an amount equivalent to one tablespoon of the powdered form. One granular form is available in drugstores; the powdered form is usually available only at health-food stores, which is a pity because it is probably one of the cheapest high-protein, high Vitamin B foods available and contains no animal fats, starches, or sugars. But it is definitely an acquired taste, and a beginner should start with small quantities (best disguised by dissolving it in fruit juice), both to get accustomed to the taste and to make sure that his or her digestion can take it (lemon juice will smooth out the digestive problem somewhat until you get used to it).

**THE QUESTION OF HEALTH FOODS**    For reasons perhaps having to do with their own past condonement of food adulteration in processing, the medical and bureaucratic establishments get remarkably enraged at the mention of health foods and are unanimous in vilifying them.

But "health food" is only the latest name for the kind of food that outside the large metropolitan areas, is simply known as wholesome food. In most parts of the country, the "health-food store" does not exist—for equivalent products you would go to a rural general store; to a country store; to a smokehouse; to local outlets for a religious settlement's products; to small stores in restored towns; to cooperative and regular supermarkets in university towns, chic suburbs, and wealthy resorts; to state, county, and local fairs, where homemade produce is sold. The product may not be labeled "health food" but it is characteristically free of pesticides and preservatives, minimally processed, and often grown without use of chemical fertilizers.

Many experts maintain that pesticides and preservatives are more desirable than the huge losses of food before and after harvesting which would occur without them. In terms of filling bellies, they are probably right, and a low level of vitality and health is certainly better than starvation. But you must also consider the quality of what you put in your belly. The pros and cons of chemical vs. nonchemical fertilizers seem pretty evenly balanced. The pesticides are in another league altogether—they are known to be harmful and the worst ones accumulate in the soil as they are washed off the plants. Therefore, while bowing your head to their possible necessity in large-scale production, you should do your best to avoid them in your own food. Not that this is easy: many supposedly pesticide-free foods have been discovered to have them after all; sometimes this is pure villainy by the grower or trader; often it is unavoidable because the pesticides are blown and washed onto the farmer's crops from neighboring fields.

Preservatives, too, have definite harmful effects, although there is much argument about the amounts that are harmful and about the possibilities of accumulation. If you want to be on the safe side, avoid these, too—look for the products (increasingly available on ordinary supermarket shelves) labeled as containing none.

Unprocessed foods are apt to contain more nutrients than their processed equivalents. White bread, for instance, is made with a bleached flour from which the germ has been removed; the nutrients added to the flour after processing never give it the same value as before. The taste is also different: processed foods are quite bland (many of them taste fake, in fact) compared with nonprocessed foods.

If you live in a metropolitan area, your chief source for these goods has to be a health-food store. Do a lot of exploring before deciding that you have found the best. Prices in these stores (and in the health-food departments of supermarkets) are higher than you would pay for conveyor-belt food, but they should not be *very* much higher. If they are, the owner is either incompetent or greedy and you should avoid his store. The prepared foods, meats, and vegetables do cost a lot more, however, and most people couldn't hope to do all their food shopping here. But if you stick to the grains, flours, dried legumes, and vegetable oils, you will be able to pick and choose among a great assortment not otherwise to be found away from the farm! Make sure that the proprietor's information about his goods is sound—many owners are pure faddists and will sell you the cure for life if you let them overwhelm you. If his store is good and you want to use it anyway, you'll have to keep your skepticism and sales resistance at the ready.

Make sure that the foods you buy are fresh and that you don't buy so much that they will go stale before you can eat them. Since most of the foods contain no preservatives, you should scan them very carefully and leave them if they show signs of age. A month's supply is probably the most you should buy.

**LOSSES IN STORAGE**   If you have a deep freezer, see Chapter 5 for additional information on storage.

**Flesh Foods**   Meats, poultry, and fish lose few nutrients in the refrigerator or freezer provided they are well wrapped. They keep well for about a week in the freezer compartment of the refrigerator; for longer storage they must be kept in a freezer at zero degrees Fahrenheit.

**Vegetables**   Most fresh vegetables can be stored in the refrigerator for several days without any great loss of nutrients if they are kept humid enough. Potatoes, onions, and rutabagas should *not* be stored in the refrigerator; these are best kept in a cool, dark place.

Leafy vegetables, salad greens, and cabbage are best kept in the vegetable crisper section or wrapped in moisture-proof bags elsewhere in the refrigerator. Carrots, beets and radishes should have their greenery removed to postpone wilting. Peas and beans keep best if left in their pods until used; if shelled, they should be wrapped in moisture-proof bags. Green or pale-red tomatoes keep best by ripening out of the sun at room temperature and then storing in the refrigerator.

Dried legumes keep indefinitely in cool, dry storage.

**Fruit**   Fresh fruit—except for berries, cherries, and bananas—can be kept in the refrigerator for several days and does not have to be covered. Berries and cherries lose their nutrients quickly, once bruised; they also rot quickly after washing. Bananas should be kept at room temperature. Dried fruit can be stored, tightly covered, in maximum temperatures of 70° F.; it should be refrigerated in hot, humid weather.

Fruit juices can also be kept for several days in the refrigerator. They do not have to be covered to retain their nutrients, but covering them keeps out the smells of other foods.

**Grains**   Whole-grain flours and cereals with no chemical preservatives can be kept in a cool dry place in well-sealed containers for up to a month without undue nutritional losses. If no such storage is available, they should be refrigerated.

**Dairy Foods**   Fresh milk should be covered and protected from strong light, which destroys riboflavin. Dried milk can be kept in a closed container in temperatures up to 75° F.; nonfat dried milk keeps better than dried whole milk. Once reconstituted, it should be stored like fresh milk.

Cheeses keep well for two weeks or so in the refrigerator.

Eggs stored large end up in the refrigerator keep well for a week or more. Leftover yolks should be covered with water and stored in a tightly sealed container; leftover whites should be tightly covered; both should be stored in the refrigerator.

**Fats**   All animal fats should be refrigerated. Vegetable oils should be refrigerated after opening, as should salad dressings and mayonnaise. Hydrogenated (hardened) vegetable shortening can be kept at room temperature if covered.

**Canned Food** Except for canned meats (which lose 30% of their thiamine by six months), these can be kept in a dry place at a maximum temperature of 70° F. for about 12 months with a loss of only 10% of nutrients.

**LOSSES IN PREPARATION** **Meats** In cooking, meats lose mostly water and some fat. Protein loss is small: about 10% will come out in the liquid during stewing, for instance. Some Vitamin $B_6$ and thiamine are lost through heat. Rare meat has more thiamine than does well-done.

**Vegetables** Some Vitamin C is lost in washing vegetables and fruit, but the alternative is ingestion of insect sprays. Vegetables should therefore be washed, but as briefly as possible.

The less cooking, the more nutrients are conserved. If you cannot digest salad or need a change from it, try sautéing Chinese-fashion: stir-fry the chopped vegetables in a little vegetable oil for two or three minutes with salt, or a little soy sauce, sherry, or broth for seasoning; almost any vegetables can be cooked this way with little nutrient loss.

Another good way to avoid losses in cooking is to cook the vegetables, tightly covered, in just enough water to prevent scorching and for just long enough to make them tender. When you have to use more water (as with whole potatoes, for instance) or cook for longer, many of the nutrients are extracted; keep the water for gravies, sauces, and stocks.

Baking and boiling root and tuber vegetables in their skins preserves more nutrients than if they are peeled first.

Rice should not be washed before cooking because this removes up to 25% of its thiamine. It should be picked over for faulty grains and foreign matter, then soaked in the water in which it is to be cooked; dirt will float to the top during soaking and can be scooped off. If the soaking water turns gray and dirty, you are getting your rice from the wrong merchant. Only the amount of water that can be absorbed in cooking should be used, i.e., double the quantity of rice.

## A BALANCED DIET

Your body should get every day a sufficient amount of complete protein, vitamins, minerals, and roughage (to help elimination). The Food and Drug Administration has issued standard recommendations for daily intake of nutrients by the normal adult: 70 grams of protein (thought to be too much by some nutritionists) plus certain minimums of vitamins and minerals. These are amply supplied by the following servings per day:

**Meat Group**   Two servings from the meat group, which includes the red meats, poultry, organ meats, fish, eggs, soybeans, and certain combinations of legumes. A serving would be two or three ounces of cooked lean meat, boneless poultry, or fish; two eggs; one cup of cooked soy beans, and certain combinations of legumes.

**Milk Group**   Two servings from the milk group, which includes cheese and ice cream. A serving would be one cup of milk, one and one-half cups of cottage cheese, a two-inch cube of cheddar-type cheese. You would need two cups of ice cream and two cups of cream cheese to get the equivalent of one cup of milk—an inedible amount in one serving.

**Grain Group**   Four servings from the grain group, which includes cereals, pastas, whole-grain rice, wheat, and baked goods. A serving would be one slice of bread, about two thirds of a cup of cooked cereal, pasta, cornmeal, rice or other whole grain, or one ounce of ready-to-eat cereal.

**Fruit and Vegetables Group**   Four servings of the vegetable and fruit group, one or two of which should be a good Vitamin C source and a half serving of which should be a good Vitamin A source. The rest should provide roughage. One serving would be a medium-size apple, banana, orange, or potato; half of a medium-size cantaloupe or grapefruit; or half a cup of any fruit or vegetable.

**Individual Variations**   These recommendations are at best a very rough guide and must be adapted to your needs:

Different bodies metabolize food differently and call for different nutrient values. Digestive and other physical problems rule out certain foods for some people, who must adjust their diet accordingly. Calorie needs differ sharply between very active and very sedentary people. Needs in the same person change from day to day, from season to season, and from decade to decade. Only you can know yourself well enough to be fully aware of your current needs and to adjust your diet accordingly.

**CALORIES**   Calories are a measurement of the amount of energy in a food; since the body's energy needs diminish somewhat with age, it is wise to reduce the number of calories, preferably by cutting down on the least nourishing items in the diet—sugar, candies, pastries, refined food, and the like.

It has been roughly estimated that, given normal habits, in her 60's a woman requires from 1500 to 2000 calories a day with no excess storage, and a man from 2400 to 2800 calories. These estimates should be reduced for those of sedentary habits, increased for very active people.

Fat people on the whole have a shorter life-span than do people of normal weight. If you consistently eat more than you need for present fuel, your body becomes choked from overload. The kidneys are overworked. So is the pancreas, because the demand for insulin is so high. Deposits of fat within the muscles and under the skin make muscular play difficult. Even more detrimental are those globs of fat on the internal organs. Fat also requires you to cart around useless baggage—just think of the strain on your heart and lungs if you were to carry a 20-pound (or 30- or 50-pound) suitcase all day. All of this makes the obese person most susceptible to the degenerative diseases: hypertension, coronary artery disease, atherosclerosis, and diabetes.

A good rule of thumb to avoid unneeded calories is to increase the amount of protein, vegetables, and fruit you get, and to decrease your carbohydrates and fats.

# 23
# Keep Moving

In a two-year study of 300,000 men over 45 years old, it was found that the death rate among the completely sedentary was four to five times that of the men who had a consistently high exercise pattern.

This is only one proof of what geriatric specialists have known for a long time—that the body, at any age, deteriorates without proper exercise. This doesn't mean you have to jog ten miles a day or exhaust yourself on a tennis court. Sports are fine if you enjoy them and are fit enough to undertake one on a regular basis. But if you don't enjoy sports, there are suggestions below for exercises you can do in the privacy of your home or as you go about your daily activities.

Exercises aid posture by keeping your muscles in good tone; stimulate digestion and elimination; maintain good blood circulation and respiration, and help keep your heart strong; keep your joints flexible, deferring the possible onset of arthritis. Once you have reached your proper weight, exercise will help maintain it.

While exercise relaxes the body, easing nervous tension so that you sleep deeply and more easily, it also relaxes the mind. With relief of anxiety and boredom comes alertness.

**FINDING YOUR OPTIMUM**  If you have led a sedentary life, you'll have to take it easy at first, to let your muscles, joints, heart, and lungs build up strength and endurance. If you have a specific ailment, consult your doctor about the type and extent of exercise you should undertake. Apart from such limitations, it is never too late to get moving.

If you have been unusually athletic, you may have to cut down on the amount and vigor of your exercise. An early indication of this might be breathlessness persisting for too long after finishing an exercise, or your heart still pounding several minutes after its accustomed time. Take warning at these signs and cut back a little to the point at which your heart and lungs are comfortable again.

It is wise to warm up each time to strenuous exercise. This loosens up your muscles and increases your breathing and circulation so you can perform without strain. If you are about to play tennis, for instance, do some stretching and flexing exercises, walk about for a while at a gradually increasing pace. If you are going swimming, play about in the water for a while, swim for short distances, and so on, before embarking on pool-length spurts.

When you are finishing off a strenuous exercise, taper off; don't come to a sudden halt or you will find your muscles knotting and your heart working overtime. If you can, take a lukewarm shower (not with soap every time unless you are very sticky).

**USING EVERYDAY MOVEMENTS** Ordinary everyday movements can be made into useful exercises. You can turn picking something up off the floor into a back stretch-and-bend exercise. Reaching up to a top shelf is an opportunity for a full tiptoe stretch of the whole body. Toe flexing and clenching, ankle flexing and rotation, and knee flexing are all practical in sitting and standing positions; doing at least one of them several times an hour shifts you out of long-held positions and thus helps circulation.

Workshop, kitchen, or garden activity gives you a chance for many variations. Simply by taking each working motion to its extreme you will eventually involve almost every muscle: one journey on tiptoe; another with knees bent and toes forward; another with two steps on tiptoe, one step with knees bent (a straight-line waltz step, in fact); another with knees bent, toes out, heels down. Unless you are carrying a heavy object you can get in some arm movements also to use your back and shoulders. The possibilities are endless.

**RECREATIONAL EXERCISES** Brisk walking is frequently recommended by doctors, partly because it is easy to fit into a daily routine. If you are more ambitious, you might try hiking or jogging. And, unless you live in a mountainous area, bikes are fun for shortish errands which you would otherwise have to make by car.

While many older people dismiss swimming as too vigorous, it can be taken at any speed you wish, from paddling on up. Among its advantages is that the water supports your body so that you can move in ways not normally possible; you can do exercises in the water that you would have to avoid out of it.

All of these you can do by yourself; games and sports you can engage in with others are dealt with in Chapter 14.

**EASY EXERCISES**   Here is a way of getting to all those muscles and joints that your favorite outdoor exercises may miss. Calisthenic exercises can supplement an outdoor exercise or replace it during the week if you can only get to golf or swimming, say, on weekends. They can also ensure flexibility and relaxation of specific muscles and joints with which you may be having trouble. Calisthenics does not consist merely of push-ups and weight lifting. Ideally, it includes exercises for relaxation, flexibility, muscle tone, and strength, with the emphasis on whatever you need most.

The following 15-minute set of exercises, starting with a relaxing massage, is designed to loosen up rusty joints and mobilize stiffened muscles.

The exercises should not be attacked: they are gentle in themselves and should be done gently and slowly. Every muscle, including the ones being used, should be as relaxed as possible. Be lazy, in fact. Breathing should be kept going steadily throughout—this is hard to do at first, you'll have a tendency to hold your breath while concentrating on a movement. Wear loose clothing that lets you move freely, or none at all in hot weather.

Lie on a thick rug or thin pad. While lying down, support your head with a paperback book of comfortable thickness—your head should not be sticking way above your body, but it should be up slightly off the floor for better neck posture.

If you can find someone to do the massage for you (in return for the same favor, perhaps), all the better: it is much easier to relax completely. If you are being massaged, stay completely passive and give your whole weight and responsibility for movement over to your masseur or masseuse.

Lie on your back, feet flat on the floor and about nine inches apart, knees up to impose the least possible strain on your lower back muscles and stomach. Your knees will probably keep falling over as you relax. You can circumvent this by propping them against each other, feet a little farther apart. Once you have practiced, you will find it easier to hold your knees vertical without muscular tension.

Massage the back of your neck, the upper vertebrae from about level with the top of the shoulder blades, up to where the spine goes into the skull. Pull up on the neck muscles on either side of your spine up to the top of your neck.

Massage around your ears and pull the ears outward.

Massage around your eyes; pull the skin of your nose forward all down the center of your nose; knead your gums through the cheeks;

run your thumbs along under the jawline with a slight kneading motion.

Rub the roots of your hair, then move the skin of your scalp.

Massage your shoulder muscles; push your shoulder joints down toward the floor with your hands.

Slide your hands, palms up, under your back on either side until the fingertips meet at the spine (don't lift your back at all for this). With a slight digging motion of your fingers, pull the back muscles out and away from either side of the spine—you should feel your back move into the floor. Repeat at two or three places down the back.

Slide your hands under the small of your back and pull them down under your buttocks, moving the buttocks down toward the feet and stretching the spine.

At this point the massage is finished and you are moving into gentle exercises.

Draw your knees up toward your chest and tug them gently with your hands.

Place your arms out flat on the floor, palms down, at right angles to your body.

Trying to keep both arms outstretched as much as possible, roll your knees (still bent up) over to the floor—first to one side, raise to center, then to the other side. This will give a good stretch across your back. When you first try this, your knees probably won't touch the floor without the opposite side of your body and arm coming up off the floor. If so, stop before your knees touch the floor—don't let your back give way. Your muscles will stretch in time.

Bring your knees back to center and lower your feet to the ground.

Bring your right knee up to the chest and tug it gently with your right hand, keeping your shoulders and neck relaxed and your elbows out to the sides. Lower your right foot to the ground while bringing your left knee up to the same position. Repeat two or three times with each leg.

Repeat the same movement, this time stretching the lowered leg out straight on the floor, foot easily pointed. Repeat rhythmically several times.

When you get stronger, do the same movement stretching the lowered leg out just *off* the floor. Do this rhythmically several times.

Tug both knees gently to your chest; lower your feet flat to the floor, knees bent; repeat three or four times.

Feet flat on the floor, knees bent, breathe in—and at the same time push the arch of your lower back into the floor; let go as you breathe out. Repeat several times, pushing your lower back into the floor on the out-breath for half the times.

Lie comfortably, feet flat, knees bent; massage your hands by digging the fingertips of one hand between the knuckles of the other; pull out on each finger in turn and rotate it; bend each finger at each joint with the other hand; press each finger back with the other hand. Treat each hand.

Make tight fists, then release your hands strongly to a splayed-out position; repeat several times. Pinch gently up the underside of each arm, taking large pieces of flesh between your fingers. Roll the flesh of the outer arm outward, all up and down your arms.

Hold your arms straight out and flex the wrists back, fingers held straight; pull your hands back toward your arms (keeping arms straight) several times. Make fists and roll your hands forward at the wrists several times. Hands open, make full circles at the wrist, two or three in each direction. Shake your hands out loosely.

(These hand and arm exercises can be done from a sitting position if you find it more comfortable.)

Sit up into as near a cross-legged (tailor's) position as possible, back straight, head balanced on top of the spine. Reach the top of your head toward the ceiling to keep your back straight—but beware of extended chest, raised shoulders, arched back. If your legs cramp, unfold them and shake them out, then return to the cross-legged position. If they still cramp, loosen the folds of your legs until you are comfortable. It will get easier with practice.

Make as many faces as possible, moving quickly from one to another and being as extreme as possible. Make whatever noises come to you with the faces (warn companions within hearing).

Screw your face up tight, bringing your facial features as close to center as possible; hold for a couple of seconds, let go to wide-open eyes and loose mouth. Repeat.

Sitting up straight, nod your head forward from the top of your spine three times; back three times; lean your left ear toward the left shoulder three times, right ear toward right shoulder three times. Still straight-backed, hang your head forward and roll it side–back–other side–forward in a full circle; and again. Repeat in the other direction.

Hold your arms out horizontally from the sides, slightly bent at the elbow and wrist, palms forward. Pull one shoulder blade in toward your spine, keeping your arm extended; pull the second shoulder blade in similarly. Pull the first shoulder blade out, extending your arm even further; pull your second shoulder blade out similarly. Repeat several times.

Uncross your legs and shake them out to remove cramps. Massage your feet the same way as you did your hands, but also run your knuckles over the bottoms of your feet several times and massage around your anklebones.

Pinch up and down the backs of your legs and thighs (the way you did your arms). Roll the flesh of the fronts of your legs outward around the leg bones.

With one leg held up over a sling made from both your arms grasped at the elbows, rotate your foot at the ankle, making full circles in each direction. Arch your foot, pointing your toes toward the ground. Flex your ankle, pulling your toes back toward the front of your leg. Repeat several times, toes clenched for half the times. Shake your foot out loosely. Repeat for the other leg.

Stretch your legs straight out on the floor in front of you, feet together, back and neck straight. Arch your foot and point your toes, keeping your knees as straight as possible; flex your ankles, pulling your toes back and keeping your knees as straight as possible. Repeat several times. Shake out your legs.

In doing these exercises, pay close attention to your reactions. You can work gently with the kind of pain that comes from long disuse. Don't push hard into any of these positions or movements; if you push hard you may, at the very least, cramp a muscle, which is painful. If you find that a position or movement is not easing up with practice, avoid it and work around it.

After several months of doing these exercises (preferably daily, but at least two or three times a week) you may want gradually to introduce tougher calisthenic exercises into the set. If you find that you are not sufficiently well disciplined to keep calisthenics up alone, or that it is too boring by yourself, look around your area for a class you can attend, making sure that it is geared to fairly easygoing exercises, at least at first. You are quite likely to find classes specially designed for older people.

## SPECIAL TECHNIQUES

**YOGA**   If you are agile, you might look into yoga, especially if you can find a class designed for older people. But be sure you get an instructor who knows his business—you don't want to tie yourself in a knot following thoughtless instructions. If you do find a good one, you will discover all kinds of emotional and mental benefits flowing from the discipline as well as the more obvious physical ones. People with faulty backs or necks, however, should stay away from yoga.

**KARATE**   Provided your body has no major muscular or joint problems, karate can help build up strength and self-confidence, as well as
teach you discipline and good exercise techniques. It has the added
advantage of teaching you to defend yourself in threatening situations.

**TAI CHI CHUAN**   Rather less well-known, this is nevertheless particularly suited to older people. It seems to have been, in the far past,
the forerunner of the Eastern martial arts, and until a few years ago
this discipline was confined to the Chinatowns of the larger cities.
Now it is to be found in increasing numbers of adult physical-educa-
tion courses.

For older people it is the near-perfect exercise: its movements are
slow-paced, circular, done with a relaxed body and a calm mind.
None of the movements imposes any muscle or joint strain and they
flow into each other so that in the end, when you know the sequence,
they perform a stately dance.

It is a dance, however, that demands correct posture, balance,
breathing, and concentration and which in the end confers strength,
vitality and a tranquil mind. In its more advanced stages it becomes
a form of self-defense that so uses your opponent's movement that
little strength of your own is needed.

If you can find a class, try it. If not, ask your local adult-education
supervisor if a class can be arranged.

# 24
# Afterword

## GRAY POWER

Thanks to their enforced segregation from the rest of society, people over 64, particularly those who have retired, form an interest group with important concerns. These concerns have already carried older people as a group into the political arena, where the jousting has only just begun. Forming, as they do, almost 10% of the total population, this is a group with potential political clout.

## ISSUES

**HOUSING**   The housing problem is felt by the whole population (except the rich) but is more onerous for the poor and for people living on fixed incomes. Although reassuring statistics show that most retired people own their own homes or are paying off mortgages on them, those statistics say nothing of the quality of their housing. Another statistic says that 30% of people over the age of 64 inhabit substandard housing.

Older people who don't own a house have special problems. Their age militates against their getting a mortgage to buy a home, even if they can afford the skyrocketing mortgage rates. Thanks to the general shortage of housing, rents are high almost everywhere except in isolated rural communities.

State and city housing authorities have attempted to help poor older people by setting aside sections of public housing for them. The federal government used to contribute annually to the local housing authorities' capital funds and also subsidized the rents of needy people in that housing. In January, 1973, however, a moratorium was declared on federal housing subsidy grants; while the federal government has continued to pay those subsidies already established, no new ones have been undertaken. As even public housing rents are being driven up by inflation, new difficulties are introduced for older people.

Federal subsidies to nonprofit low-income housing in the private sector have also been suspended. The suspension was supposedly for a review and evaluation of the programs, but this seems not to have taken place; there is now little hope that programs will ever be revived in their previous form. However, the housing shortage is serious enough to make some sort of subsidized housing program inevitable eventually.

Another aspect of the housing problem concerns the million older people who are living in institutions, mostly nursing homes. As is now notorious, large numbers of these institutions are of very low standards. Despite many honorable exceptions, cost cutting and efficiency are prime directives for a great many institutions. Many crowd patients together in cramped quarters with few or no recreational facilities. Many encourage passivity, often dragooning residents into complete conformity with the institution's requirements. Care is almost always custodial, with little or no attempt at rehabilitation.

This would be bad enough if their residents were always people with no other possibility in life. But estimates are that some 25% to 30% of these people could, with a little outside help, be living in their own homes. They might need cleaning help, transport to outpatient clinics, a nurse on call (by telephone) for sudden illness, someone to bring or cook a hot meal every day. While some of these services are becoming available to older people through various outreach programs, only one or two isolated attempts have yet been made to extract that 25% or 30% of institutionalized older people and establish them in homes of their own. If a network of home-maintenance plans, such as now exist in several northern European countries, could once be set up, these people, now slowly dying, could be given a new lease on life.

Shared housing has rarely been attempted by older people unless they have been friends, and even then the group has often been limited to two or three people. But a commune, particularly the urban type, could be a solution to problems of cost and company. A fairly loosely knit group whose common interest lies in the maintenance of decent living quarters could convert one large house or several smaller houses into a group residence with private studio apartments and common kitchen and bathroom facilities. Rent or mortgage, utilities and service costs, and food purchases shared among the group would lower the burden considerably for each member. The group would provide company or help in case of accident or illness for those who wanted or needed it, while the individual rooms would assure privacy.

Among the few existing examples are two set up by outside sponsors rather than by groups of older people, but, if they work, more independent groups may be encouraged: In Philadelphia, the Gerontological Research Institute of the Philadelphia Geriatric Center bought nine small houses through FHA mortgages and converted them into small apartments; each house had three or four people. Rents, set for low income levels, covered utilities and heavy cleaning, as well as the usual services, plus specific ones needed by individual tenants. In Kansas City, the Institute of Community Studies is establishing cooperative living arrangements in medium to largish houses that are converted to provide individual private quarters and group "family" areas and facilities. The residents share household expenses, duties, and responsibilities.

**SOCIAL SECURITY AND WORK** As Social Security payments are made out of contributions by workers and employers, payments may be considered a right, not a charity from a benevolent government. Contrary to general belief, your contributions are not held for you. They are mostly paid out to current recipients of Social Security. When you become eligible to collect payments, your payments will be made from contributions by other workers at that time.

Social Security was not originally intended to be a pension: it was seen as a kind of supplement to private pensions and to income from the workers' own savings. Considering that it was originated during the Depression, this seems to have been a rather foolish way of viewing the realities of life. In any case, it never worked as a supplement. For most retired people it was, and is, the only income during retirement.

Although the niggardly payment leaves people at the brink of poverty, penalties are imposed on anyone who supplements Social Security by working for more than very low wages. Only if your supplementary income is from investments, interest on savings, annuities, rentals, or other nonworking sources are you not penalized (on the grounds that this is income from money earned during, not after, your permitted working life). So if you were rich enough to accumulate a great deal of money during your working life, you will not be penalized after retirement; if you never earned enough to put aside these kinds of savings, you will continue not to earn enough.

To compound the predicament, about half of the people retiring during their 60's are doing so under mandatory retirement plans.

Most of them are perfectly capable of doing their work, often at a higher standard of quality than younger workers. Many of those who find their current job taxing could easily continue if the job were re-designed to their continuing abilities or if they were transferred to less onerous work. But older workers are not considered as individuals under these compulsory retirement plans.

The earnings limitation on Social Security payments, plus the com-pulsory retirement plans, are obviously efforts to limit the number of people in the labor force. (At the other end of the age span, school-leaving age was raised and attendance at college encouraged for much the same purpose.) With this constriction of the labor force, unem-ployment figures can be minimized and labor unions are in a stronger bargaining position.

But the labor force is the group out of whose Social Security taxes (and they are true taxes because they are compulsory) Social Security payments are currently made. If the number of retired people is not too large compared with the number of workers, the tax burden is bearable. If the number of retired people grows and the number of workers does not, or shrinks, the burden gets heavier.

What changes might be made to the present system to ease the lot of retired people (who form 20% of the poor in the United States and are the only section of the poor whose numbers are actually growing) without overburdening the labor force?

1. Social Security payments could be raised to the level of an ade-quate pension and tied to a cost-of-living index based on essential consumer goods (housing, clothing, food, medical expenses).

This would discourage swelling of the labor force since presumably more people would choose to retire to an adequate income. It would also increase the tax burden on the labor force unless the contribu-tions were invested and payments made out of the workers' own contributions plus interest from the investment. Initially, there would have to be government subsidies to those who had to retire before their own contributions could support them; these subsidies would continue at a diminishing rate until workers with a full working-life history of invested contributions were reaching retirement age.

Administratively, the cost of keeping track of individual contribu-tions would be overwhelming. Contributions could be pooled for in-vestment, and payments made at a flat rate which might be based on age at retirement. The pool of available funds would match the size of the retired population because it would be formed of their own contributions.

2. Social Security could be paid at a certain age whether or not you retired (this is already done at age 72 in the United States and

earlier in several other countries); it would not be increased to an adequate pension level.

This would swell the ranks of labor since people would need to supplement their Social Security income. By not retiring, however, they would still be paying contributions to Social Security funds, thus spreading the burden over a larger number of people.

People who could not go on working for health reasons would be faced with low income levels, but this could be mitigated by special supplements.

3. Compulsory retirement could be abolished; Social Security payments would not be raised to adequate pension level. The same results as under (2) would prevail.

4. Social Security payments could be raised to adequate pension level; mandatory retirement would be abolished; Social Security payments would begin at a certain age for those who retired then, and only on retirement for those who continued working.

Here, nonpayment of Social Security could be regarded as a penalty for working; this and higher benefit rates would tend to keep the labor force from swelling. The penalty could be offset by payment of higher Social Security rates at later retirement, as is done now.

**TRANSPORTATION** Many people now over the age of 64 have never learned to drive an automobile. Others give up driving because they cannot afford a car or because a physical disability makes driving too dangerous. Others limit their driving to local roads because highways or city streets confuse them and make them nervous. In all, only about 15% of people over 64 have a driver's license.

Very few people indeed can afford a chauffeured limousine and few more can afford to take taxis (those who can, by the way, take almost 70% more trips than those who can't). The only thing left, then, is public transportation.

Yet outside the larger cities and a few well-organized towns, a long-distance Greyhound is often easier to find than a local bus to your three-miles-distant shopping center. Even where public transportation is available, the cost is high—prohibitively so for people managing on near-poverty-level budgets. Finally, available transport is often not well suited to older people who have the kind of health problems that prevent their driving cars.

The problem of insufficient public transportation is not confined to older people, of course. But public-transport systems are held to be uneconomical in any but densely populated areas and must usually be subsidized.

Efforts to get public transportation for older people must usually be made through the municipalities, through local social- and voluntary-service agencies, or by groups of older people seeking financial support from federal funds, state funds, and local merchants. For example, a transportation cooperative was formed in Missouri which has a membership of over 3000 older people in 18 counties. Once a region has reached this degree of organization and has sufficient members, it can apply to the state Office on Aging for a matching-fund grant (under the Older Americans Act) for minibuses.

Successful systems do exist. They are usually small-scale. Some, particularly those subsidized by municipalities, do not restrict passenger eligibility; others are intended only for older people. They usually involve small (between eight and 20 passengers) vehicles which have shallow steps and lots of handgrips. Drivers may be specially trained and are friendly, patient, and helpful. Routes usually lie between residences and frequently used amenities like shopping, medical, and recreational centers, parks, and downtown areas. Schedules usually avoid rush hours and may be regular or on call at, say, 24 hours' notice; some run every day, others for two or three days a week. The service may be free or for a low fare per trip. Some that are run by voluntary agencies (the Senior Citizens Mobile Service in Chicago, for instance) actively seek out dejected and withdrawn older people and encourage them to use the service.

Such systems have given previously confined older people a feeling of independence. Opportunities for outside activities and for friendly encounters have broadened their horizons a hundredfold. For many it has meant a new lease on life and release from isolation and loneliness.

Where older people have to rely on general public transportation, ID cards for special low fares (often half fare) on local trips have been introduced in many cities, towns, and counties throughout the country. Traveling times on low fares are often limited to nonrush hours.

The unsuitability of much public transportation is open to correction, given enough awareness by manufacturers and designers plus a big push from the riding public. *Transportation and Aging: Selected Issues,* DHEW Publication No. (SRS) 72-20232, available from the Superintendent of Documents, is an excellent source of data on transportation and its effect on the lives of older people.

**HEALTH CARE   Costs**   Medical prices increased by 40% during the first six years after the introduction of Medicare, compared with 20% in the six years immediately preceding it. Physician's fees increased at twice the rate of the consumer price index during the 1960's, with the largest increase occurring at the time Medicare and Medicaid went into effect. Both programs reimbursed doctors according to their "usual and customary fees."

The increased cost of hospital care can be attributed to increased outlay on labor and materials, and on the high cost of modern technological apparatus and procedures; duplication of equipment, care, research, and many services is also a culprit, although much of it can be exonerated on humanistic grounds.

It is unfortunate that about 25% of all patients and some 50% of older patients are estimated to be receiving hospital care unnecessarily: it may be more convenient for their doctor; they may need less intensive care such as home help or nursing-home care which is not available in their community; or being an inpatient may be the only way for them to qualify for insurance benefits.

Demand for health care increased sharply with the coming of Medicare and Medicaid, largely because of an influx of sick people who had previously been unable to afford medical help. The increased demand, in the face of the already short supply, has also helped drive costs up.

Medicare, which was intended to pay about 80% of the cost of covered benefits, pays only about 40% of an older person's medical costs, according to recent estimates. Partly this is because so many medical items—glasses, hearing aids, consultations with physicians, most hospital emergency care, drugs, and long periods in hospitals and nursing homes—are not covered by Medicare and because of the deductibles and coinsurances for which the patient is also liable under the plan. Many older people, in fact, are paying out more than they did before Medicare.

Private health-insurance plans pay an average of 24% of health services costs.

Group medical practices in which the patients, whether sick or not, pay regular premiums that do not increase during periods of sickness can prevent crippling expenses. In this type of practice, there are about half as many hospitalizations as in other types.

**Availability** Even if you can pay for them, you may have a hard time finding medical services, depending on which part of the country you are in and which service you need. The U. S. Public Health Service estimated that in 1971 we were short almost 50,000 physicians (as well as 17,000 dentists, 150,000 nurses, 105,000 environmental-health specialists, and 161,000 other health professionals). California had a high rate of 160 doctors per 100,000 population in

1972, whereas Alaska had only 63 per 100,000. (The American Medical Association figures differ since they include physicians not active in patient care.)

The shortage is largely because of the limited number of places in medical schools—100,000 qualified applicants were turned down in the 1960's for this lack. Part of the lack stems from the "professional birth control" exercised by the professional associations on the total number of graduates per year since 1932, when the AMA began to fear an oversupply of doctors. Some can be attributed to the unwillingness of poorer states to finance further places, since, as they claim, most of their medical-school graduates leave to practice in more profitable or more medically interesting parts of the country.

Paraprofessional assistance for less skilled medical jobs is one possibility now being explored in areas of gross shortage; this frees physicians for more demanding tasks. The widespread use of paraprofessionals, however, requires a remodeling of medical education and of malpractice insurance.

**Quality** The most frequent complaint from patients about their doctors is the latter's apparent unwillingness to spend time or words on them; patients consequently get a general feeling their doctor doesn't want to be bothered with them. This has been attributed partly to the depersonalizing effects of medical training. Many doctors, of course, are very rushed and have little time to give elementary explanations over and over again to patients. Yet some doctors, and very busy ones at that, seem able to satisfy their patients' need to feel cared for. For those doctors without this fortunate facility, the use of paraprofessionals to talk to patients might alleviate the problem.

Several studies (at the University of California and the Columbia University School of Public Health, for two) indicate that many surgical operations are performed unnecessarily, particularly hysterectomies, tonsillectomies, and adenoidectomies. The first category involves older women, in particular, and the Columbia study found that one third of hysterectomies performed in New York City were unnecessary while another 10% were questionable.

Thanks partly to methods of financing whereby private and public health insurance covers only catastrophic illness, preventive-care services have scarcely been born under the present health system. Because prices for medical checkups are so high and free clinic services often don't include preventive checkups, people with low incomes tend to wait until their condition is quite bad before they seek medical help. Thus medical services have become oriented to this acute type of care and have failed to develop effective programs for such preventive measures as lay education, health screenings, outreach programs, and coordination among the various health agencies.

**National Health-Care Plans**    Almost everyone agrees on the need for a national health scheme. The preferred type in this country is an insurance plan, which basically assures the payment of medical practitioners for their services and ensures that sick people don't get turned away because they can't pay. It is a financial scheme which does not address itself to the other problems discussed above.

Some proposed insurance plans limit eligibility, usually to older people and the poor. Proposed coverage varies greatly. All of the plans include some kind of cost-sharing by the recipient: deductibles and usually coinsurance (the patient pays a percentage of the rest of the bill.) All propose federal funding through payroll taxes; some retain Social Security taxation and state contributions. Some plans propose fee schedules; others stay with a "reasonable charge" basis. Institutions would be reimbursed more or less as at present. They all, also, give the administration of the plan over to insurance companies—a large factor in the increasing acceptance of such plans— usually under some federal or state supervision.

A more radical approach proposes government control and administration not only of the financing of health care, but also of its delivery: the training and distribution of medical professionals; the supply and maintenance of health-service facilities (hospitals, home help, extended-care services, and the like); some control, at least, of the drug industry; and the ordering of medical research. The most radical health-service plans give total eligibility; no member of the population would be excluded. Benefits would be comprehensive and would not be subject to deductibles, coinsurance, or any other form of direct payment by recipients. Financing would be through progressive taxation of income for the specific purpose.

**Pros and Cons**    The main objection to any reform on a national scale is to the control of the health services by federal and state governments. Partly this is a matter of principle—such control is seen as leaping socialism. The medical professions also maintain that administration by nonmedical professionals would lead to inefficiencies and bad procedures. The fact is, however, that their own record as administrators of health services is not very good.

Patient overload is dreaded, and with good reason, considering the shortage of most health services even now. This can only be remedied by increased medical-school enrollment and by giving incentives for medical professionals to move into underserved communities. Even if these remedies were fully applied immediately, it would take another decade to see the results; and, while medical-school enrollment is being increased somewhat, this is not yet enough. Thus, full coverage for full benefits might well produce chaos. Against this must be weighed the sufferings of people who must do without services until such coverage is introduced.

With the overload, the loss of the one-to-one relationship between doctor and patient is feared. As noted above, many patients—even middle-class patients—don't find that relationship very satisfactory now, and poor patients find it mostly nonexistent.

The amount of paper work involved in a national health-care plan is often said to be overwhelming for medical personnel. However, they already face quite large amounts of paper work with the current private insurers, and the likelihood of a significant increase is debatable. Group practice with shared administrative work and costs is a solution to this problem for many doctors.

The cost of a large bureaucracy necessary to administer health-care plans is another objection. But we already pay for the large (and, by government standards, rather luxurious) bureaucracies of the insurance companies. Selected essays on the whole subject can be found in *The Nation's Health*, The Reference Shelf, Vol. 43, No. 3, edited by Stephen Lewin (Wilson, 1971).

## ORGANIZATIONS

Recent years have seen an awakening to these problems (and many others—nutrition, legal aid, job opportunities, education—some of which have been discussed in various chapters of this book) on the part of both older people themselves and the federal, state, and local governments.

One result has been a burgeoning of voluntary groups of older people in attempts to tackle the problems themselves rather than wait for outside help. Some groups are purely local and address themselves to specific local issues. Others are national and use both political lobbying and local problem-solving in their approaches.

**LOCAL**   The local independent groups are too many and too various to name. They include groups formed to solve local transportation shortages; to set up employment opportunities for older people; to provide telephone assurance services for homebound older people; to provide senior teachers' aides to local schools; to provide day-care services for elderly people; to contact isolated elderly people and bring them back into society; and so on, ad infinitum. The successful programs can, and usually do, apply for financial help from federal and state governments; many others find ways to continue on voluntary financing from private sources.

**NATIONAL**   The chief national independent groups are the American Association of Retired Persons, the National Council of Senior Citizens, and the Gray Panthers.

**American Association of Retired Persons**   Founded by a retired teacher whose initial concern, health insurance for retired teachers, blossomed into concern for a larger spectrum of older people's problems, AARP is a nonprofit organization. It and its sister organization, the National Retired Teachers Association, have a combined membership of over 5 million. Anyone over the age of 54, retired or not, can join for a nominal fee, although membership is largely middle-class.

The organization offers many services to its membership. These include health, life, and automobile insurance; a travel service with group tours; a low-cost pharmacy service; adult education; an employment service for temporary jobs; community work projects; a tax-aid program; a health-education program; discounts on certain hotels and automobile rental services; hospitality lounges; a consumer-information program; help in preretirement planning; a bimonthly magazine; and a monthly news bulletin.

The stance of the AARP is one of activity and involvement, and its 1300-plus chapters work for local community welfare. AARP has a strong lobby in Washington which keeps a finger on the legislative pulse. It has a particular interest in health-care costs, insurance, and work opportunities for older people.

Write to: 1225 Connecticut Ave., N.W., Washington, D.C. 20036.

**National Council of Senior Citizens**   This, too, is a nonprofit organization. It is nonpartisan and has a national membership of over 3 million people over the age of 54. Affiliated to it are more than 3000 senior citizens' clubs, divided fairly evenly among church groups, social-welfare and recreation groups, and trade-union groups (Michigan, in particular, has a large trade-union membership in the United Auto Workers).

The aims of NCSC are the restoration of dignity and independence to older people through such measures as adequate income levels, comprehensive health services, decent housing at feasible prices, property-tax relief, adequate low-cost transportation, and good nutrition. Its methods are those of political action: a strong lobby in Washington (trade-union affiliations help there) and a chain of involvement from there on out to the local clubs by means of local delegates to the national organization.

The NCSC was founded in 1961 and its first goal was to get a Medicare plan enacted. After a hard struggle, with the AMA as its chief opponent, it succeeded—and then shifted its attention to retirement-income levels. The result was an increase in Social Security benefits and greater efforts at providing community service employment for poor older people.

The Council offers its members life and health insurances, a low-cost pharmacy service, travel discounts, and a monthly newspaper. Through local groups, the Council sponsors outreach programs and other community services. Members do not have to belong to affiliated clubs, and fees are nominal. Write to: 1511 K St., N.W., Washington, D.C. 20005.

**Gray Panthers**   This is a movement that claims no membership; it is, rather, a network of social activists who act as organizers, enablers, and catalytic agents at the grass-roots level, making older people conscious of the discrimination they suffer and encouraging reform.

Its aims are radical: direct participation in all institutions which affect the lives of older people; the cessation of compulsory retirement based on age; reform of both public and private pension systems and of government and service agencies as a whole; the redirection of national priorities from war to domestic problems; and the abolition of poverty in the United States. A large order, but then, in the view of the Gray Panthers, society needs a total overhaul.

The original name of the group was Coalition of Older and Younger Adults, which better describes it than does the present, catchier name. The group was formed in Philadelphia in 1970. By 1972 it had attracted sufficient response to make a nationwide organization feasible. The presence of younger people in the group is explained by the fact that age discrimination begins very early in our culture. The coalition is loose-knit, with no formal membership and no dues, but with a mailing list some 5000 strong.

Recent spheres of action have been opposition to a housing project in New Mexico; an ecology drive, a ghetto food stores' boycott, and work for better pension plans in Washington, D.C.; organization of patients' rights committees in nursing homes, reduction of mass-transit fares, and introduction of free banking services in Philadelphia. The New York branch is working on the elimination of compulsory retirement laws in the state. Health-care reform is a continuing major activity of all branches.

Write to the Gray Panthers at 3700 Chestnut St., Philadelphia, Pa. 19104. Closely affiliated with the Gray Panthers is Ralph Nader's Retired Professional Action Group (2000 P St., N.W., Washington, D.C. 20036), which is chiefly concerned with consumer problems.

**Senior Advocates International**   (1825 K St., N.W., Washington, D.C. 20006) works toward reform in such areas as health insurance, pension, and employment. For a small fee, members are offered insurance, drug, travel, and other services at discount prices.

**GOVERNMENT** Almost every federal government department has policies that affect older people. The Older Americans Act, 1965, and the Older Americans Comprehensive Services Amendments, 1973, delineated several spheres for special governmental action, usually in conjunction with other agencies. These spheres include: state, area, and community programs (under Title III); research and development programs and manpower training (under Title IV); Foster Grandparents, RSVP, and similar service projects (under Title VI); and a nutrition program (under Title VII).

**Administration on Aging** This division of the Department of Health, Education, and Welfare was set up by the Act as the principal agency for carrying out these programs. It serves as a clearinghouse for information on aging, provides consultative help at central and regional offices, and makes grants to assist local and state agencies with local community programs.

State Offices on Aging are the administrators of funds for community projects. Direct grants go to national or regional research or demonstration projects.

Many counties have an Office on Aging at their county seat; otherwise the state Office on Aging at the state capital is the place to approach for information on any programs in your area. If the Office on Aging itself is not involved, it should be able to refer you to the appropriate government department, state agency, or voluntary agency.

## CONCLUSION

Much attention is being given (most of it only recently) to ways of helping older people.

For a long time, ideas and proposals tended to take the form of handouts: older people were seen as passive. While this may be appropriate for the ancient and helpless, nothing could be more unsuitable for the majority of people under the age of, say, 80. While life expectancy for a 65-year-old has not improved much, health levels certainly have: they are equal to those of a 40-year-old of 50 years ago. For this we can thank the technology which relieves us of so many backbreaking jobs. We can thank the great strides made in medicine for preventing and curing a multitude of diseases which laid our recent ancestors low. We can thank the widespread dissemination and better quality of education and the greatly increased information from the public media; with this intellectual activity, our minds are kept livelier for a longer time than was ever before possible for any but the privileged and exceptional.

But even apart from these considerations, the handout approach is based on wrong assumptions. Old age is not just a period of greater or lesser physical deterioration, it is also one more of life's periods of growth. The help really needed is in developing our individual abilities to deal with the process of transition that will enable that growth to take place.

Recreational centers are all very well, but far more effective would be a system of values which included aging as an integral part of life. Instead, what we have had is a segregation of older people out of the effective web of society (sometimes of their own volition, and not surprisingly, seeing the widespread lack of welcome from the general population), accompanied by a spoon-feeding of palliatives whose main function seemed to be to salve the conscience of the younger members of society.

The causes and organizations outlined above are strong signs that, as at all levels of our society, passivity among older people is breaking up; that they are stepping forward to take active roles in what is, after all, their own community. With their accumulated experience and skills and historical perspective, the chances are good for real change.

# Further Reading

*The Ages of Life: A New Look at the Effects of Time on Mankind and Other Living Things.* Lorus J. Milne and Margery Milne. Harcourt, Brace & World, 1968.

*The Aging American: An Introduction to Social Gerontology and Geriatrics.* Milton L. Barron. Crowell, 1961.

*Aging in America.* Bert Kruger Smith. Beacon Press, 1973.

*The Coming of Age.* Simone de Beauvoir. Putnam, 1972.

*Free Time: Challenge to Later Maturity.* Eds. Wilma Donahue, Woodrow W. Hunter, Dorothy H. Coons, and Helen K. Maurice. University of Michigan Press, 1958.

*Growing Old: The Process of Disengagement.* Elaine Cumming and William E. Henry. Basic Books, 1961.

*Nobody Ever Died of Old Age.* Sharon Curtin. Atlantic Monthly Press, 1973.

*Normal Aging.* Reports from the Duke Longitudinal Study, 1955–1969. Ed. Erdman Palmore. Duke University Press, 1970.

*Nothing to Lose.* Margaret E. Kuhn. Warner Paperbacks, 1975.

*Planning the Older Years.* Eds. Wilma Donahue and Clark Tibbitts. University of Michigan Press, 1950.

*Processes of Aging: Social and Psychological Perspectives.* Eds. Richard A. Williams, Clark Tibbetts, and Wilma Donahue. Atherton Press, 1963.

*The Retirement Trap.* Leland Frederick Cooley and Lee Morrison Cooley. Doubleday, 1965.

U. S. government publications, available from the Superintendent of Documents (Government Printing Office, Washington, D.C. 20402), are many; they include: *The Retirement Process* (report of conference, Gaithersburg, Md., 1968, ed. Frances M. Carp; Department of Health, Education, and Welfare), and the series of booklets on background and issues for White House Conference on Aging, February, 1971.

Bibliographies include *A General Bibliography on Aging, Retirement*

*Planning: A Bibliography,* and *Multi-Service Centers for Older People: A Bibliography* (The Library of the National Council on the Aging, 200 Park Avenue South, New York, N.Y. 10003) and *Publications Available to the Public* (Administration on Aging, HEW, 330 Independence Avenue, Washington, D.C. 20201—also available from the Superintendent of Documents).

Periodicals include *Aging* (monthly newsletter of the Administration on Aging [address immediately above], also available from the Superintendent of Documents); *Retirement Living* monthly (Harvest Years Publishing Company, 150 East 58th Street, New York, N.Y. 10022); *Modern Maturity* and *Dynamic Maturity* bimonthlies (published for members of the American Association of Retired Persons, 1225 Connecticut Avenue, N.W., Washington, D.C. 20036); *Senior Citizens News* (monthly newsletter of the National Council of Senior Citizens, Inc., 1511 K Street, N.W., Washington, D.C. 20005); *Contact* (newsletter of the Projects on Aging, School of Social Work, University of Washington, 1417 Northeast 42nd Street, Seattle, Wash. 98105); *International Senior Citizens News* (membership newsletter of the International Senior Citizens Association, 11753 Wilshire Boulevard, Los Angeles, Calif. 90025); *The Gerontologist,* bimonthly, and *Journal of Gerontology,* quarterly (Gerontological Society, 1 Dupont Circle, Washington, D.C. 20036); *Current Literature on Aging* (The Library of the National Council on Aging, 200 Park Avenue South, New York, N.Y. 10003); and *Senior Advocate* (monthly magazine of Senior Advocates International, 1825 K Street, N.W., Washington, D.C. 20006).

# Index